INTERNATIONAL DEVELOPMENT IN FOCUS

Transforming Agribusiness in Nigeria for Inclusive Recovery, Jobs Creation, and Poverty Reduction

Policy Reforms and Investment Priorities

ELLIOT MGHENYI, CORA DANKERS, JAMES THURLOW,
AND CHIDOZIE ANYIRO

Contents

Boxes

Figures

Map

Tables

Acknowledgments

This book was written by Elliot Mghenyi, Cora Dankers, James Thurlow, and Chidozie Anyiro, with contributions from World Bank staff and external partners: Kwaw Andam, Jeremy R. Strauss, Anne-Christelle Ott, Tran C. Thang, Nome Sakane, Xiaoyue Hou, and Adetunji Oredipe. It draws from background papers prepared by some of the authors and by JMSF Agribusiness Consulting in Nigeria.

The book is an output of the World Bank's Agriculture and Food Global Practice in collaboration with the Finance, Competitiveness, and Innovation Global Practice.

The study was taken under the overall guidance of Shubham Chaudhuri, Rachid Benmessaoud, Marianne Grosclaude, Chakib Jenane, Rashmi Shankar, and Kofi Nouve. Special thanks to Martien van Nieuwkoop and Simeon Ehui for their invaluable support.

The team benefited greatly from the excellent guidance of the following peer reviewers: El Hadj Adama Toure, Christopher Brett, and Kofi-Boateng Agyen. The team also benefited from the useful suggestions provided by Alberta Mascaretti, Jean-Christophe Maur, Indira Konjhodzic, Hardwick Tchale, Farbod Youssefi, Sandra Broka, Parmesh Shah, Eme Essien Lore, Vengai Chigudu, Ibrahim Adamu, Samjhana Thapa, Geeta Sethi, Sheu Salau, and members of the Agriculture Donor Working Group in Nigeria.

The team thanks government officials for very productive engagements that really shaped the scope of the study. Special thanks to H. E. Dr. Kayode Fayemi, Governor of Ekiti State and Chair of Nigeria Governors' Forum; Mr. Alhaji Sabo Nanono, former Hon. Minister for Agriculture and Rural Development; and Dr. Andrew Kwasari, Senior Special Assistant to the President on Agriculture. The team expresses sincere thanks to Dr. Muazu Abdulkadir, former Permanent Secretary, Federal Ministry of Agriculture and Rural Development (FMARD); Mr. Aliyu Ahmed, Permanent Secretary, Ministry of Finance Budget and National Planning; Mr. Isiaka Olarewaju, Director, National Bureau of Statistics; Dr. Baba Madu, Head of National Accounts, National Bureau of Statistics; Mr. S. O. Eloho, Director Economic Growth, Ministry of Budget and National Planning; Dr. Bright Wategire, Director of Programs Coordination, FMARD; Dr. Abdulrahman

Balarabe, National Coordinator for Fadama; and honorable commissioners responsible for agriculture in Ekiti, Kaduna, Kogi, Ogun, and Osun.

The team also thanks the private sector organizations that participated in discussions regarding the challenges faced by agribusinesses across the country. Special thanks go to members of the Nigeria Agribusiness Group and private sector agribusinesses in Kaduna, Kogi, Lagos, Ogun, and Osun.

About the Authors

Chidozie Anyiro is an agriculture economist at the World Bank's Sustainable Development Practice Group, where he supports the Agriculture and Food Program in Nigeria. He has led and worked with advisory and analytics teams to prepare agricultural policy and investment plans, agricultural public expenditure review, and flagship reports on transforming agribusiness, improving agriculture service delivery, and disruptive agricultural technologies. He has also worked with operational teams on the preparation and supervision of multisectoral investment projects in Liberia and Nigeria. He is a trained agricultural economist with broad expertise in agribusiness, agricultural finance, environmental economics, and impact assessment of agricultural projects. He has published widely in this field and holds a PhD in agricultural economics.

Cora Dankers has been working for the Food and Agriculture Organization (FAO) since 1999 on projects that promote farmer-market linkages and agribusiness development in domestic and international value chains. She has conducted research on the impact of voluntary standards on market access for smallholder farmers. She has experience working with farmers' cooperatives and small- and medium-scale agricultural enterprises and with contract farming. Since she joined the FAO Investment Centre in 2017, she has participated in implementation support and project design missions in Bangladesh, Nepal, Pakistan, the Philippines, and Vietnam. She has conducted pre-investment research into wholesale markets, aquaculture development pathways, and value chains, and she has supported a matching grant facility in Suriname. She holds an MSc in tropical agronomy from Wageningen University, the Netherlands.

Elliot Mghenyi is lead agriculture economist at the World Bank. He is responsible for leading policy dialogue, coordinating investment projects, and providing advisory services and analytics in complex countries. He has worked extensively across East Asia, South Asia, and Sub-Saharan Africa on agribusiness and food systems, climate-smart agriculture, food price policies, natural resource management, public expenditure management, and impact evaluations. He has published widely in this field and holds a PhD in agricultural, food, and resource economics from Michigan State University.

James Thurlow is a development economist whose research focuses on the interactions among policies, economic growth, and poverty, primarily using computable general equilibrium and microsimulation modeling. His past research focuses on evaluating public investments and policies; rural, regional, and urban development; and climate change and other external risks. He has worked with governments and researchers throughout Sub-Saharan Africa and in Bangladesh, Peru, Tunisia, and Vietnam.

Abbreviations

AFS	agrifood system
CMD	cassava mosaic disease
CRIN	Cocoa Research Institute of Nigeria
DDGE	dietary diversity growth elasticity
DOC	day-old chick
ECOWAS	Economic Community of West African States
ERGP	Economic Recovery and Growth Plan
ESP	Economic Sustainability Plan
FI	financial institutions
fintech	financial technology
FMARD	Federal Ministry of Agriculture and Rural Development
FRILIA	Framework for Responsible and Inclusive Land-Intensive Agricultural Investments
GAP	good agricultural practice
GDP	gross domestic product
ha	hectare
HPAI	highly pathogenic avian influenza
HQCF	high quality cassava flour
ILO	International Labour Organization
IOT	input-output table
KOR	kernel outturn rate
LBA	licensed buying agent
MFN	most favored nation
MRD	Mekong River Delta
NASC	National Agricultural Seeds Council
NCAN	National Cashew Association of Nigeria
NEPC	Nigerian Export Promotion Council
NESS	Nigeria Export Supervision Scheme
NIRSAL	Nigeria Incentive-Based Risk-Sharing System for Agricultural Lending
NPV	net present value
NXP	Nigeria Export Levy
PGE	poverty growth elasticity

R&D	research and development
RCN	raw cashew nuts
RIAPA	Rural Investment and Policy Analysis (model)
SAM	social accounting matrix
SMEs	small and medium enterprises
SUT	supply-use table
TCDUs	Tree Crops Development Units
TFP	total factor productivity
VINACAS	Vietnam Cashew Association
WRS	warehouse receipt system

Executive Summary

Modern economic policy making in Nigeria has placed enormous emphasis on diversifying the economy to nonoil productive sectors. For example, long before the 2015–16 recession, the National Economic Empowerment and Development Strategy (2004) outlined a strategy for private sector development focusing on diversification to nonoil sources of growth, among other objectives. Agriculture has always been considered an important sector for diversification, most recently as outlined in the Economic Recovery and Growth Plan (ERGP) 2017–20 and the Economic Sustainability Plan (ESP) 2020. With the aim to restore economic growth following the 2015–16 recession and lay the foundations for long-term structural change, the ERGP recognized the need to diversify the economy to nonoil productive sectors such as agriculture and agro-allied industries in order to build an economy that can generate inclusive growth and create jobs. More recently, the government launched the ESP in July 2020 to mitigate the adverse impacts of the COVID-19 (coronavirus) crisis and lay the ground for a robust recovery. Among the major interventions proposed in the ESP is a Mass Agriculture Programme "to create millions of job opportunities, directly or indirectly, over a 12-month period." Similar programs were proposed in roads, renewables, and housing.

Why has diversification preoccupied modern economic policy making in Nigeria? It is mainly because growth has largely been noninclusive and without jobs. Furthermore, the dependence on oil has severely limited the ability of the economy to absorb external shocks, such that falling global oil prices have led to two recessions in the last five years. A key feature of Nigeria's economy is that high oil prices lead to strong economic growth and vice versa. Nigeria experienced strong and stable economic growth during 2000–10, with an annual gross domestic product (GDP) growth rate of more than 6 percent, well above its population growth rate. Oil prices rose during this period. However, the strong years of growth did not appreciably reduce the unemployment rate, which remained nearly flat at about 4 percent.

Nigeria's dependence on oil can be traced to the 1960s, when exports of crude oil and gas increased sharply to provide a stream of enormous revenues to the government. The oil boom diverted attention away from nonoil sectors such as agriculture and manufacturing, and those sectors have become less competitive over time. Although the agriculture and manufacturing sectors feature prominently in policy dialogue around diversification, there is not enough clarity or consensus on the parts of agriculture (or manufacturing or services) to diversify into or on the expected outcomes on jobs, poverty reduction, and so on. Without clarity on investment priorities and expected outcomes, declarations that agriculture should drive diversification have often failed to persuade budget holders to allocate resources. That lack of clarity has also deprived policy makers and practitioners of the information, inspiration, and conviction to develop and execute sector plans that could operationalize diversification.

This book aims to improve understanding of the potential of Nigeria's agribusiness sector (primary agriculture plus off-farm agribusiness) to accelerate inclusive recovery from the 2020 recession, create jobs, reduce poverty, and improve nutrition outcomes. A key early finding of the book is that the agribusiness sector is critical to accelerating inclusive recovery and creating jobs. The book builds on this evidence to identify the specific value chain groups that have the most potential to create jobs, reduce poverty, and improve nutrition outcomes. Next, the book highlights the complex set of factors that mediate the performance of agricultural value chains, distinguishing among issues that pertain to upstream primary agriculture, those that affect downstream off-farm agribusiness, and cross-cutting challenges. The agribusiness-enabling environment takes center stage in this part of the book, focusing on policy reforms around seed regulations, fertilizer quality control, warehouse receipts, agricultural trade, and land reforms. Finally, the book takes deep dives to identify reforms to increase competitiveness in the value chains found to have the most potential to create jobs, reduce poverty, and improve nutrition outcomes. The detailed value chain studies include cashew nuts (representing traditional cash crops), rice, cassava, and poultry (representing livestock value chains). The approach taken in this part of the study is to benchmark performance of these value chains with those in Vietnam, a country that has within the past two decades emerged as a global leader in agribusiness and a top exporter in several commodities and products that are important in Nigeria's agribusiness sector. The strong performance of the agribusiness sector in Vietnam provides a model of structural transformation that could serve Nigeria very well.

WHAT CAN AGRIBUSINESS DO FOR INCLUSIVE RECOVERY AND JOBS?

The agribusiness sector includes all farms and firms involved in producing, harvesting, packing, processing, preserving, distributing, marketing, and disposing of food and nonfood agricultural products. Those activities could be classified into the following categories: agriculture, processing, trade and transport, food services, hotels, and inputs. The agriculture segment of agribusiness includes all of the classical agriculture sector GDP: the primary production of all crops, livestock, forestry, and fishing. The processing segment includes the part of the manufacturing sector GDP that involves processing, value addition, and preservation of food and nonfood agricultural products. Examples include food processing, beverages, tobacco, cotton yarn, and timber. The trade and transport segment includes the part of the services sector GDP that entails transportation, storage, logistics, and trading for agricultural commodities and products between farms, firms, and final consumers. The food services segment is the part of the classical services sector GDP that involves the preparation and sale of food outside the home (for example, restaurants and street vendors). The hotels segment includes the part of the hotels and accommodation GDP associated with food. The inputs segment includes all GDP generated during domestic production of the inputs used by farmers and processors, excluding the inputs produced by the above five segments.

Agribusiness is a large part of Nigeria's economy, directly providing more than 50 percent of jobs and contributing more than 35 percent to the national GDP. It has enormous potential for transformation because primary agriculture is much larger than off-farm agribusiness. Primary agriculture accounts for 21 percent of the national GDP, whereas off-farm agribusiness contributes 14 percent. The 1.5 ratio of primary agriculture to off-farm agribusiness GDP indicates that transformation is still in the early stages. Therefore, there are enormous opportunities to design policies and investments to accelerate transformation and create more and better jobs. With the current low level of transformation, primary agriculture provides more jobs (about 21 million) than off-farm agribusiness (about 8 million jobs). However, off-farm agribusiness provides better jobs than primary agriculture does, with GDP per worker at least 1.6 times higher than in primary agriculture and comparable to the economywide average. Within agribusiness segments, labor productivity is highest in input supply and processing and lowest in hotels, food services, and primary agriculture. Labor productivity in primary agriculture tends to be underestimated, however, when measured as GDP per worker because workers in primary agriculture are engaged seasonally and not throughout the year. The GDP attributable to these workers is generated only during the cropping season; therefore, the average annual labor productivity measure is biased downward unless corrected for seasonality. Furthermore, primary agriculture also tends to be a residual employer that absorbs low-skilled rural individuals who cannot find jobs elsewhere.

An early conclusion of the book is that the agribusiness sector provides perhaps the best opportunities to accelerate inclusive recovery from the 2020 recession while generating more and better jobs. This conclusion is based on analysis of the growth, jobs, and labor productivity outcomes in the past decade (2009–18). The experience of this decade is quite instructive because it was marked by prerecession volatility, recession, and postrecession recovery—similar to the current economic situation and the near-term challenges going forward. During this period, the off-farm agribusiness sector outperformed the overall economy in GDP growth, jobs creation, and labor productivity growth. In particular, GDP in off-farm agribusiness segments grew on average by 5.3 percent annually compared to 3.7 percent economywide, jobs in off-farm agribusiness grew on average by 3.5 percent annually compared to 2.5 percent economywide, and labor productivity (GDP per worker) in off-farm agribusiness grew on average by 1.8 percent annually compared to 1.2 percent economywide. Similarly, primary agriculture outperformed the overall economy in terms of GDP growth (4.3 percent versus 3.7 percent) and the creation of better jobs as labor productivity grew by 2.8 percent compared to 1.2 percent economywide. Within off-farm agribusiness, GDP growth and jobs creation were fastest in hotel and food services followed by trade and transport. The processing segment and primary agriculture led all agribusiness segments in the creation of better jobs.

Successful transformation will depend on productivity growth on the farm and stronger links between on-farm and off-farm agribusiness. Future opportunities for growth and jobs will increasingly be in off-farm segments, in particular processing, hotels and food services, and input supply segments. However, these growth and job creation opportunities cannot materialize without better coordination of agriculture/agribusiness value chains to reduce fragmentation and establish stronger links between upstream primary production and downstream value addition segments. In addition, a growth and transformation strategy for agribusiness should aim for (1) raising productivity in the on-farm segment (primary agriculture) to reduce the costs in downstream off-farm segments; (2) effective coordination of agricultural value chains, including moving away from fragmented spot markets to strong forms of vertical arrangements; (3) expanding processing of higher-value farm products such as cash crops, livestock products, and livestock and fisheries feeds through value chain development approaches that establish strong links with primary agriculture; (4) diversifying farm production and moving away from root crops that have low value-added and processing potential and low nutritional value (the 59 percent of root crops that don't include cassava and potatoes); (5) and increasing domestic production of the inputs used in farming and processing, including seeds, agrochemicals, vaccines, and fertilizers.

HOW MUCH GROWTH IS NEEDED FOR AGRIBUSINESS TO CREATE 6 MILLION JOBS?

Assessment of the growth required to meet specific jobs targets and identification of value chains with the most potential for jobs, poverty reduction, and nutrition is conducted using the Rural Investment and Policy Analysis (RIAPA) model.[1] RIAPA is a computable general equilibrium model, and its core database is a social accounting matrix that captures all income and expenditure flows between all economic actors in the country—including producers, consumers, and the government—and between these economic actors and the rest of the world. The model estimates how the speed and structure of growth in different subsectors affect consumption and income and their knock-on effects on various outcomes of interest such as jobs and poverty. These estimates reflect the differences in consumption patterns for different households and their factor endowments and demand for resources. For example, because poor households tend to depend on incomes from low-skilled workers, growth in sectors that have high intensity of low-skilled labor is likely to have a relatively larger impact on their incomes. In the same vein, because poor households tend to spend a relatively higher share of their food budget on staples, productivity growth in staple sectors would lower prices, raise food consumption among the poor, and potentially transition some of them out of poverty. Outcome indicators in the RIAPA model include economic growth, employment, poverty, dietary diversity score, poverty-growth elasticity, dietary diversity growth elasticity, and economy/sectoral growth employment elasticity. The model is updated with data from 2018—the base year.

The whole agribusiness sector needs to grow by 5.4 percent annually to create 6 million jobs through 2024.[2] The growth burden to meet this jobs target is higher if either on-farm or off-farm agribusiness stagnates. For example, if left alone to achieve the jobs target, the on-farm segment will have to grow by 8.4 percent annually through 2024 to create 6 million jobs. The off-farm segment will have to grow even faster—by 13 percent annually—to create the 6 million jobs on its own by 2024. The same target of 6 million jobs can be achieved with lower growth rates if the target year for achieving the result is pushed further into the future; for example, only 3.9 percent growth is required to meet the jobs targets in 2026. The agribusiness sector in Nigeria was growing 3.4 percent in 2018 and will need to surpass these levels by about 2 percentage points to meet the 6 million jobs target by 2024. The COVID-19 pandemic has slowed growth considerably, and it is estimated that primary agriculture grew by 1.7 percent in the first three quarters of 2020 compared to 2.4 percent during the same period in 2019. Despite the increased growth burden to meet the jobs targets, analysis of agribusiness growth rates in developing countries suggests that it is possible for the sector to grow at rates higher than 5 percent. For example, the agribusiness sectors in Ethiopia, Mali, and Niger grew at 8.0, 9.0, and 10.2 percent, respectively, between 2013 and 2018.

WHICH VALUE CHAINS HAVE THE MOST POTENTIAL TO CREATE JOBS?

Traditional cash crops emerge as the value chains with highest potential to create jobs, followed by cassava, rice, oil seeds, and pulses. The jobs attributed to these value chain groups come not only from the direct effects of productivity growth in the value chain but also from the indirect effects through incentives created outside the value chains. For example, increasing cassava productivity may allow farmers to reallocate resources to other crops, thereby diversifying production and creating more jobs in other agricultural enterprises. Similarly, increasing incomes of workers in a value chain also allows households to purchase products from other sectors or value chains, thereby generating economy-wide spillovers. The results for rice and cassava highlight policy trade-offs on the location of new jobs. On the one hand, cassava is significantly stronger than rice in creating jobs within agribusiness sectors—it has a higher agribusiness growth employment elasticity relative to rice. On the other hand, rice creates relatively more jobs in the broader economy than cassava but actually contributes negatively to jobs within the agribusiness segment. The larger economywide links in rice are through the milling industry as well as through the hotels and food services segments. Within the edible oil seeds group, sesame is emerging as an important commodity for growth and exports. Nigeria has the highest sesame yields globally, which has laid strong foundations for competitiveness in global exports markets. Sesame seed was the most exported agricultural commodity in the first quarter of 2019, accounting for 40.4 percent of Nigeria's agricultural exports—with about 70 percent of exports going to major consuming countries such as China, Japan, and Turkey.

WHICH VALUE CHAINS HAVE THE MOST POTENTIAL TO REDUCE POVERTY?

The value chain groups with highest potential to reduce Nigeria's national poverty headcount rate are pulses, goats and sheep, poultry and eggs, fish and aquaculture, cattle and dairy, and traditional cash crops. These pro-poor value chain groups have semi-poverty growth elasticity of more than –1, which means that a 1 percentage change in agricultural GDP arising from productivity growth in any of those value chains will reduce the national poverty headcount ratio by more than 1 percentage point. However, not all of the value chains are as effective in reducing poverty in rural areas. Specifically, productivity growth in fish and aquaculture and cattle and dairy reduces national poverty more than rural poverty, indicating that the benefits of their growth accrue more to the urban poor relative to rural poor. The links with urban poverty are primarily through off-farm postproduction management of the products and lower consumer prices. Those livestock products tend to have high income and price elasticity of demand. With productivity growth, the prices for such products fall and demand increases, especially among the urban poor. The extent to which the rural poor benefit partly depends on the trade-off of growth and prices. Clearly, the instantaneous effect of productivity growth is to increase the incomes of producers, but this effect appears to be dampened by falling farm gate and consumer prices. In addition to the direct income and consumption effects, increased production and demand create employment opportunities for the poor and low-skilled workers to move commodities from the farm to the market.

WHICH VALUE CHAINS HAVE THE MOST POTENTIAL TO IMPROVE NUTRITION?

Food groups with the highest potential to improve nutrition are cattle and dairy, fruits, poultry and eggs, goats and sheep, fish and aquaculture, and vegetables. Assessment of the potential of value chain groups to improve nutrition relies on estimates of dietary diversity growth elasticity, which measures the percent change in the dietary diversity score of poor households divided by the per capita GDP growth rate. The dietary diversity score is calculated for household groups using food expenditure shares. Diversity is estimated using a generalized entropy measure across six food categories: cereals and roots, vegetables, fruits, meat, fish and eggs, milk and dairy, and pulses and oil seeds. A more diverse diet is associated with better nutrition outcomes. Food groups that dominate production and consumption—the main staples—perform poorly in the dietary diversity score, primarily because such foods already occupy a large share of the consumption basket and productivity growth makes them more available and cheaper, which further reduces the diversity of diets and leads to poor nutrition outcomes. Not surprisingly, staple foods such as sorghum and millet have the worst dietary diversity growth elasticity, followed by yams, cassava, maize, bananas, rice, and edible oil seeds.

MAJOR CHALLENGES IN PRIMARY AGRICULTURE AND OFF-FARM AGRIBUSINESS

Working with smallholder farmers presents several challenges to agribusinesses. Perhaps the foremost of those challenges, at least from the perspective of downstream agribusinesses, are variable quality of production and low productivity. These challenges occur because of weak access to improved technology of production and quality inputs, weak access to credit and risk-sharing services leading to investments in assets with poor returns, high ex post transaction costs for contract enforcement, and weak farmer organizations that cannot effectively monitor disparate smallholders to ensure they adhere to their obligations under vertical coordination arrangements. Despite a long history of development projects organizing smallholder farmers into groups, farmer organizations tend to be ineffective mainly because they are formed primarily to pursue livelihoods objectives. It takes significant capacity building to transition such groups into growth-oriented farmer organizations, such as cooperatives or producer companies, that can form long-term relationships with growth-oriented agribusinesses and incentivize member farmers to invest in appropriate technology of production to achieve the quality desired by remunerative markets.

Most farmers in Nigeria use fertilizers inefficiently and without improved seeds, primarily because of inadequate supply of these inputs and poor design of input subsidy programs. On the one hand, under well-functioning input markets, farmers are unlikely to purchase fertilizers at full cost only to combine them with traditional seeds because the returns to fertilizer are significantly lower with traditional seeds compared to with improved seeds. On the other hand, farmers could end up using inorganic fertilizers together with traditional seeds if farmers can access fertilizers at less than full cost through subsidy programs that don't provide fertilizers as a package with improved seeds. Efficiency in the use of inorganic fertilizers can be improved by reforms in the fertilizers and improved seed delivery systems to increase the market supply of these inputs and enforce quality standards. In addition, any fertilizer subsidy programs should be transitioned to adapt the principles of smart subsidies. The two key principles of smart subsidies are (1) targeting farmers who need to learn about proper use of fertilizers or those who could use them profitably but cannot because of working capital constraints and (2) delivering the subsidy through the private sector by adopting voucher systems that require farmers to purchase a package of fertilizers and improved seeds together. Smart subsidies will need to be accompanied by effective extension and service delivery to enable farmers to learn about nutrient deficiencies in their plots, nutrient requirements for different crops, crop water requirements, critical irrigation periods, and so on.

Total factor productivity (TFP) in primary agriculture has not improved for decades. TFP captures differences in productivity that are not due to differences in use of inputs but are rather attributable to factors such as technological progress and efficiency in the conversion of inputs to outputs. The lack of progress on TFP is mainly explained by (1) underinvestment in the agricultural research required to generate high-yielding and climate-resilient crop varieties and livestock breeds and (2) weak farmer extension and advisory services required to disseminate proper crop and livestock management practices that would enable farmers to use existing technologies efficiently. Nigeria's investment in agricultural research as a share of agricultural GDP fell from an already low 0.39 percent in 2008 to 0.22 percent in 2017. In comparison, Ghana's share is 0.99 percent, and South Africa's is 2.79 percent (Beintema, Nasir, and Gao 2017). In the face of changing climate, targeted agricultural research and development and effective advisory and extension services are critical to deliver the triple wins of improved productivity, enhanced resilience and adaptation, and reduction of greenhouse gas emissions.

Smallholder farmers have weak access to credit, leading to underinvestment in improved technologies for primary production and postharvest management. The commercial lending sector tends to consider smallholder agriculture too risky, primarily because lenders face challenges in distinguishing between good and bad borrowers. Furthermore, lenders incur significant costs in processing a large number of relatively small loans to smallholder farmers. Smallholders have weak land rights and face difficulties using land as collateral for commercial credit. They are less likely to have their lands formally registered compared to medium- and large-scale farmers, primarily because most smallholders acquire land through inheritance, and the land is often subdivided among siblings without passage of full rights. In addition, smallholders tend to demand small and high-frequency loans that don't match the financial products available. Access to credit is also a challenge for small and medium enterprises (SMEs) in off-farm agribusiness segments, limiting their ability to invest in productive assets, capacities, and technologies that increase competitiveness and growth.

Coordinated value chain financing arrangements can address the financing needs faced by both farmers and to off-farm agribusinesses. The factors contributing to weak access to credit by agribusiness SMEs are varied and include structural issues in the financial services sector, weak competitiveness of agribusinesses in domestic and export markets, high risk of failure and stunted growth, lack of financing instruments such as warehousing receipt systems, and the structure of primary agriculture, which is dominated by smallholders perceived as bad risks by banks. Addressing these challenges requires a multipronged approach that includes reforming the financial services sector, improving the agribusiness-enabling environment, and disrupting the financial services sector with financial technology (fintech) products that meet the needs of agribusiness SMEs and smallholders while generating information on creditworthiness of the farmers and riskiness of specific agricultural enterprises. In addition to those reforms, evidence suggests that coordinated value chain financing arrangements can be very successful in Nigeria because they take a "whole-of-agribusiness" approach to address financing needs across multiple actors in the value chains. Without value chain financing, SMEs that face relatively more severe financial constraints cannot invest in innovative technologies and risk being eliminated from the value chains.

Digital technologies have enormous potential to improve access to finance through fintech and mobile money and to enable delivery of various other services. Governments can support digital agriculture through various types of foundational public investments and policy and regulatory reforms. Although the federal government has implemented various schemes to de-risk the sector,[3] much unfinished business remains. In particular, there is enormous scope for disruption in the financial sector through fintech, mobile money, and innovations that deepen financial inclusion, generate information on creditworthiness of entrepreneurs, and increase return on investments in specific value chains. Recent advances in fintech and mobile money (for example, M-PESA in Kenya) have enabled smallholders and informal enterprises across sectors to access small and high-frequency loans with repayment terms that match their cashflow profiles. In addition, fintech and mobile money applications have proven effective in generating credit records for smallholders, and this information can be harnessed by traditional banks to identify good risks among smallholder farmers. The main areas for public interventions include policies that lay the foundations for innovation and scaling out of digital technologies, expansion of rural broadband and supporting infrastructure, and collecting and digitizing plot-level data on farmers to provide the foundations for building platforms and innovations for service delivery.

REFORMING THE AGRIBUSINESS-ENABLING ENVIRONMENT

Nigeria has made significant improvements in the overall business-enabling environment and agriculture sector policies. Recent policy reforms must be fully operationalized to generate results and maintain the momentum to address the remaining gaps. The climate for doing business is improving,[4] but Nigeria ranks 131 out of 190 in the World Bank ease of doing business survey 2020, far behind the top countries in Sub-Saharan Africa—Rwanda (38) and Kenya (56). In addition, the agribusiness-enabling environment has improved significantly with the passage of the National Agricultural Seeds Council Act 2019 and the National Fertilizer Quality (Control) Act 2019, and with significant progress on the Plant Variety Protection Bill and the legal and regulatory framework for warehouse receipts (table ES.1). Because those acts have not been fully operationalized, however, there is important unfinished business to translate the legal and policy frameworks into action plans for implementation. Specific issues in the enabling environment are discussed in the following paragraphs, focusing on seed development and quality control, fertilizer quality control, the warehouse receipt system, agricultural trade, and land reforms.

TABLE ES.1 Critical actions to operationalize reforms in Nigeria and expected impacts of reforms

	CRITICAL ACTIONS TO OPERATIONALIZE REFORMS	POTENTIAL IMPACTS OF REFORMS
Seed development and quality control	• NASC to develop and publicize written **procedures and guidelines for the private sector to access germplasm from public sources** for carrying out research to generate early generation seeds and for seed multiplication. *(Currently no guidelines are available, but two seed companies have accessed germplasm; there's also need for wholistic review of NASC operational standards to ensure consistency with international standards, especially ISTA and UPOV.)*	• Increased private sector participation in seed development, multiplication, and marketing to farmers
	• NASC and private sector seed companies to **jointly develop and implement business models for PPPs** in the production of early generation seed to alleviate the persistent problem of inadequate supplies *(various PPP options are currently being considered).*	• Removal of low-quality and fake seeds from the market • Increased availability of quality seeds, including imported seeds
	• NASC to develop and roll out **protocols for decentralizing seed quality assurance through third parties** such as private seed inspectors and laboratories *(currently only cassava is covered on a pilot basis).*	• Increased crop productivity and production
	• NASC to finalize and roll out the implementation of **regulations and SOPs (and technical capacity) to recognize and protect breeders' intellectual property rights,** consistent with the Plant Variety Protection Bill, especially as it relates to conducting distinctiveness, stability, and uniformity tests required to grant property rights.	
	• The Seed Registration and Release Subcommittee should **develop and publicize (1) the testing requirements for varieties imported for seed production and (2) the requirements for seeds imported for commercialization, distinguishing between ECOWAS countries versus outside the ECOWAS region.** The advisory is needed because of the lack of a functional and verifiable seed catalogue system in ECOWAS region.	
	• NASC to assess the **efficiency, transparency, and cost-effectiveness of its variety release system** and update the system to ensure consistency with international best practice.	
	• FMARD and NASC to finalize and roll out implementation of **SOPs for seed inspectors** to carry out the duties and obligations specified in the National Agricultural Seeds Council Act 2019.	

continued

TABLE ES.1, *continued*

	CRITICAL ACTIONS TO OPERATIONALIZE REFORMS	POTENTIAL IMPACTS OF REFORMS
Fertilizer quality control	• FMARD has established digital platforms for fertilizer companies (manufacturers, blenders, and agro-dealers) to apply for registration, provide feedback, and capture activities of field inspectors. **But sensitization of the end user of fertilizers—farmers and farmer organizations—remains weak. The platform could be expanded with modules that enable sensitization and education of these stakeholders on the fertilizer reforms**—as well as feedback mechanisms. • **Integrate the feedback and information generated from the digital platforms with extension services** to provide continuous communications campaigns targeted to farmers and farmer organizations on effective quality control of fertilizers, the concept of plot-specific fertilization based on small area soil testing, and the opportunities available with fertilizer blending to meet plot specific nutrient requirements. • **Finalize and disseminate the SOPs for fertilizer testing** so that testing protocols are harmonized between the reference lab in the country and private sector labs to ensure comparability of results, especially in cases where litigation is involved. • FMARD to **develop SOPs for fertilizer inspectors** to carry out the duties and obligations specified in the National Fertilizer Quality (Control) Act 2019, including inspections of premises handling fertilizers and taking official samples for analysis. • FMARD to develop **regulations that require fertilizer manufacturers and blenders to put satisfactory security features on product packages to enable tracing the source of adulteration.**	• Increased private sector importation and marketing of fertilizers • Improved fertilizer availability, especially to smallholder farmers • Improved quality of fertilizers in the market • Increased crop productivity and production
Warehouse receipt system	• **Gazettement of rules developed by the Securities and Exchange Commission** to provide the regulatory environment for warehouse receipts in lieu of the Warehouse Receipts (and Other Related Matters) Bill 2019. • Provide for certification of warehouses based on existing rules and regulations, **in a manner that is credible and based on the independent assessment of reliable evaluators of assets, usually by private sector agencies.** • **Enable admission of warehouse receipts in the collateral registry** so that the financial instrument could be registered in a designated, reliable, easy-to-register, and easy-to-search registry. • **Build capacity of farmers organizations** to understand how to use the warehouse receipt instruments, their rights and obligations, grades and standards for commodities, proper postharvest handling before warehousing, and so on.	• Increased private sector investments in warehousing and improved standards of collateral management and quality of facilities • Increased farmer access to finance through warehouse receipts • Increased farmer access to large buyers • Reduced transaction costs • Improved price discovery, especially for farmers who tend to have less market information • Reduced postharvest loss and waste
Agricultural exports	• **Establish electronic phytosanitary system to streamline export procedures and issue phytosanitary certificates on site.** • Reduce the time and cost of obtaining mandatory, agriculture-specific, per-shipment export documents. • Rationalize fees on exports levied by the Nigeria Export Levy and the Nigeria Export Supervision Scheme to avoid double taxation and remove bureaucratic hurdles for obtaining support from the Nigerian Export Promotion Council.	• Increased exports of agricultural commodities • Improved service delivery and confidence of actors in export value chains

Source: Original compilation for this book.
Note: ECOWAS = Economic Community of West African States; FMARD = Federal Ministry of Agriculture and Rural Development; ISTA = International Seed Testing Association; NASC = National Agricultural Seeds Council; PPP = public-private partnership; SOPs = standard operating procedures; UPOV = International Union for the Protection of New Varieties of Plants.

Seed development and quality control

Among the major reforms embedded in the National Agricultural Seeds Council Act 2019 is that it empowers the council to encourage the establishment of seed companies for the purpose of carrying out research, production, processing, and marketing of seed. The act recognizes plant breeders' rights but has no specific measures to protect those rights beyond empowering the council to approve and implement programs and measures to protect the rights. Private companies can access early generation seed if their registration allows handling of the seed. The act does not allow varieties already registered in another country to be automatically approved for commercialization; however, it empowers the Minister of Agriculture and Rural Development to, on the advice of the Seed Registration and Release Subcommittee, waive the testing requirements if an imported variety is already registered under a regional variety release system. For foreign varieties not registered under a regional release system, the subcommittee is empowered to determine the required "limited multi-locational verification trial" according to its rules and procedures. The new act does not require varieties for exports or varieties to produce commodities for exports to be subject to variety release or registration requirements unless required by the importing country. However, the related legislation on phytosanitary and bio-safety controls apply.

Several aspects of the seed quality control system will be strengthened when the new act is operationalized. The reforms would ultimately enable the removal of poor-quality seeds from the market and increase transparency in quality control processes. In particular, the new act clarifies the functions of seed inspectors and provides them sufficient powers to take samples of any seeds of any variety from any person or entity marketing or purchasing seed, carry out seed testing, search premises handling seed, and carry out field inspections necessary to monitor seed production and certification. The act not only encourages random market inspections but also stipulates clear penalties for sale of mislabeled seed bags. However, private seed companies or third parties, including private laboratories, still cannot certify seed in Nigeria nor is a fee schedule for seed certification published, potentially constraining the provision of high-quality seeds to producers throughout the country.

Fertilizer quality control

The National Fertilizer Quality (Control) Act 2019 sets the framework for effective quality control of fertilizers, and its full operationalization is critical. Under the old policy regime, the permit for fertilizer blending, marketing, and distribution was valid for only one year, and the process to obtain it took three months. The brief validity and length of time to obtain the permit were major disincentives for private sector participation in fertilizer business. With the new act, the time to process fertilizer permits decreases from three months to 30 days. Furthermore, the duration of the permit has been increased from one year to three years, and the owner of a permit need not apply again after three years but instead pays a renewal fee. This provision creates stable expectations among the private sector and has the potential to catalyze more investments in the fertilizer business. The act also provides elaborate procedures and timelines for conflict resolution when a permit or certificate of registration is canceled. In addition, the act sets a framework for effective quality control of fertilizers.

It provides a detailed account of prohibited activities, offenses, and penalties in fertilizer handling and trade, including operating without registration, selling fertilizers that contain destructive ingredients or properties that are harmful to a plant group, repurposing fertilizers to other uses, and obstructing duly authorized officers from carrying out their enforcement and regulatory functions. The new law specifies inspection and enforcement actions, including the power to enter and inspect, take official samples for analysis, and issue orders that stop the sale or disposal of fertilizers whenever there is a reasonable cause. It stipulates labeling requirements, including the maximum allowable quantity deviations between the label and the physical samples.

Warehouse receipt system

Completion of the legal and regulatory framework for a warehouse receipt system (WRS) is critical. A WRS enables farmers and traders to access finance by liquidating part of the value of their nonperishable commodities while searching for better prices. The system is composed of the following parties: depositors of commodities—mainly farmers, farmer organizations, and traders; warehousing facilities and collateral management services; banks and financial institutions; and buyers of commodities and warehouse receipts, including traders, millers, exporters, and so on. The laws and regulatory frameworks for the WRS do not operate in isolation but rather work in parallel with broader laws defining negotiable instruments, passage of title for goods, use of assets as collateral, bankruptcy laws, contract laws, and so on. The Warehouse Receipts (and Other Related Matters) Bill 2019 did not receive presidential assent because some stakeholders were concerned that the bill ignored existing legislation that was already regulating some aspects of WRS . The lack of support for the bill means that there are still gaps in the legal and regulatory framework, and any warehouse receipts issued are not negotiable instruments and cannot be used as collateral in the commercial banking sector.

Land reforms to facilitate responsible agribusiness investments

The framework for land administration is ambiguous and nonuniform across states and lacks sufficient protections for the large number of agricultural households that derive livelihoods directly from the land. The lack of standardized requirements for land transfers and the uncertainty of property rights contribute to thin land markets and weakened incentives for long-term investments by landholders. The legal framework for land administration consists of the Land Use Act of 1978 and the Urban and Regional Planning Act, Decree No. 88, of 1992. The state governments control land administration within their state boundaries through executive governors who have legal authority to make any decisions on land administration in their states. In addition to the acts and the authority vested with the executive governors, legitimate customary and religious practices and norms often have the force of law. The ambiguous framework for land administration has encouraged informal land transfers that do not afford enough protections to the parties and do not create stable expectations to encourage investments on land. It is estimated that nearly 70 percent of land transactions are informal (Butler 2012) and only 3 percent of the land is formally registered.[5] Even private sector companies face enormous challenges when allocated land by state governments because in many cases the land is encumbered with competing claims. For example, out of about 140,406 hectares of land allocated to the private sector by the Ogun state government, investors have been able to occupy only 30 percent[6]—the remaining 70 percent is contested by the communities, and investors have not been able to move in.

The adoption and implementation of the Framework for Responsible and Inclusive Land-Intensive Agricultural Investments (FRILIA) is critical to addressing challenges in land administration for agricultural (and nonagricultural) purposes. Currently, only Ogun and Kaduna states have embarked on the process of adopting FRILIA[7] through the support of World Bank–financed projects.[8] The scaling-out of FRILIA to more states will afford enormous economies of scale and provide communities, investors, and other stakeholders with a modern framework to guide responsible land-based agricultural investments. In particular, the adoption of FRILIA would enable state governments to enhance regulatory, institutional, and operational systems and provisions for land administration to attract private sector investments while protecting existing land-based agricultural livelihoods; addressing competing claims on land without leaving any claimants worse off; and mitigating social and environmental impacts related to land acquisition, resettlement of claimants, and new investments. FRILIA comprises 33 principles organized into the following four principles/pillars: (1) overarching principles, (2) principles on recognizing and protecting land rights, (3) principles on state land acquisition and resettlement, and (4) principles related to environmental and social sustainability (table ES.2).

The four FRILIA principles aim to achieve the following:

- Creation of an enabling environment for investments and improved investor confidence, thus mitigating conflicts arising from competing claims on land allocated to investors.
- Sustainable economic development and growth rooted in environmental and social stability. FRILIA enables complementary investments on land in growth clusters (for example, agribusiness, roads, waste management, and educational institutions) and observes environmental and social safeguards.
- Protection of the rights and economic opportunities of local communities to ensure they benefit optimally from large-scale investments, thus enhancing shared prosperity and broad-based welfare gains from land-based investments.
- Participation of all stakeholders in decision-making around land acquisition and utilization. This approach facilitates capacity building and transfer of technical know-how to local communities and empowers the communities to participate in their own development.
- Establishment of mechanisms for accountability of government institutions by providing toolkits and checklists to formalize the decision process on land acquisition and allocation.
- Effective mitigation of potential environmental and social risks associated with land-intensive investments.

The principles are derived from two internationally negotiated agreements on responsible land-based investments: (1) the Voluntary Guidelines on the Responsible Governance of Tenure of Land, Fisheries, and Forests in the Context of National Food Security; and (2) the United Nations Committee on World Food Security's Principles for Responsible Investment in Agriculture and Food Systems. (Espinosa, Myers, and Vhugen 2019).

TABLE ES.2 Summary of principles of the Framework for Responsible and Inclusive Land-Intensive Agricultural Investments

OVERARCHING FRILIA PRINCIPLES: TRANSPARENCY AND CONSISTENCY WITH DEVELOPMENT POLICY OBJECTIVES	PRINCIPLES ON RECOGNIZING AND PROTECTING LAND RIGHTS	PRINCIPLES ON STATE LAND ACQUISITION AND RESETTLEMENT	PRINCIPLES RELATED TO ENVIRONMENTAL AND SOCIAL SUSTAINABILITY
• Investments should be consistent with and contribute to policy objectives, including poverty eradication, food security, sustainable land use, employment creation, and support to local communities. • Investments should occur transparently. • Land acquisition and related adverse impacts will as much as possible be minimized or avoided. • A range of investment and production models should be considered, including alternatives to large-scale transfer of land. • Investments should be subject to consultation and participation and should include the disadvantaged and vulnerable, who will be informed of their rights and assisted to negotiate. • Communities have opportunity and responsibility to decide, on the basis of informed choices, whether to make land available. • Investments should be monitored.	• Investments should safeguard against dispossession of legitimate tenure-rights holders. • Existing legitimate rights, including customary and informal, and rights to common property resources, should be systematically and impartially identified. • Provide for protection of rights through grievance redress mechanisms that provide accessible and affordable procedures for third-party settlement of disputes, including but not limited to disputes arising from displacement or resettlement. These mechanisms should consider the availability of judicial recourse and community and traditional dispute resolution mechanisms.	• Compensation standards are to be disclosed and applied consistently. • Economic and social impacts caused by land acquisition or loss of access to natural resources shall be identified and addressed, including for people who may lack full legal rights to assets or resources they use or occupy. • Adequate compensation will be provided to purchase replacement assets of equivalent value and to meet any necessary transitional expenses before taking land or restricting access. • Supplemental livelihood improvement or restoration measures will be provided if taking land causes loss of income-generating opportunities. • Public infrastructure and community services that may be adversely affected will be replaced/restored. • Displaced persons with land-based livelihoods should be offered an option for replacement land unless equivalent land is not available. • Principles specific to compensation, resettlement, and livelihood restoration.	• Safeguard against environmental damage, unless adequately mitigated. • Investments should be preceded by independent assessments of potential positive and negative impacts on tenure rights, food security, livelihoods, and environment. • Consider potential adverse impacts on physical cultural property, and, as warranted, provide adequate measures to avoid, minimize, or mitigate such efforts. • Promote community, individual, and worker safety. • Promote fair treatment, nondiscrimination, and equal opportunity of workers; prevent all forms of forced and child labor. • Promote use of recognized good practices related to hazardous materials generated.

Source: Based on Espinosa, Myers, and Vhugen 2019.
Note: FRILIA = Framework for Responsible and Inclusive Land-Intensive Agricultural Investments.

COMPETITIVENESS AND INVESTMENT PRIORITIES IN SELECTED VALUE CHAINS

With the aim to identify sources of competitiveness and policy priorities in selected value chains in Nigeria (table ES.3), the analysis benchmarks yields, costs, prices, and other aspects of competitiveness with similar value chains in Vietnam. Vietnam was chosen as a comparator because the Southeast Asian nation has within the past two decades emerged as a global leader in agribusiness and a top exporter in several commodities and products that are important in Nigeria's agribusiness sector. In 2019, Vietnam generated export earnings of at

TABLE ES.3 **Investment priorities for cashew nuts, rice, cassava, and poultry value chains, Nigeria**

VALUE CHAIN	RECOMMENDED POLICY PRIORITIES
Cashew nuts	• Optimally replace old orchards with improved, higher-yielding, and early maturing varieties. Nigeria lost its leading position in global cashew nut production primarily because it did not replace old orchards.
	• Develop a strategy for the cashew nut subsector in Nigeria that considers removing barriers to importation of RCN from neighboring West African countries to be processed in Nigeria for export markets.
	• Reduce the import tariff regime for RCN to enable the domestic processing industry to access RCN produced from neighboring countries. Nigeria levies a flat 20 percent import duty for both RCN and processed kernel imports. In contrast, in Vietnam the import duty is 5 percent for RCN and 25 percent for processed kernels (most-favored nation rate).
	• Investors in cashew nut processing could aim to move up the value chain and develop niche, branded, and differentiated cashew nut products for direct selling to supermarkets in western countries, including organic and fair-trade labeled products.
	• Embark on strategic improvements in the institutional and enabling environment for the cashew nut subsector. Part of doing so will require strengthening and improving coordination between the federal Cocoa Research Institute of Nigeria (responsible for research and development) and state agencies responsible for transferring seedlings and plant materials to farmers (for example, the state Tree Crops Development Units).
	• Develop a specific policy and strategy for cashew production and export promotion.
	• Establish electronic phytosanitary system to streamline export procedures and issue phytosanitary certificates on site and reduce the time and cost of obtaining mandatory, agriculture-specific, per-shipment export documents.
	• Rationalize fees on exports levied by the Nigeria Export Levy and the Nigeria Export Supervision Scheme to avoid double taxation and remove bureaucratic hurdles for obtaining support from the Nigerian Export Promotion Council.
Rice	• Develop a strategy to increase competitiveness of domestic rice. The supply response from import ban has waned, and trade policy alone will not improve competitiveness in the domestic market.
	• Invest in research and development to develop high-yielding varieties and improve quality attributes of local rice (taste, aroma, texture, and so on) under local growing conditions, coupled with broad-based dissemination to farmers.
	• Coordinate investments between farmers and millers to expand the milling capacity while improving the varieties with desired attributes can increase competitiveness of domestic rice.
	• Transform old cooperatives into new generation cooperatives modeled as producer companies that can take a long-term investment approach to asset building and service provision in critical areas such as input supply, irrigation management, extension management, and marketing.
	• Improve the technology of postharvest drying by farmers to increase rice quality and reduce postharvest losses.
Cassava	• Pursue a dual strategy for transformation of the cassava sector, focusing on increasing the competitiveness of the industrial starch value chain and modernizing the food product value chains to improve quality of garri and high-quality cassava flour.
	• Transform the industrial starch value chain through coordinated investments between researchers, farmers, and the processing sector so that farmers can access varieties that yield high starch content and produce for the specific needs of starch processors under vertical coordination schemes.
	• Complement research and development work with an effective system to transfer clean planting materials to farmers while removing old plants contaminated with cassava mosaic disease, treating soils and providing effective extension to ensure farmers apply correct agronomic practices and proper fertilization.
	• Modernize the value chains for cassava food products with the aim to deliver healthy garri and high-quality cassava flour to meet increased demand for healthy diets and meet the needs of the milling and baking industries.
	• Coordinate investments between the cassava flour milling sector and upstream segments (farmers and researchers) to help expand the market for high-quality, differentiated garri products, including by supplying farmers with varieties that are low in starch and with better taste.

continued

TABLE ES.3, *continued*

VALUE CHAIN	RECOMMENDED POLICY PRIORITIES
Poultry	• The government may revisit the policy of banning chicken imports because it has slowed growth of the poultry consumption market. Annual per capita consumption of chicken meat in Nigeria considerably lags countries with comparable per capita incomes.
	• Vertical coordination between poultry production in the South and the feed segment in the North provides significant opportunities for regional collaboration and growth.
	• Priority reforms for the poultry feed segment include specification and enforcement of standards to ensure the quality of feeds, including standards for maximum allowable levels of mycotoxins, heavy metals, and microorganisms in feed ingredients and compound feeds as well as regular inspection, sampling, and testing of feeds by the Ministry of Agriculture and Rural Development and market inspection agencies.
	• Collaboration between private investors and public veterinary health authorities would expand investments in breeding for high-yielding birds and production of vaccines and drugs.
	• Access to energy is a major constraint faced by the poultry industry in Nigeria. There are enormous investment opportunities in efficient poultry waste management to generate biogas energy and soil fertilizers.

Source: Original compilation for this book.
Note: RCN = raw cashew nuts.

least US$3 billion from each of the following commodities—cashew nuts, rice, cassava, fish, coffee, tea, black pepper, and rubber—resulting in total agricultural export revenue of US$40 billion (World Bank 2020). Those eight value chains have experienced strong export growth, founded on productivity growth in on-farm and off-farm segments and improved coordination of investments across the value chains. Access to remunerative export markets has generated broad-based gains in the incomes of farmers and higher returns for agribusinesses, thus increasing foreign exchange earnings and public revenues.

The strong performance of the agribusiness sector in Vietnam has ushered in a model of structural transformation that could serve Nigeria very well. Agricultural wage rates and farmer incomes increased rapidly between 2010 and 2018, contributing to about 75 percent of the poverty reduction in rural areas (World Bank 2019). The strong performance of agricultural value chains has spurred the rural economy as farm incomes have been invested in rural sectors and created job opportunities outside farming. Perhaps the most interesting feature of Vietnam's model of structural transformation is that labor released from farming has been productively absorbed in the rural nonfarm sector, unlike the usual pattern in which labor migrates to urban sectors leaving rural sectors without the skills or demand for services and goods necessary to catalyze rural development. Although about 80 percent of rural households in Vietnam continue to engage in agriculture, many of those households are increasingly involved in the rural nonfarm sector, and the diversification of income sources has not only raised rural incomes but also increased the resilience of households to economic shocks.

NOTES

1. RIAPA was developed by the International Food Policy Research Institute.
2. This target was set by the government policy document, "Delivering on the Government's Priorities 2019–2023," for the second term of the Buhari presidency.

3. Recent programs include the Nigeria Incentive-Based Risk-Sharing System for Agricultural Lending, Commercial Agriculture Credit Scheme, and Anchor Borrowers Program; however, this study could not obtain data on the performance of those programs.

4. In May 2018 the Senate passed the Companies and Allied Matters Act, which included several major reforms, including new business ownership forms such as sole proprietorships and limited liability companies, improved company registration procedures (including e-signatures for registration), improved insolvency process, and enhanced protection of minority investors. However, it has yet to be passed by the House of Representatives and approved by the Presidency.

5. Data from the Doing Business data set (World Bank, Washington, DC), https://www.doing-business.org/en/data/exploreeconomies/Nigeria.

6. Data provided by Ogun State government during consultations on the World Bank financed Ogun State Economic Transformation Project. The project is supporting (among other investments) the adoption of the Framework for Responsible Investments in Land-Intensive Agriculture Investments (FRILIA).

7. The state of Jigawa has adopted the Land Acquisition and Resettlement Framework (LARF).

8. Kaduna State Economic Transformation Program for Results and Ogun State Economic Transformation Project.

REFERENCES

Beintema, Nienke, Abdullahi M. Nasir, and Lang Gao. 2017. "Agricultural R&D Indicators Factsheet: Nigeria." International Food Policy Research Institute and Agricultural Research Council of Nigeria.

Butler, S. 2012. "Nigerian Land Markets and the Land Use Law of 1978." Focus on Land in Africa, Gates Open Research. https://gatesopenresearch.org/documents/3-1414.

Espinosa D., G. Myers, and D. Vhugen. 2019. "Towards Responsible Agricultural Investment in Kaduna State." Unpublished manuscript.

World Bank. 2019. "Better Opportunities for All: Vietnam Poverty and Shared Prosperity Update," World Bank, Washington, DC.

World Bank. 2020. "Improving Agricultural Interventions under the New National Target Programs in Vietnam." World Bank, Washington, DC.

1 Introduction: Agriculture in the (Elusive) Diversification Agenda

Nigeria has for a long time placed enormous emphasis on diversifying its economy to nonoil productive sectors.[1] Agriculture has always been considered an important part of the nonoil sectors to drive diversification, most recently as outlined in the Economic Recovery and Growth Plan (ERGP) 2017–20 and Economic Sustainability Plan (ESP) 2020. The ERGP aimed to restore economic growth following the 2015–16 recession and to lay the foundations for long-term structural change. It recognized the need to diversify the economy to nonoil productive sectors such as agriculture and agro-allied industries in order to create an economy that can generate inclusive growth and jobs. In particular, the ERGP identified the following key execution priorities: stabilizing the macroeconomic environment, achieving agriculture and food security, ensuring energy efficiency (power and petroleum products), improving transportation infrastructure, and driving industrialization focusing on small and medium enterprises. The ESP was launched in July 2020 to mitigate the adverse impacts of the COVID-19 (coronavirus) crisis and provide the foundation for a robust recovery. The ESP lays out a package of policy measures and short-term programs over 12–18 months, including a Mass Agricultural Programme to bring between 20,000 and 100,000 hectares of new farmland under cultivation in every state of the federation "with the aim to create millions of job opportunities, directly or indirectly, over a 12-month period." Similar programs are envisioned in roads, renewables, and housing.

Why has Nigeria's diversification agenda remained elusive? The lack of progress could be blamed on weak implementation and misalignment of public spending but often reflects more profound underlying issues. One perspective worth considering is that there is a real lack of clarity or consensus on which nonoil sectors are worth diversifying into, the specific segments to target, and the expected outcomes on jobs, poverty reduction, and so on. For example, simply proclaiming that agriculture should be central to the diversification agenda without providing sound assessment of expected outcomes does not do anything to advise policy makers and budget holders. It also fails to provide development practitioners with the information, inspiration, and conviction to develop and execute reforms and programs that could help operationalize the diversification agenda.

This book offers to advance understanding of the potential of the agribusiness sector (primary agriculture plus off-farm agribusinesses) to contribute to economic diversification in Nigeria. The book comes at a time when the country is recovering from the worst recession in four decades (World Bank 2020). The evidence presented here can inform policy reforms and help set investment priorities to accelerate inclusive recovery, create jobs, and reduce poverty. First, drawing on unique data from national accounts and supply-use tables, chapter 2 recalibrates national accounts to identify and estimate the size of various segments of the agribusiness sector—primary agriculture, input supply, agricultural processing, agricultural trading and transportation services, food services, and hotels. The enriched data enable the assessment of the performance of these agribusiness segments, individually and collectively, in generating growth, jobs, and labor productivity over the past decade (2009–18). This period was marked by prerecession volatility, recession, and postrecession recovery, similar in many ways to the current economic situation and the near-term challenges going forward. Performance in this period is quite instructive and provides useful evidence on the economic segments that can drive inclusive recovery from the 2020 recession. The main finding is that the agribusiness sector provides perhaps the best prospects to accelerate inclusive recovery and growth while generating more and better jobs.

Second, building on the evidence that the agribusiness sector is critical to accelerating inclusive recovery and jobs, chapter 3 proceeds to identify the specific agricultural value chain groups that have the most potential to create jobs within the agribusiness sector and in the broader economy. In addition to job creation, the agribusiness sector plays other important roles in development, including supporting the livelihoods of poor and vulnerable households and providing nutritious foods to support human capital development. Because Nigeria has a poverty headcount ratio nearly three times higher in rural areas than in urban areas and a majority of its rural poor derive their livelihoods from agriculture, a plausible approach to reduce poverty could consider catalyzing productivity in the activities that the poor are engaged in and in the areas where they live. A key finding in chapter 3 is that the specific value chains with the most potential to create jobs are not necessarily the most effective in reducing poverty or improving nutrition, clearly calling for selectivity of value chains depending on policy objectives. Another important finding is that the growth burden to meet any specific jobs targets is lower when both on-farm and off-farm segments of agribusiness grow in tandem and higher if either segment stagnates. Clearly, a whole-of-agribusiness approach is needed to accelerate inclusive recovery and jobs creation.

Third, this work highlights the complex set of factors that mediate the performance of agricultural value chains, distinguishing between issues that pertain to primary agriculture and those that mainly affect off-farm agribusiness. Analysis of the agribusiness-enabling environment takes center stage in chapter 4, drawing from ongoing consultations on policy reforms with government and stakeholders around seed development and quality control, fertilizer quality control, warehouse receipt systems, and responsible land administration for agricultural investments. In addition, chapter 4 focuses on competitive factors that operate within the broader macroeconomic environment, trade policies, and sectoral policies and institutions to ultimately determine the performance of the primary agriculture and off-farm agribusiness segments in terms of productivity, growth, jobs creation, competitiveness, and so on. The analysis of competitive factors draws from recent household surveys and multicountry Enterprise Surveys. A major conclusion of the chapter is that, although the agribusiness-enabling environment has improved substantially, a significant reforms agenda still needs to be operationalized.

Fourth, the book builds on the foregoing evidence to dive deeper into assessing opportunities for increasing the competitiveness of specific value chains with the most potential to create jobs and reduce poverty. The specific commodities are cashew nuts (chapter 5), rice (chapter 6), cassava (chapter 7), and poultry (chapter 8). The approach taken in these chapters benchmarks performance of these commodities with Vietnam, a country that has within the past two decades emerged as a global leader in agribusiness and a top exporter in several commodities and products that are important in Nigeria's agribusiness sector. Furthermore, the strong performance of the agribusiness sector in Vietnam has ushered a model of structural transformation that could serve Nigeria very well.

The remainder of this introductory chapter discusses the main reasons why diversification has preoccupied economic policy making, including the history of noninclusive growth without jobs and its limited impact on the World Bank's twin goals of poverty reduction and shared prosperity. The centrality of agriculture in the diversification agenda is founded on its inclusiveness and resilience, which is discussed briefly as a prelude to a more compelling analysis in the rest of the book. This introductory chapter ends by assessing progress on the agriculture targets in the most recent diversification policy—the ERGP 2017–20.

WHY DIVERSIFICATION PREOCCUPIES ECONOMIC POLICY MAKING

Growth in Nigeria has been noninclusive, illustrating a weak association between growth and jobs. Nigeria's growth patterns in the last two decades could be grouped into the following four periods: consistent growth (2000–10); prerecession volatility (2010–14); recession and recovery (2015–19); and the COVID-19 pandemic (2020). During the first period, the economy grew on average by more than 6 percent annually; however, the unemployment rate hardly responded and instead remained nearly flat at about 4 percent (figure 1.1). Next, the prerecession period was marked by annual growth declining for the first time in nearly a decade by more than 4 percentage points: from 8.0 percent in 2010 to 3.7 percent in 2012. Although growth recovered by about 3 percentage points by 2014, the recovery was short lived and lasted for only about two years before the economy went into recession. The volatile and declining growth trend in this prerecession period is associated with an upward trend in the unemployment rate, starting around 2013. That the unemployment rate was relatively flat during the strong growth period but rose during the volatile and declining growth period demonstrates an asymmetrical response of unemployment to growth. The patterns suggest that, with the current structure of the economy, sustained growth may not reduce the unemployment rate, but declining growth leads to rising unemployment. The economy worsened after 2014, leading to the recession of 2015–16. The unemployment rate continued to increase with negative growth, with unemployment reaching about 8 percent in 2016 and remaining flat in the recovery period (2017–18). The COVID-19 pandemic has plunged the economy to its worst recession in four decades (World Bank 2020), and many jobs will be lost in manufacturing and services.

FIGURE 1.1

A decade of strong economic growth did not reduce the unemployment rate, but volatility and declining growth quickly led to rising unemployment, Nigeria, 2000–21

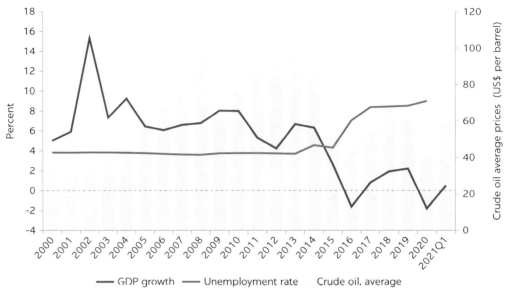

Sources: World Development Indicators and World Commodity Price Data.

The dependence on oil severely limits the ability of the economy to absorb shocks. A key feature of Nigeria's economy is its dependence on oil, a commodity that has faced rapidly fluctuating prices in the last five years alone. This dependence can be traced to the 1960s when exports of crude oil and gas increased sharply, providing a stream of enormous revenues to the government. The oil boom diverted attention away from other sectors like agriculture and manufacturing, and these sectors became less competitive. For example, in 2019 agriculture contributed 2 percent to exports and manufacturing contributed less than 7 percent. By contrast, oil contributed about 90 percent of export earnings, 30 percent of banking sector credit, and more than 50 percent of the revenue of federal and state governments in 2011–15, although its share in gross domestic product (GDP) was about 10 percent. High oil prices lead to strong economic growth and vice versa. The COVID-19 pandemic reduced global demand for oil, leading to a rapid fall in prices. Government revenues are projected to drop by US$12 billion (3 percent of GDP) or more because of falling oil prices, and the contraction of economic activities will further reduce internally generated revenues (World Bank 2020). The loss of revenues severely constrains the ability of the government to respond with fiscal measures to protect economic activity and accelerate recovery.

Global experience shows that economies that record significant growth with limited job creation—as often happens in resource-rich countries—tend to have limited poverty reduction and increasing inequality, primarily because the benefits of growth are narrowly shared and hardly benefit the poor. Poverty is a major problem in Nigeria, and previous years of robust economic growth have had little impact (map 1.1). The national poverty headcount ratio was 40 percent in 2019 based on the national poverty line (NBS 2019), which is relatively high by middle-income country standards yet masks even higher rates of poverty in rural areas and northern parts of the country. For example, the poverty headcount

MAP 1.1

The poverty headcount rate was more than 61 percent in many northern states in Nigeria, 2019

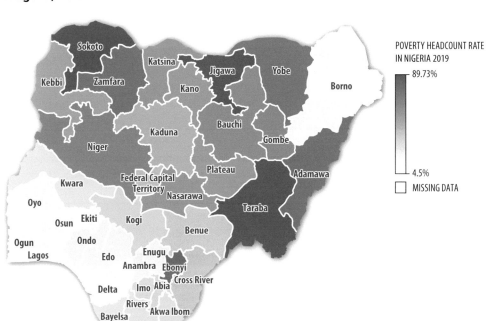

IBRD 46204 | OCTOBER 2021

Source: Based on data provided by National Bureau of Statistics, Nigeria.

ratio in rural areas is 52 percent compared to 18 percent in urban areas and is more than 61 percent in most northern states compared to less than 20 percent in most southern states.

Nigeria's history of growth without inclusion and jobs has not only had limited impact on reducing poverty and inequality but also created conditions for social unrest. The national poverty rate is expected to increase from 40 percent in 2019 to 42.5 percent in 2020 as the economy contracts because of the COVID-19 pandemic. Experience around the world shows that persistent poverty and joblessness, especially among youth, can lead to social unrest and civil strife. The last quarter of 2020 witnessed social disturbances that betray a sense of hopelessness and despair among youth who lack opportunities to pursue their aspirations.

WHY AGRICULTURE FEATURES STRONGLY IN THE DIVERSIFICATION AGENDA

Agriculture is the most resilient sector in Nigeria, which helps to protect the livelihoods of millions during tough economic times. Its resilience, however, is partly due to weak links with the rest of the economy. Agriculture was the only sector without negative growth during the 2015–16 recession and was the most stable sector in the turbulent years preceding it (figure 1.2). The relative stability of agriculture compared to other sectors (manufacturing, services, and industry) helps to protect the more than 70 percent of the population either directly employed in the sector or dependent on it for their livelihoods. Experience from

FIGURE 1.2

Agriculture is the most resilient sector, protecting livelihoods and jobs during tough economic times

Sectoral growth patterns, Nigeria, 2004–21

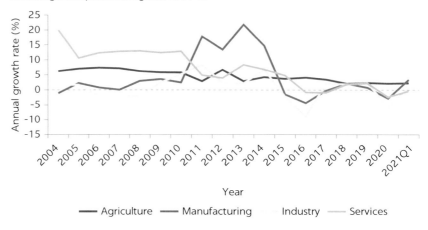

Source: World Development Indicators, World Bank.

previous economic downturns shows that many jobs are lost in the more volatile sectors—manufacturing, industry, and services—during hard economic times. Many people losing jobs in those sectors retreat to productive employment in agriculture, making it a productive safety net for vulnerable workers across the country. Agriculture is the most pro-poor sector in Nigeria and has unrealized potential to deliver broad-based, inclusive economic growth and poverty reduction. A competitive agriculture sector can contribute to foreign exchange savings and earnings through import substitution and exports. Nonoil exports are dominated by agricultural products, representing up to 70 percent of the value of nonoil exports.[2] In addition, agriculture contributes significantly to national food security, by accounting for a large proportion of total food consumption requirements, and to livelihood resilience in conflict and postconflict environments.

The resiliency of the sector was harshly tested by the COVID-19 pandemic. Social distancing and restrictions on movement led to contraction in the supply of labor for agriculture production. The effects were more pronounced in labor-intensive farming systems that depend on migrant and hired labor and smallholder farms that rely on "labor-go-round" arrangements in which villagers descend on one farm at a time to carry out land preparation and planting activities. Restrictions on interstate movement disrupted supply networks for seeds, fertilizers, agrochemicals, and technical advice. These inputs became less available and more costly, reducing farmers' demand for the inputs and leading to reduced area under cultivation.

The functioning of food supply chains was disrupted as movement restrictions left farmers without buyers, whereas consumers experienced food shortages in the markets. Farm-level food loss and waste increased because farmers could not find markets, especially for perishable commodities such as fruits and vegetables, tomatoes, dairy and meat products, and fish. A household survey conducted in May–April 2020 shows that 80 percent of rural and urban households faced an increase in prices of major food items consumed, 55 percent of rural respondents faced increases in prices of farming/business inputs, and nearly 30 percent of rural households faced falling prices of farming/business outputs

(Lain et al. 2020). A follow-on survey conducted in the middle of the planting season showed that about 38 percent of households engaged in agriculture made significant changes because of the pandemic. Of these affected households, about 52 percent reduced area planted, 30 percent cultivated crops that take less time to mature, and 25 percent did not plant on time (Siwatu et al. 2020). Primary agriculture grew by an estimated 1.7 percent in the first three quarters of 2020 compared to 2.4 percent during the same period in 2019.

PERFORMANCE ON ERGP AGRICULTURE TARGETS

Performance on the ERGP agriculture targets has been weak. The ERGP set specific targets related to growth in agriculture GDP, achieving food self-sufficiency, and transitioning from importer to exporter in selected commodities; however, most of the targets have not been achieved. Specific targets for agriculture GDP growth were 5.03 percent in 2017, 7.04 percent in 2018, 7.23 percent in 2019, and 8.37 percent in 2020. Reaching those targets would have meant increasing agricultural GDP from 16.0 trillion Nigerian naira (N) in 2015 to N21.0 trillion in 2020 at an average annual growth rate of 6.92 percent. Agricultural GDP growth in 2017–19 missed the targets by wide margins (figure 1.3). Furthermore, agricultural GDP growth in 2020 contracted because of the COVID-19 pandemic, missing the higher 2020 target by an even wider margin. In addition to growth, the ERGP aimed for self-sufficiency in rice (2018), tomato paste (2017), and wheat (2019/2020), and improved terms of trade that would turn the country into a net exporter of fish, poultry meat, palm oil, groundnuts, cashew nuts, and other edible oil. The goal of becoming self-sufficient in rice was achieved in 2019 on the back of supply response to import restrictions but has been missed for tomato paste and wheat. The goal to become a net exporter for various commodities has been missed for tomatoes, vegetable oil, groundnuts, cassava, poultry, fish, and livestock.

FIGURE 1.3

Nigeria's ERGP targets on agriculture growth were missed by wide margins in 2017–19

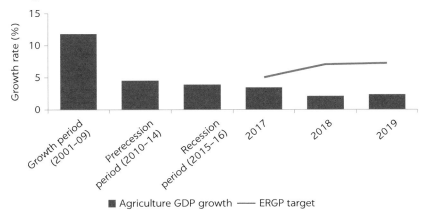

Source: Economic Recovery and Growth Plan (ERGP), 2017–19; National Bureau of Statistics, Nigeria.

Agricultural growth in the postrecession recovery period was driven by a broad range of subsectors, including cereals, cash crops, and vegetables. The fastest average annual production growth occurred in millet, a cereal food staple grown mainly in the northern parts of the country (figure 1.4). Growth was from a relatively low base because the crop had recorded negative growth in the prerecession period. A turnaround occurred during the recession and production soared to more than 20 percent average annual growth in the postrecession period. Other agricultural subsectors that performed well in the postrecession period include sesame, which has emerged as a major export crop in recent years, and soybean. The latter are grown mostly in Nigeria's Middle-Belt and are becoming an increasingly important source of animal feed for the poultry and fish sectors in the southern states. Both sesame and soybean performed well before the recession, but growth dipped during the recession and then recovered by more than 10 percent in 2017–18. Tomato and wheat recorded significant growth—8 percent and 5 percent, respectively—in the postrecession period, a remarkable expansion considering that these subsectors contracted by –8 percent and –17 percent, respectively, during the recession.

Expansion of area under cultivation was the dominant source of production growth, except for tomatoes and sesame because growth in those subsectors was driven by higher yields. Yields for tomatoes increased by 27.4 percent, but area under cultivation contracted by about –14 percent. Sesame had a more balanced increase in yields (6.96 percent) and expansion in area under cultivation (5.99 percent), indicating that both sources of growth are important in a commodity that is becoming increasingly significant for exports. In contrast, there was a major drop in yields for wheat (–11.1 percent) although area under cultivation rapidly expanded by 17.6 percent. Yields for the rest of the commodities did not change appreciably—cocoa beans (–1.58 percent), millet (1.41 percent), soybean (0.78 percent).

Rice contracted after the recession, which is notable because the subsector grew rapidly before and during the recession, driven by expansion of area under cultivation. Average annual production growth in the postrecession period

FIGURE 1.4

Agricultural subsectors that drove growth after the 2015–16 recession in Nigeria

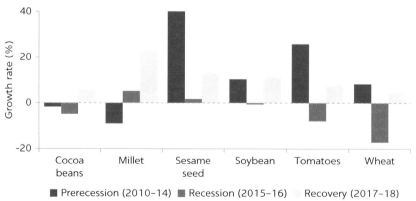

Source: FAOSTAT (Statistics Division, Food and Agriculture Organization of the United Nations) and National Bureau of Statistics, Nigeria.

FIGURE 1.5

Agricultural subsectors that contracted after the 2015–16 recession in Nigeria

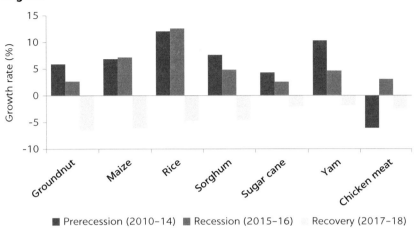

Source: FAOSTAT (Statistics Division, Food and Agriculture Organization of the United Nations) and National Bureau of Statistics, Nigeria.

contracted to about –5 percent after growing steadily by more than 12 percent between 2010 and 2016 (figure 1.5). The earlier growth was fueled by import restrictions that not only resulted in a steep decline in official imports to near zero by 2019 but also increased domestic production. The production growth, however, was driven by expansion in area under cultivation, which increased from 6.74 percent in 2010–14 to 10.63 percent during the recession. Clearly, the expansion of area under cultivation could not be sustained, and there was negative growth of –5.23 percent in cultivated area in 2017–18. It is important to note that rice yields have remained persistently low relative to major producers in the world. In addition to rice, several major food and industrial commodities posted growth before and during the recession but then contracted afterward. These commodities include maize, sorghum, groundnuts, sugarcane, and yams. Production growth in chicken meat has been quite uneven, recording negative growth of about –6.1 percent in 2010–14, followed by mild recovery during the recession and back to negative growth afterward.

NOTES

1. For example, long before the 2015–16 recession, the National Economic Empowerment and Development Strategy (2004) outlined a strategy for private sector development focusing on diversification to nonoil sources of growth, among other objectives.
2. World Bank Group staff calculation based on online data from Nigeria's National Bureau of Statistics (NBS).

REFERENCES

Lain, Jonathan W., Julie T. T. Perng, Tara Vishwanath, M. Abul Kalam Azad, Gbemisola O. Siwatu, Amparo Palacios-Lopez, Kevin R. Mcgee, Akuffo Amankwah, and Ivette M. Contreras Gonzalez. 2020. "COVID-19 from the Ground Up: What the Crisis Means for Nigerians." World Bank, Washington, DC.

NBS (National Bureau of Statistics, Nigeria). 2019. "Poverty and Inequality in Nigeria: Executive Summary." National Bureau of Statistics, Abuja.

Siwatu, Gbemisola O., Amparo Palacios-Lopez, Kevin R. Mcgee, Akuffo Amankwah, Tara Vishwanath, M. Abul Kalam Azad, and Jonathan W. Lain. 2020. "Impact of COVID-19 on Nigerian Households: 2nd Round Questionnaire." World Bank, Washington, DC.

World Bank. 2020. "Nigeria in Times of COVID-19: Laying Foundations for a Strong Recovery." Nigeria Development Update, June 2020. World Bank, Washington, DC.

2 Agribusiness for Inclusive Recovery and Jobs

Basic knowledge on the relative size and structure of the agribusiness sector (primary agriculture and off-farm segments) in Nigeria remains sketchy. This is not uncommon because few countries systematically track the size of agribusiness segments in their national accounts. However, because policy dialogue on missed opportunities in Nigeria's agriculture often suggests Nigeria's potential to become the Brazil of Africa, it is worth noting that Brazil actively tracks the dynamics of growth in its agribusiness segments. Brazil has used that information to develop growth strategies that have propelled the country to become a major player in global food and nonfood agricultural systems. In Nigeria, a lack of basic knowledge about the relative size, structure, and dynamics of the agribusiness segments has created uncertainty about the potential of these segments to providing inclusive growth (recovery) and jobs—the key outcomes of the diversification agenda.

What is the potential of the agribusiness sector to accelerate inclusive recovery and create jobs in the economy? That is the overarching question addressed in this chapter. To facilitate the discussion, the analysis begins with an assessment of the size and structure of the sector. By providing this basic yet previously unavailable information, the book enables a better assessment of the extent to which current policies, institutions, and investments have affected transformation. The analysis also compares the structure and size of the sector in Nigeria with middle-income structural peers, regional peers in Sub-Saharan Africa, and high-income aspirational comparator countries that have already achieved transformation. The findings lay a strong foundation to help identify the policy and investment priorities to "build back better" and retool the sector to accelerate recovery from the pandemic and serve the needs of an advanced modern economy. The data and methodology used for the analysis are described in appendix A.

DYNAMICS OF AGRIBUSINESS DURING ECONOMIC TRANSITION

The agribusiness sector includes all farms and firms involved in producing, harvesting, packing, processing, preserving, distributing, marketing, and disposing of food and nonfood agricultural products (figure 2.1). These activities could be classified into the following categories: agriculture, processing, trade and transport, food services, hotels, and inputs. The agriculture segment of agribusiness includes all of the classical agriculture sector gross domestic product (GDP): the primary production of all crops, livestock, forestry, and fishing. The processing segment includes the part of the manufacturing sector GDP that involves processing, value addition, and preservation of food and nonfood agricultural products. Examples include food processing, beverages, tobacco, cotton yarn, and timber. The trade and transport segment includes the part of the services sector GDP that entails transportation, storage, logistics, and trading for agricultural commodities and products between farms, firms, and final consumers. The food services segment is also a part of the classical services sector GDP, involving the preparation and sale of food outside the home (for example, restaurants and street vendors). The hotels segment includes the part of the hotels and accommodation GDP that is associated with the sale of food. The inputs segment includes all GDP generated during domestic production of the inputs used by farmers and processors, excluding the inputs produced by the other five segments.

The off-farm agribusiness segment provides opportunities for more and better jobs during economic transition. As countries transition from lower to higher income, the off-farm agribusiness segment grows much faster than primary agriculture and creates more and better jobs (figure 2.2). These patterns are driven mainly by growing per capita incomes and urbanization. As per capita incomes rise, consumers demand less of the traditional staples and more of the high-value foods like fruits, vegetables, and animal proteins, creating demand and growth in postharvest management services such as sorting, grading, cold storage, packaging, and so on. Food expenditures increase even as the share of food in total expenditure declines (Bennet's Law).

At the same time, increased urbanization concentrates consumer demand in urban areas that are often far from the rural areas where most of food production occurs, creating demand for food transportation, trading, logistics, and value preservation. Workers in urban areas increasingly demand processed foods that are ready to eat or easy to prepare because their time working is more valuable than their time cooking. Increased urbanization and the shift in consumer demand lead to expansion of the agribusiness sector, including cold chains, aggregation and food storage, food processing and nutrition enrichment, logistics and transport, modern retailing, restaurants, food services, and so on. The overall business of providing safe and nutritious food grows rapidly, much faster than primary agriculture, and becomes an engine for transformation, jobs, income growth, and poverty reduction. It is estimated that a successful transformation converges on-farm and off-farm agribusiness GDP at about US$4,000 per capita such that countries at this point on average earn US$1 of agribusiness GDP off the farm for every US$1 earned on the farm (figure 2.2).

Successful transformation depends on productivity growth on the farm and stronger links between on-farm and off-farm agribusiness segments. Agriculture productivity growth creates the conditions necessary for transformation,

FIGURE 2.1

Agribusiness includes primary agriculture and nonfarm food and nonfood agricultural businesses

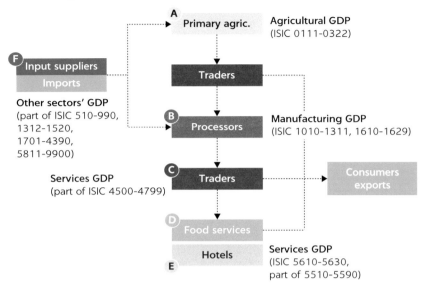

Source: International Food Policy Research Institute.
Note: ISIC refers to the International Standards Industrial Classification, which is the United Nations system used to classify all economic activities. Agric. = agriculture.

FIGURE 2.2

At about US$4,000 per capita, countries earn US$1 of agribusiness GDP off the farm for every US$1 earned on the farm

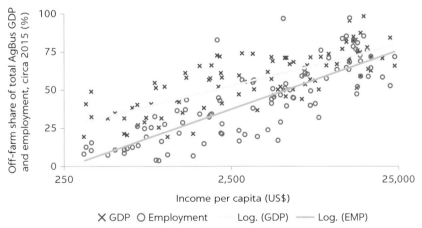

Source: Original calculations for this book using the International Food Policy Research Institute's Rural Investment and Policy Analysis (RIAPA) model and social accounting matrix (SAM).
Note: AgBus = agribusiness.

consistent with the development experience of all countries that started with a large agricultural sector (Christiansen, Demery, and Kuhl 2011; Gollin, Parente, and Rogerson 2007; Johnston and Mellor 1961; McMillan and Headey 2014; Mellor 1995; Timmer 1988). Higher labor productivity in primary agriculture releases agricultural labor from the farm to off-farm agribusiness segments and the broader economy. It stimulates higher wages and creates demand for high-value and more nutritious foods—as well as for other goods and services.

Productivity growth reduces the cost of food, thus increasing real incomes of consumers. Income opportunities for producers increase because they can produce more with fewer resources and at a lower cost. Similarly, agribusinesses in the food processing industry experience lower costs of raw materials, allowing for greater margins and more investments in capital goods that can increase competitiveness in domestic and export markets. In addition to productivity growth, transformation is dependent on stronger links between upstream primary agriculture and the off-farm agribusiness segments. Agribusinesses increasingly move away from spot markets and establish backward linkages, for example contract farming in which farmers produce to meet specific quantity and quality in exchange for better technology of production and services.

AGRIBUSINESS IS CRITICAL FOR INCLUSIVE RECOVERY AND JOBS

Agribusiness is a large part of Nigeria's economy, directly providing more than 50 percent of jobs and contributing more than 35 percent to the national GDP. Primary agriculture is larger than off-farm agribusiness, indicating enormous potential for transformation. Primary agriculture accounts for 21 percent of the national GDP, and off-farm agribusiness contributes 14 percent (figure 2.3). The 1.5-to-1.0 ratio of primary agriculture to off-farm agribusiness GDP indicates that transformation is still in the early stages. Therefore, there are enormous opportunities to design policies and investments to accelerate transformation and create more and better jobs. Currently, a large majority of agribusiness jobs is in primary agriculture (about 21 million), whereas off-farm agribusiness generates about 8 million jobs. The largest off-farm agribusiness segment, in terms

FIGURE 2.3

Agribusiness is a large part of the national economy, with enormous scope for transformation to create more and better jobs

GDP and employment estimates, Nigeria, 2018

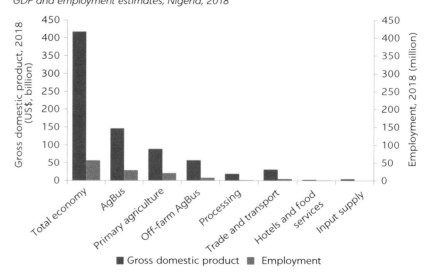

Source: Original calculations for this book using the International Food Policy Research Institute's Rural Investment and Policy Analysis (RIAPA) model and social accounting matrix (SAM).
Note: AgBus = agribusiness.

of both GDP and jobs, is trade and transport; it accounts for 57 percent of the off-farm agribusiness GDP and 62 percent of jobs. The importance of this segment is partly driven by the North–South divide between major production areas and consumption markets—and the segment will likely continue to grow with increased commercialization and urbanization. The processing segment is a relatively small share of off-farm agribusiness, accounting for 31 percent of the off-farm agribusiness GDP and 20 percent of jobs. The input supply segment is about twice the size of the services segments (hotels and food services) in terms of share of off-farm agribusiness GDP. However, the services segments provide three times more jobs than the input supply segment.

Labor productivity (GDP per worker) in agribusiness processing and input supply segments is respectively 1.5 and two times higher than in an average job in the economy. But there are significant differences in labor productivity within the off-farm agribusiness segments (figure 2.4). Labor productivity is highest in the input supply segment (more than twice the economywide average), which indicates that this segment has the highest potential to create better jobs. Agribusiness processing is another segment with enormous potential for better jobs because jobs in this segment are at least 1.5 times more productive than the economywide average. The hotels and food services segments create more jobs per GDP than all other off-farm agribusiness segments, but labor productivity is lowest in hotels and food services. The trade and transport segments have

FIGURE 2.4

Better jobs can be created in agribusiness input supply and processing, Nigeria

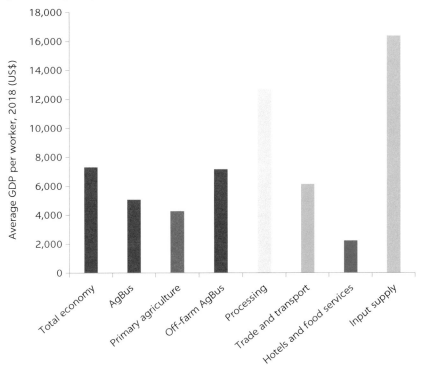

Source: Original calculations for this book using the International Food Policy Research Institute's Rural Investment and Policy Analysis (RIAPA) model and social accounting matrix (SAM).
Note: AgBus = agribusiness.

relatively lower labor productivity than the input supply and processing segments, but trade and transport create more jobs per GDP. For example, figure 2.5 shows that agribusiness trade and transport account for about 40 percent of GDP and nearly 40 percent of jobs in the overall trade and transport segment—whereas agribusiness processing represents nearly half of manufacturing GDP but accounts for about 36 percent of jobs in manufacturing.

With the current low level of transformation, primary agriculture provides more jobs than off-farm agribusiness, but going forward more and better jobs will be created in off-farm agribusiness segments. Primary agriculture currently accounts for about 70 percent of all agribusiness jobs, whereas off-farm segments contribute 30 percent. Off-farm segments generate better jobs, however, because labor productivity off-farm is nearly 1.75 times higher than in primary agriculture, even though calculations of labor productivity for primary agriculture tend to be underestimated when measured as GDP per worker. Because workers in primary agriculture are engaged seasonally and not throughout the year, the GDP attributable to these workers is generated only during the cropping season. It means that the average annual labor productivity measure is biased downward unless corrected for seasonality. Furthermore, primary agriculture also tends to be a residual employer that absorbs low-skilled rural individuals who cannot find jobs elsewhere.

The growth, jobs, and labor productivity outcomes from 2009 to 2018 suggest that the agribusiness sector provides perhaps the best opportunities to accelerate inclusive recovery and jobs creation. That experience is quite instructive and

FIGURE 2.5

More jobs can be created in agribusiness trade and transport and in hotels and food services, Nigeria

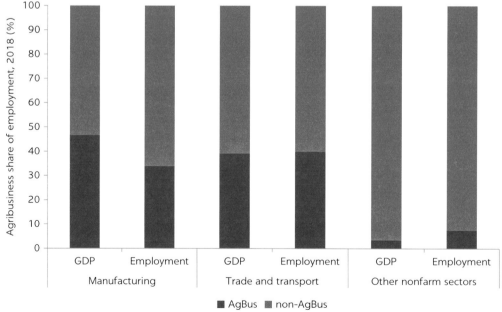

Source: Original calculations for this book using the International Food Policy Research Institute's Rural Investment and Policy Analysis (RIAPA) model and social accounting matrix (SAM).
Note: AgBus = agribusiness.

provides useful lessons on what sectors can drive recovery now that the economy is in a recession. The 2009–18 period was marked by prerecession volatility, recession, and postrecession recovery—similar to the current economic situation and the near-term challenges going forward. During this period, the off-farm agribusiness sector outperformed the overall economy in GDP growth, jobs creation, and labor productivity growth. In particular, GDP in the off-farm agribusiness segments grew on average by 5.3 percent annually compared to 3.7 percent economywide, jobs in off-farm agribusiness grew on average by 3.5 percent annually compared to 2.5 percent economywide, and labor productivity (GDP per worker) in off-farm agribusiness grew on average by 1.8 percent annually compared to 1.2 percent economywide. Similarly, primary agriculture outperformed the overall economy in terms of GDP growth (4.3 percent versus 3.7 percent) and creation of better jobs as labor productivity grew by 2.8 percent compared to 1.2 percent economywide (figure 2.6). Within off-farm agribusiness, GDP growth and jobs creation were fastest in hotel and food services, followed by trade and transport. The processing segment and primary agriculture led all agribusiness segments in the creation of better jobs. A major conclusion from these results is that the agribusiness sector as a whole (on-farm and off-farm) provides the best prospects to accelerate recovery and create more and better jobs.

Many agribusinesses operate in the informal sector and lack the incentives to invest in appropriate technologies for food handling, leading to high food loss and waste and to foodborne diseases that pose huge economic costs. The 2017 national survey[1] of micro, small, and medium enterprises in Nigeria shows that

FIGURE 2.6

Agribusiness segments grew faster and created more and better jobs than the overall economy in Nigeria, 2009–18

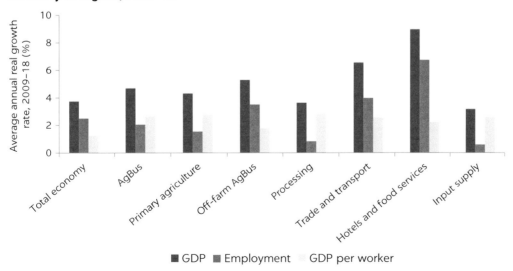

Source: Original calculations for this book using the International Food Policy Research Institute's Rural Investment and Policy Analysis (RIAPA) model and social accounting matrix (SAM).
Note: AgBus = agribusiness.

the number of microenterprises in Nigeria is more than 500 times the number of small and medium enterprises (SMEs).[2] Agribusiness microenterprises (and many of the small enterprises) tend to operate in the informal sector, serving low-income consumers who cannot sufficiently reward food quality and safety. For this reason, agribusinesses in the informal food sector tend not to invest in appropriate technology for food handling and processing or in skilled workers, leading to significant food safety risks and foodborne diseases.

The economic cost of foodborne diseases is enormous and disproportionately affects low-income consumers, but support for informal enterprises could have important impacts. It is estimated that foodborne diseases cost Nigeria more than US$6 billion in 2016, placing it behind China, India, and Indonesia in terms of economic losses originating from foodborne diseases (Jaffee et al. 2019; see figure 2.7). Food safety is an important public good that can be generated by supporting the large informal segment to invest in appropriate technology of food handling and processing, skilling workers, and integrating into formal value chains. Support to the informal sector would also promote gender goals because female entrepreneurs are twice as likely to be in microenterprises than in SMEs. In 2013, female entrepreneurs accounted for 43.32 percent of the ownership structure of microenterprises—compared to 22.75 percent for SMEs.

FIGURE 2.7

Nigeria ranked behind only China, India, and Indonesia in terms of economic losses originating from foodborne diseases in 2016

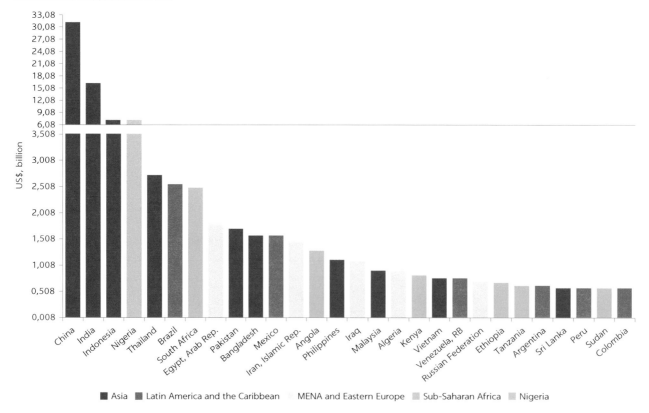

Source: Jaffee et al. 2019.
Note: MENA = Middle East and North Africa.

COMPARING AGRIBUSINESS IN NIGERIA WITH COMPARATOR COUNTRIES

A comparison of the structure and performance of the agribusiness segment in Nigeria with other countries enables a better understanding of the opportunities available for growth of the agribusiness segment. Nigeria is a middle-income country with per capita income of US$2,030 (2019). Its degree of transformation could be compared to middle-income structural peers, high-income aspirational comparators, and Sub-Saharan African regional peers (figure 2.8). Middle-income peers resemble Nigeria in key elements of their economic structure and overall performance in recent years. The cohort includes lower-middle-income countries with nominal income per capita of at least 50 percent that of Nigeria and upper-middle-income countries with nominal income per capita less than double that of Nigeria. Middle-income structural peers include Indonesia, Pakistan, and Vietnam. Aspirational comparators are advanced countries and higher-middle-income countries that have achieved rapid transformation in the last few decades. The aspirational comparators have successfully transformed such that their off-farm agribusiness GDP is larger than on-farm agribusiness GDP by a factor of more than one. Countries that fit this description include Brazil, Chile, South Africa, and Thailand. Nigeria could also be compared to regional peers in Sub-Saharan Africa—such as Ethiopia, Ghana, and Kenya—that have already achieved middle-income status or those that have high populations and are growing fast.

Analysis of the structure of agribusiness during economic transition shows that the processing, input supply, and food services segments are larger in

FIGURE 2.8

Off-farm share of agribusiness GDP and employment in Nigeria is comparable to middle-income structural peers and regional peers in Sub-Saharan Africa

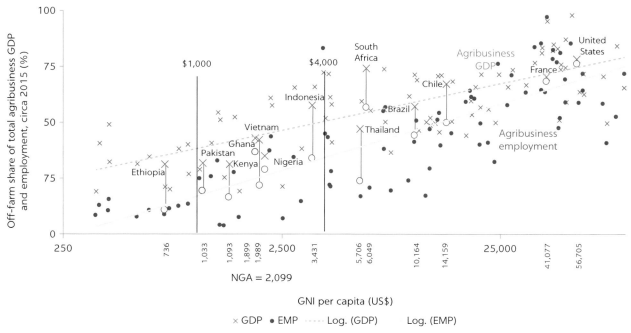

Source: Original calculations for this book using the International Food Policy Research Institute's Rural Investment and Policy Analysis (RIAPA) model and social accounting matrix (SAM).
Note: EMP = employment; GNI = gross national income; NGA = Nigeria.

countries that are further along in the transformation process—the aspirational comparators (figure 2.9). Currently, trading and transportation is the largest off-farm agribusiness segment in Nigeria, and it can continue to grow with increased urbanization and commercialization of agriculture. However, the largest gains as the sector transforms will increasingly be in the processing, input supply, and food services segments. The overall growth in off-farm agribusiness will depend on establishing stronger intrasectoral links with the on-farm segment (primary agriculture).

As the sector transforms, there will be more job opportunities in off-farm agribusiness segments, especially processing, food services, and input supply segments. Figure 2.10 illustrates the dynamics of sources of agribusiness jobs as countries transform their agribusiness sectors. At the lower end of the spectrum are low-income countries such as Ethiopia where agriculture contributes about 34 percent to national GDP and directly employs about 66 percent of the labor force.[3] Primary agriculture is the single most important source of jobs in Ethiopia, with off-farm agribusiness contributing only about 11 percent of agribusiness jobs. The share of primary agriculture jobs in agribusiness declines steadily as countries move along the transformation path—to about 76 percent in lower-middle-income countries, 61 percent in upper-middle-income countries, and 41 percent in high-income countries. At the same time, the shares of most off-farm segments grow steadily during transformation, with processing growing from 3 percent in low-income countries to 21 percent in high-income countries; hotels and food services growing from 2 percent in low-income countries to 15 percent in high-income countries; and input supply growing from 1 percent in low-income countries to 10 percent in high-income countries.

Better coordination between primary agriculture and off-farm agribusinesses would help unlock the growth and job opportunities in processing, food services, and input supply segments. Key elements of a growth and transformation strategy for agribusiness could aim for the following:

FIGURE 2.9

Aspirational comparators have larger shares of processing, input supply, and food services segments in agribusiness GDP than Nigeria does

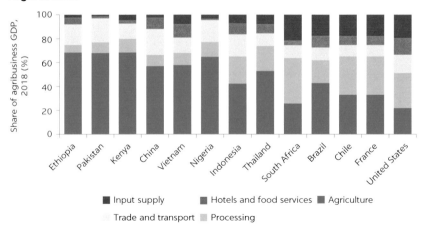

Source: Original calculations for this book using the International Food Policy Research Institute's Rural Investment and Policy Analysis (RIAPA) model and social accounting matrix (SAM).

FIGURE 2.10

Transformation of the sector will bring about more job opportunities in processing, hotels and food services, and input supply segments

Share of jobs in agribusiness (%)

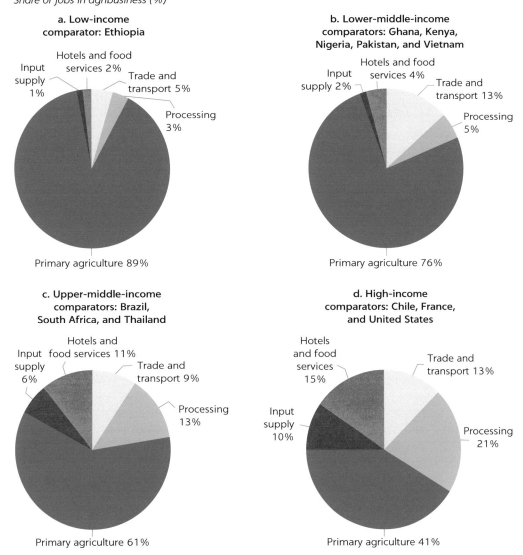

a. Low-income
comparator: Ethiopia

Input supply 1%
Hotels and food services 2%
Trade and transport 5%
Processing 3%
Primary agriculture 89%

b. Lower-middle-income
comparators: Ghana, Kenya, Nigeria, Pakistan, and Vietnam

Input supply 2%
Hotels and food services 4%
Trade and transport 13%
Processing 5%
Primary agriculture 76%

c. Upper-middle-income
comparators: Brazil, South Africa, and Thailand

Input supply 6%
Hotels and food services 11%
Trade and transport 9%
Processing 13%
Primary agriculture 61%

d. High-income
comparators: Chile, France, and United States

Hotels and food services 15%
Trade and transport 13%
Input supply 10%
Processing 21%
Primary agriculture 41%

Source: Original calculations for this book using the International Food Policy Research Institute's Rural Investment and Policy Analysis (RIAPA) model and social accounting matrix (SAM).

- Raising productivity in the on-farm segment (primary agriculture) to reduce the costs in downstream off-farm segments
- Effective coordination of agricultural value chains, including moving away from fragmented spot markets to strong forms of vertical arrangements
- Expanding processing of higher-value farm products such as cash crops, livestock products, and livestock and fisheries feeds through value chain development approaches that establish strong links with primary agriculture
- Diversifying farm production and moving away from root crops that have low value added, processing potential, and nutritional value (the 59 percent of root crops that don't include cassava and potatoes)
- Increasing domestic production of the inputs used in farming and processing, including seeds, agrochemicals, vaccines, and fertilizers

CONCLUSIONS

This chapter has examined the potential of the agribusiness sector to accelerate inclusive recovery and create jobs in the economy. The main conclusion emerging from this analysis is that the growth, jobs, and labor productivity outcomes in the last decade (2009–18) indicate that the agribusiness sector provides perhaps the best opportunities to accelerate inclusive recovery from the 2020 recession while generating more and better jobs. The 2009–18 period is instructive because it is similar to the current economic situation and the near-term challenges going forward. During that period, the off-farm agribusiness sector outperformed the overall economy in GDP growth, generating jobs and labor productivity growth. Similarly, primary agriculture outperformed the overall economy in terms of GDP growth and creation of better jobs as labor productivity growth in primary agriculture grew twice as fast as the economy-wide average.

Future opportunities for growth and jobs will increasingly be in the off-farm segments—in particular, processing, hotels and food services, and input supply segments. However, these growth and job opportunities cannot materialize without better coordination of agriculture/agribusiness value chains to reduce fragmentation and establish stronger links between upstream primary production and downstream value-addition segments.

The key elements of a growth and transformation strategy for agribusiness would involve (1) raising productivity in the on-farm segment (primary agriculture) to reduce the costs in downstream off-farm segments; (2) effective coordination of agricultural value chains, including moving away from fragmented spot markets to strong forms of vertical arrangements; (3) expanding processing of higher-value farm products such as cash crops, livestock products, and livestock and fisheries feeds through value chain development approaches that establish strong links with primary agriculture; (4) diversifying farm production and moving away from root crops that have low value added, processing potential, and nutritional value; and (5) increasing domestic production of the inputs used in farming and processing, including seeds, agrochemicals, vaccines, and fertilizers.

The next chapter will advance the analysis presented here by looking at the potential of specific value chain groups to generate jobs, reduce poverty, and improve nutrition outcomes. This is important because the agribusiness sector in Nigeria is composed of a wide range of commodities and value chains, and the potential of different value chain groups to achieve development outcomes could vary greatly. It's critical from a policy and investment perspective to understand which value chain groups are most effective in achieving the critical development outcomes.

NOTES

1. The survey was carried out by the Small and Medium Enterprises Development Agency of Nigeria and National Bureau of Statistics.
2. The classification of micro, small, and medium enterprises in Nigeria is based on the number of persons employed and the value of assets, excluding land and buildings. Enterprises that employ 10–49 persons and have assets valued at 5 million to 50 million naira (N) are considered small. Enterprises employing 50–199 persons and with assets valued at N50 million to N500 million are considered medium. At the upper end of this classification are

large firms with a workforce greater than 199 and assets of more than N500 million. At the lower end are the microenterprises—firms employing between 1 and 9 persons and with assets valued at less than N5 million. In 2013, the number of microenterprises was about 500 times higher than the number of SMEs. Nigeria had about 37 million microenterprises (of which more than 3 million were in agriculture) and only 68,168 small and 4,670 medium enterprises.

3. According to the World Bank's World Development Indicators.

REFERENCES

Christiaensen, L., L. Demery, and J. Kuhl. 2011. "The (Evolving) Role of Agriculture in Poverty Reduction—An Empirical Perspective." *Journal of Development Economics* 96: 239–54.

Gollin, D., S. Parente, and R. Rogerson. 2007. "The Food Problem and the Evolution of International Income Levels." *Journal of Monetary Economics* 54: 1230–55.

Jaffee, S., Spencer Henson, Laurian Unnevehr, Delia Grace, and Emilie Cassou. 2019. *The Safe Food Imperative: Accelerating Progress in Low- and Middle-Income Countries.* Agriculture and Food Series. Washington, DC: World Bank.

Johnston, B. F., and J. W. Mellor. 1961. "The Role of Agriculture in Economic Development." *American Economic Review* 51: 566–93.

McMillan, M., and D. Headey. 2014. "Introduction—Understanding Structural Transformation in Africa." *World Development* 63 (November): 1–10.

Mellor, J. W., ed. 1995. *Agriculture on the Road to Industrialization.* IFPRI: John Hopkins Press.

Timmer, C. P. 1988. "The Agricultural Transformation." In *The Handbook of Development Economics*, edited by H. Chenery and T. N. Srinivasan, vol. I: 275–331. North Holland, Amsterdam.

3 Selecting Value Chains to Create Jobs, Reduce Poverty, and Improve Nutrition

The preceding chapter concluded that the agribusiness sector provides enormous scope to accelerate inclusive recovery from the recession and to generate more and better jobs. Policy makers in Nigeria are also concerned about the high rate of poverty, and the government has declared its ambition to lift 100 million people out of poverty by 2030. The prevalence of poverty—measured by the poverty headcount ratio—is more than two times higher in rural areas (52 percent) than in urban areas (18 percent). Most of the poor are directly employed in agriculture and depend on farming for their livelihoods. Therefore, efforts to reduce poverty are likely to have more success if they aim to catalyze broad-based growth in rural areas and in agriculture. The extent to which productivity growth in agriculture reduces poverty is higher in countries in the early stages of economic transformation (figure 3.1) and dissipates as countries grow richer (Ivanic and Martin 2018; Ligon and Sadoulet 2018). Nevertheless, the evidence is quite strong that productivity growth equal to a 1 percent increase in gross domestic product (GDP) reduces poverty more when that growth is in agriculture than when it is in industry and services.

How fast does the agribusiness sector need to grow to meet the sectoral jobs targets set in government policy? Which value chains provide the most potential to create jobs, reduce poverty, and improve nutrition outcomes to support human capital development? The answers to these questions will help policy makers set reasonable targets on these development outcomes, facilitate prioritization of value chains to meet specific development objectives, and ultimately enable more efficient allocation of scarce development resources. At a more operational level, the analysis can help inform the technical design of programs and identify partnerships with the private sector and other stakeholders.

FIGURE 3.1

In low-income and lower-middle-income countries, productivity growth equal to 1 percent of GDP in agriculture reduces poverty more than the same size productivity growth in other sectors

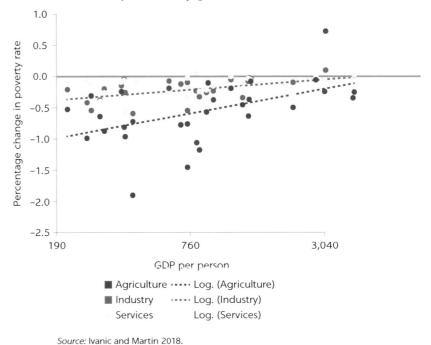

Source: Ivanic and Martin 2018.

SIZE OF VALUE CHAIN GROUPS

Table 3.1 describes the contribution of value chain groups to on-farm and off-farm agribusiness GDP and the share of specific commodities within each value chain group. Overall, root crops and horticulture account for the largest shares of agribusiness GDP, with each contributing 28 percent. The main difference between these two value chain groups is that horticulture contributes a relatively higher share to off-farm agribusiness GDP (21 percent) than root crops (15 percent), clearly indicating that horticulture provides more opportunities in downstream value addition. The next largest value chain group is cereals, contributing 14 percent to overall agribusiness GDP with balanced shares between the on-farm (13 percent) and off-farm (14 percent) segments. The traditional cash crops group is the largest in terms of contributions to off-farm GDP, with a share of about 24 percent, primarily because the commodities in this group are industrial crops that are generally not consumed on the farm and instead require a high degree of value addition outside the farm into food and nonfood products. Livestock contributes less than 10 percent to agribusiness GDP (including fishing), with most of the value generated in cattle meat, small ruminants, poultry meat, and raw milk—in that order. Pulses and oil seeds are a small subsector contributing about 4 percent, which equals the total contribution of the fish and forestry groups (2 percent each).

TABLE 3.1 Root crops and horticulture generate more than half of agribusiness GDP in Nigeria

VALUE CHAIN GROUP	SHARE IN AGRIBUSINESS GDP (%)[a]			SHARES OF COMMODITIES AND PRODUCTS IN AGRIBUSINESS GDP (%)
	OVERALL	ON-FARM	OFF-FARM	
Cereals	14	13	14	Maize 32% | Sorghum and millet 23.7% | Rice 44.1% | Wheat and barley 0.1% | Other cereals 0.1%
Pulses and oil seeds	4	3	4	Pulses 27.4% | Groundnuts 15.9% | Other oil seeds 56.6%
Root crops	28	37	15	Cassava 35.8% | Irish potatoes 1.8% | Sweet potatoes 3.6% | Other roots 58.8%
Horticulture	28	33	21	Leafy vegetables 14.4% | Other vegetables 46%
Livestock	8	8	7	Cattle meat 29.9% | Raw milk 10.6% | Poultry meat 14.7% | Eggs 7.3% | Small ruminants 20.6% | Other livestock 16.9%
Fish	2	3	2	Aquaculture 28.8% | Capture fisheries 71.2%
Traditional cash crops[b]	10	1	24	Tobacco 0.1% | Cotton and fibers 25.9% | Coffee 3.1% | Cocoa 53.9% | Cut flowers 10.7% | Rubber 3.3% | Other crops 3.1%
Forestry	2	1	4	*Cannot easily be assigned to a single activity*
Unattributable	4	—	9	
Total	100	100	100	

Source: Original calculations for this book using the International Food Policy Research Institute's Rural Investment and Policy Analysis (RIAPA) model and social accounting matrix (SAM).
Note: — = not available.
a. Some GDP from certain highly processed products (for example, beverages and baby foods) cannot be traced back to a single agricultural product chain without risking double-counting.
b. Excludes cashew nuts and sugarcane.

METHODOLOGY

The analysis to identify value chains with the most potential to create jobs, reduce poverty, and improve nutrition was conducted using the Rural Investment and Policy Analysis (RIAPA) model. RIAPA is a computable general equilibrium model, and its core database is a social accounting matrix (SAM) that captures all income and expenditure flows between all economic actors in the country, including producers, consumers, government, and the rest of the world (see box 3.1). The model estimates how the speed and structure of growth in different subsectors affect consumption and income and their knock-on effects on various outcomes of interest such as jobs and poverty. These estimates reflect the differences in consumption patterns for different households and their factor endowments and demand for resources. For example, poor households tend to depend on incomes from low-skilled workers; therefore, growth in sectors with a high intensity of low-skilled labor is likely to have a relatively large impact on those households. In the same vein, poor households tend to spend a relatively higher share of their food budget on staples, so productivity growth in the staples sector would lower prices, raise food consumption among the poor, and potentially transition some of them out of poverty. The outcome indicators in the RIAPA model include the following:

- *Economic growth* is measured by real GDP at factor cost either for all sectors (total GDP) or for specific sectors.

Box 3.1

The Rural Investment and Poverty Analysis model

The Rural Investment and Poverty Analysis (RIAPA) model is a computable general equilibrium model that simulates the functioning of a market economy, including markets for products and factors (that is, land, labor, and capital). RIAPA measures how impacts are mediated through prices and resource reallocations, and it ensures that resource and macroeconomic constraints are respected, such as when inputs or foreign exchange are limited. RIAPA provides a consistent simulation laboratory for quantitatively examining value chain interactions and spillovers at national, subnational, and household levels.

RIAPA divides the economy into sectors and household groups that act as individual economic agents. Producers maximize profits and supply output to national markets where it may be exported, combined with imports, or both, depending on relative prices, with foreign prices affected by exchange rate movements. Producers combine factors and intermediate inputs using sector-specific technologies. Maize farmers, for example, use a unique combination of land, labor, machinery, fertilizer, and purchased seeds. Workers are divided by education levels, and agricultural capital is separated into crop and livestock categories. Labor and capital are in fixed supply, but less educated workers are treated as underemployed. Producers and households pay taxes to the government, which uses these and other revenues to finance public services and social transfers. Remaining revenues are added to private savings and foreign capital inflows to finance investment (that is, investment is driven by levels of savings). RIAPA is dynamic, with past investment determining current capital availability.

RIAPA tracks changes in incomes and expenditures for different household groups, including changes in food and nonfood consumption patterns. Poverty impacts are measured using survey-based microsimulation analysis. Individual survey households map to the model's household groups. Estimated consumption changes in the model are applied proportionally to survey households, and postsimulation consumption values are recalculated and compared to a poverty line to determine households' poverty status.

Source: Benfica and Thurlow 2017.

- *Employment* includes both paid and unpaid work such as home enterprises. Workers may have multiple jobs, but only their primary job is considered, and no adjustment is made for hours worked.
- *Poverty* is measured by the poverty headcount or poverty gap. The former is the share of the population with consumption below the poverty line, and the latter is the cumulative distance between poor people's consumption levels and the poverty line (also described as depth of poverty).
- *Dietary diversity score* is calculated for household groups using food expenditure shares. Diversity is estimated using a generalized entropy measure across six food categories (cereals and roots; vegetables; fruits; meat, fish, and eggs; milk and dairy; and pulses and oil seeds). A more diverse diet is associated with better nutrition outcomes.
- *Poverty growth elasticity* (PGE) is the percentage change in the poverty rate divided by the per capita GDP growth rate. *Semi-PGEs* use percentage point changes in the poverty rate.
- *Dietary diversity growth elasticity* is the percentage change in the dietary diversity score of poor households divided by the per capita GDP growth rate.

- *Growth employment elasticity* is the percentage change in employment divided by the percentage change in GDP. It can be calculated for a specific segment of the economy, for example to capture the agribusiness GDP growth employment elasticity.

The assessment of the job creation and poverty reduction potential of alternative value chain groups begins with establishing a baseline scenario for 2018–25 using recent trends. The business-as-usual scenario is summarized in table 3.2. The initial values are for 2018, the base year for analysis from which simulations are run. The population is expected to grow at 2.45 percent annually, which is higher than employment growth (2.42 percent) and expansion of crop area. National GDP grows at nearly the same rate as the population—2.96 percent versus 2.45 percent, respectively—meaning that GDP per capita barely improves. Agricultural GDP continues to grow nearly as fast as industry but slower than services GDP. However, the agribusiness part of industry (agro-processing) grows faster than agriculture, industry, and services. These growth patterns not only reflect outcomes in the base year (2018) but also are consistent with relative performance of the sectors in the past decade (2009–18). Poverty is projected to decline marginally in the baseline scenario, with PGE of –0.13. Productivity growth is adjusted to replicate trends in sectoral GDP.

The simulations to estimate the jobs and poverty reduction effects of value chains proceed by accelerating total factor productivity growth beyond baseline growth rates, one value chain group at a time, such that total agricultural GDP is 1 percent higher in 2025 than it is in the baseline scenario.[1] The simulated expansion of agricultural production increases supply to downstream processing activities and generates demand for agricultural trade and transport services and inputs. Because agricultural subsectors differ in size, the same absolute increase in total agricultural value added is achieved across value chains if smaller value chains expand more rapidly than larger ones. The initial GDP shares of value chains are listed in table 3.1. The smallest value chain is fish, followed by pulses and oil seeds. Productivity gains in these value chains will need to be relatively large to generate the 1 percent increase in agricultural GDP compared to what would be required from larger value chains such as cassava and rice. The burden for productivity growth placed on smaller value chains may be difficult to achieve in practice; however, simulating the same absolute increase in agricultural GDP enables a consistent approach to compare impacts across value chains.

TABLE 3.2 Baseline scenario for Nigeria, 2018–25
Percent annual change

POPULATION	GDP GROWTH RATE					EMPLOYMENT	CONSUMPTION PER CAPITA	POVERTY HEADCOUNT RATE	PGE	SEMI-PGE
	TOTAL	AGRICULTURE GDP	INDUSTRY	AGRO-PROCESSING	SERVICES					
2.45	2.96	2.89	2.73	3.37	3.07	2.42	0.23	-0.06	-0.13	-0.09

Source: Original calculations for this book using the International Food Policy Research Institute's Rural Investment and Policy Analysis (RIAPA) model.
Note: PGE = poverty growth elasticity.

HOW MUCH GROWTH IS NEEDED IN AGRIBUSINESS TO CREATE 6 MILLION JOBS?

Jobs creation remains a key priority of the government and features prominently in recent government policy documents. The most recent policy documents emphasizing job creation are the Economic Recovery and Growth Plan 2017–20, Delivering on the Government's Priorities 2019–2023, and the Economic Sustainability Plan 2020. In particular, the second of those documents sets a specific target to create 6 million jobs in the agribusiness sector between 2019 and 2023. These jobs would be created through medium-term interventions to catalyze agro-based business clusters for processing, value addition, and technology support—along with accompanying investments to improve access to finance and markets, increase yields, remove barriers to exports, and promote better use of arable land. Although the COVID-19 (coronavirus) pandemic shifted the focus to short-term measures, the jobs agenda remains a priority because the economic downturn is expected to increase the unemployment rate by about 10 percentage points compared to 2018 levels—from 23.1 percent in 2018 to 33.6 percent by the end of 2020 (ESC 2020). The Economic Sustainability Plan 2020 adopted a short-term agenda to create "millions of jobs" over a 12-month period through a Mass Agricultural Programme. Going forward, jobs are expected to remain a priority in the policy documents that are currently under preparation—Nigeria's Medium-Term National Development Plans 2021–25 and 2026–30 and the Nigeria Agenda 2050.

According to projections with economic data before the onset of COVID-19, the agribusiness sector was on track to create 6 million jobs by the middle of 2027 (figure 3.2). These results are based on a linear time trend of agribusiness GDP and employment outcomes using data observed before the pandemic, with 2019 as the base year. The regressions are based on growth rates rather than levels and do not factor the COVID-19 dip because economic outcomes for 2020 have not been fully observed. Clearly, there is interest in

FIGURE 3.2

Projections from base year 2018 indicate that the agribusiness sector was on track to create 6 million jobs in Nigeria by mid-2027

New jobs created under current trends

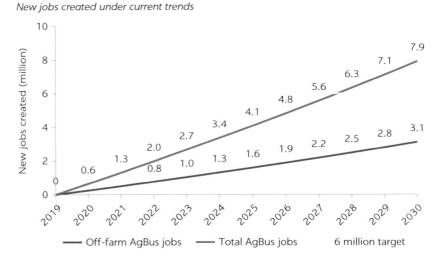

Source: Original calculations for this book using the International Food Policy Research Institute's Rural Investment and Policy Analysis (RIAPA) model.
Note: AgBus = agribusiness.

creating the 6 million jobs earlier than 2027 because previous targets had aimed to create the same number of jobs by 2023—a difference of four years that is equivalent to one full government term. The on-farm segment would contribute most of the jobs (about 3.4 million), and the balance of 2.2 million (about 37 percent) would be contributed by the off-farm segments, which is consistent with the current structure of the agribusiness sector in which on-farm is dominant.

The growth burden to create 6 million jobs is lower when on-farm and off-farm segments grow in tandem and if the target year for achieving the result is pushed into the future. In particular, the study finds that the agribusiness sector needs to grow by 5.4 percent annually to create 6 million jobs by 2024 and that higher growth would be required from either segment if the other part stagnates (figure 3.3). For example, if left alone to achieve the jobs target, the on-farm segment will have to grow by 8.4 percent annually through 2024 to create 6 million jobs. The off-farm segment will have to grow even faster—by 13 percent annually—to create the 6 million jobs by 2024 on its own. The 6 million jobs target can be met in future years with a lower growth rate—for example, only 3.9 percent growth is required to meet the jobs targets in 2026.

These estimates were calculated using the growth employment elasticity, which estimates the percentage change in employment given 1 percentage change in agribusiness GDP. The calculated elasticity for the overall agribusiness sector is 0.57. Consistent with the findings in the previous chapter, the off-farm segments create jobs relatively faster for each 1 percentage change in its GDP than the on-farm segments. The respective elasticities are 0.75 (off-farm) and 0.49 (on-farm); however, the on-farm segment is larger and currently employs more people. The higher baseline translates to more jobs in absolute numbers in the on-farm segment. More important, these results reinforce the need for coordinated investments between on-farm and off-farm segments of agribusiness so that the segments grow in tandem.

FIGURE 3.3

The whole of agribusiness needs to grow concurrently to create 6 million jobs faster

Agribusiness growth needed to create 6 million jobs in Nigeria

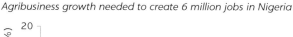
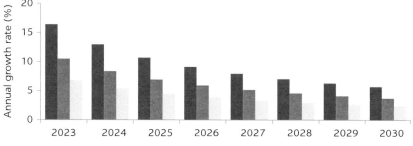

Source: Original calculations for this book using the International Food Policy Research Institute's Rural Investment and Policy Analysis (RIAPA) model.

FIGURE 3.4

The growth rate required for Nigeria's agribusiness sector to create 6 million jobs has been achieved by several Sub-Saharan African and other developing countries in recent years

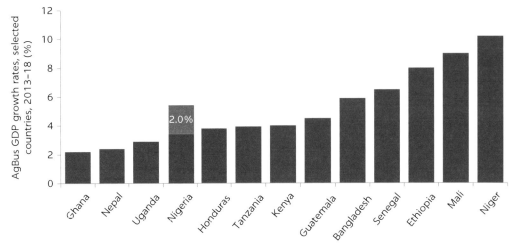

Additional AgBus GDP growth needed to achieve jobs targets (2018-23)A

Source: Original calculations for this book using the International Food Policy Research Institute's Rural Investment and Policy Analysis (RIAPA) model.
Note: AgBus = agribusiness.

Although the growth rates needed for agribusiness to create 6 million jobs are quite ambitious for Nigeria at this juncture, agribusiness sectors in several countries have grown even faster in recent years. Nigeria's agribusiness sector grew by 3.4 percent in 2018 and needs to surpass that level by about 2 percentage points to meet the 6 million jobs target by 2024. The COVID-19 pandemic slowed that growth considerably: it is estimated that primary agriculture grew by 1.7 percent in the first three quarters of 2020 compared to 2.4 percent during the same period in 2019. Although the growth burden to meet the jobs target has increased, the analysis of agribusiness growth rates in developing countries suggests that it is possible for the sector to grow at rates higher than 5 percent. For example, the agribusiness sectors in Ethiopia, Mali, and Niger grew at 8.0, 9.0, and 10.2 percent, respectively, between 2013 and 2018 (figure 3.4).

VALUE CHAINS WITH THE MOST POTENTIAL FOR JOB CREATION

Whether employment elasticity is evaluated economywide or within the agribusiness sector, the traditional cash crops emerge as the value chains with the highest potential to create jobs, along with oil seeds, pulses, rice, and cassava. The jobs attributed to traditional cash crops come not only from the direct effects of productivity growth in that value chain but also from indirect effects through incentives created outside the value chain. This is true for other value chains as well. For example, increasing cassava productivity may allow farmers to reallocate resources to other crops, thereby diversifying production and creating more jobs in other agricultural enterprises. Similarly, increasing incomes of workers in a value chain allows households to purchase products from other sectors or value chains, thereby generating economywide spillovers. Table 3.3 reports growth employment elasticities in the economy and within agribusiness. The traditional cash crops value chain group ranks first on both accounts. A key characteristic of this value chain is that it has a relatively larger share of downstream processing and trade and transport activities, with nearly 80 percent of GDP generated off the farm, which leads to higher employment multipliers (figure 3.5) (Benfica and Thurlow 2017). Traditional cash crops' employment elasticity of 0.11 implies that a 1 percent increase in agricultural GDP driven by productivity growth in traditional cash crops increases jobs in the national economy by 0.11 percent and in the agribusiness sector by 0.15 percent.

The results for rice and cassava highlight policy trade-offs on the location of new jobs. On the one hand, cassava is significantly stronger than rice in creating jobs within the agribusiness sectors—it has higher agribusiness growth employment elasticity than rice. On the other hand, rice creates relatively more jobs in the broader economy than cassava but actually contributes negatively to jobs within the agribusiness segment. The larger economywide links in rice are through the milling industry as well as hotels and food services segments. Unlike

TABLE 3.3 Traditional cash crops, edible oil seeds, pulses, rice, and cassava have the potential to create the most jobs in Nigeria

TARGETED SECTOR WITHIN AGRICULTURE	EMPLOYMENT ELASTICITY (RANK IN PARENTHESES)	
	ECONOMYWIDE	AGRIBUSINESS
Maize	0.02 (9)	0.01 (5)
Sorghum and millet	−0.01 (13)	−0.03 (7)
Rice	0.08 (2)	−0.04 (8)
Pulses	0.04 (4)	0.08 (4)
Edible oil seeds	0.07 (3)	0.15 (3)
Cassava	0.03 (7)	0.15 (2)
Yams	−0.01 (12)	−0.06 (10)
Vegetables	−0.02 (15)	−0.33 (14)
Bananas	0.01 (10)	−0.06 (11)
Fruits	0.01 (11)	−0.02 (6)
Traditional cash crops	0.11 (1)	0.15 (1)
Cattle and dairy	0.03 (5)	−0.44 (15)
Poultry and eggs	−0.01 (14)	−0.16 (12)
Goats and sheep	0.02 (8)	−0.27 (13)
Fish and aquaculture	0.03 (6)	−0.04 (9)

Source: Original calculations for this book using the International Food Policy Research Institute's Rural Investment and Policy Analysis (RIAPA) model and social accounting matrix (SAM).
Note: GDP employment elasticity is the percentage increase in total or agriculture-food system employment given a 1 percent increase in agricultural GDP originating from the targeted value chain group.

FIGURE 3.5

The contribution of on-farm and off-farm segments to the value chain GDP differs across value chain groups in Nigeria

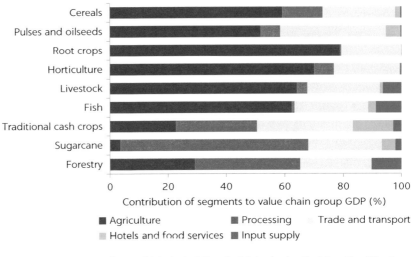

Source: Original calculations for this book using the International Food Policy Research Institute's Rural Investment and Policy Analysis (RIAPA) model and social accounting matrix (SAM).

countries in East Asia where cassava is used for starch and other industrial products, cassava is not an industrial crop in Nigeria and its use is limited to staple food products. Cassava is generally not consumed in hotels and restaurants. Cassava processing is predominantly for producing *gari* and cassava flour in small-scale processing units. As with cassava, the root crops value chain group does not involve major processing activities and most of its downstream GDP comes from trading and transportation (figure 3.5). Nearly 80 percent of GDP in the root crop value chain group is generated on the farm. In summary, these findings demonstrate that the potential to create jobs differs across value chains and depends on the links between the primary production segment of the value chains and the downstream segments of agribusiness and the broader economy. The rice and cassava value chains are studied in more detail in chapters 6 and 7, respectively.

Edible oil seeds and pulses have strong potential for jobs, and within edible oil seeds sesame is becoming a major export commodity. Edible oil seeds and pulses are ranked third and fourth, respectively, when potential is evaluated economywide and within agribusiness. Nearly half of the agribusiness GDP in these value chains is generated off the farm, with trade and transportation alone accounting for 36 percent of the agribusiness GDP. Within the edible oil seeds group, sesame is emerging as an important commodity for growth and exports (figure 3.6). Nigeria is the fifth-largest producer of sesame in the world (and third-largest in Africa) with about 550,000 metric tons in 2017, which is nearly 10 percent of the total global output. But Nigeria ranks first globally in terms of yields with more than 1 ton per hectare. The high yields have laid strong foundations for competitiveness in global exports markets. Sesame seed was Nigeria's most exported agricultural commodity in the first quarter of 2019, accounting for 40.4 percent of agricultural exports with about 70.0 percent of exports going to the major consuming countries such as China, Japan, and Turkey.

FIGURE 3.6

High yields have laid strong foundations for growth and exports in sesame seed

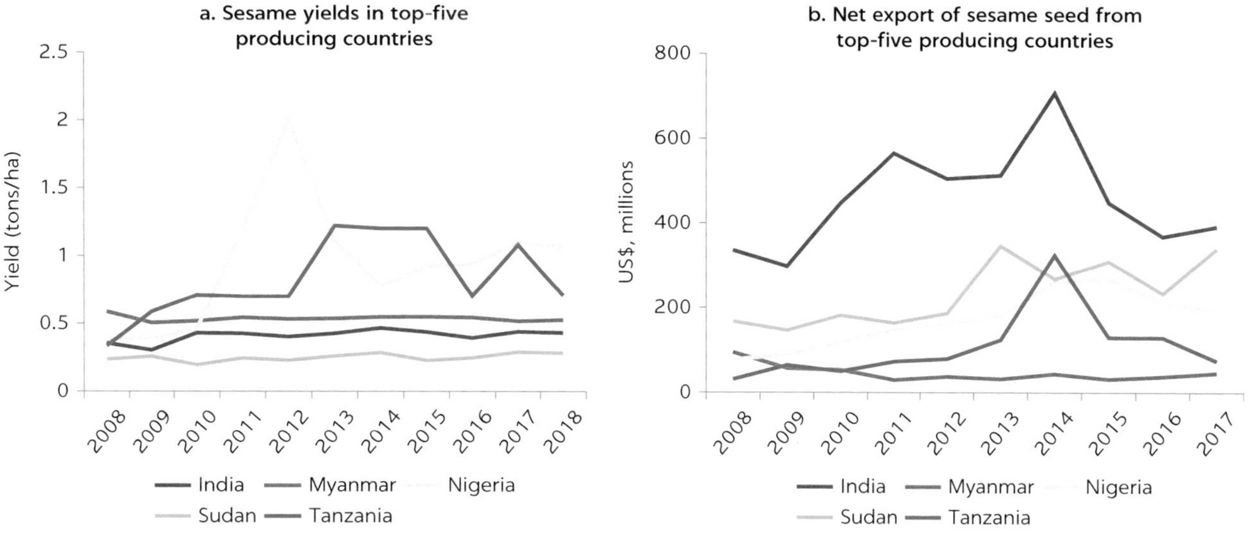

a. Sesame yields in top-five producing countries

b. Net export of sesame seed from top-five producing countries

Source: FAOSTAT (Statistics Division, Food and Agriculture Organization of the United Nations).
Note: ha = hectare.

VALUE CHAINS WITH THE MOST POTENTIAL FOR POVERTY REDUCTION

The value chain groups with highest potential to reduce the national poverty headcount ratio are pulses, goats and sheep, poultry and eggs, fish and aquaculture, cattle and dairy, and traditional cash crops, in that order. These pro-poor value chain groups have semi-PGE of more than –1, which means that a 1 percent change in agricultural GDP arising from productivity growth in any of these value chains will reduce the national poverty headcount ratio by more than 1 percentage point (table 3.4). However, some of these value chains are more effective at reducing poverty in urban areas. Specifically, productivity growth in fish and aquaculture and cattle and dairy reduce national poverty more than rural poverty, indicating that the benefits of their growth accrue more to the urban poor than to the rural poor. The links with urban poverty are primarily through off-farm postproduction management of products and lower consumer prices. These livestock products tend to have high income and price elasticity of demand. Productivity growth leads to falling prices and increased demand, especially among the urban poor. The extent to which the rural poor benefit partly depends on the trade-off between growth and prices. Clearly, the instantaneous effect of productivity growth is to increase the incomes of producers, but this effect could be dampened by falling farm gate and consumer prices. In addition to the direct income and consumption effects, the increased production and demand create employment opportunities for the poor and low-skilled workers to move these commodities from the farm to the market.

TABLE 3.4 **The value chain groups with the most potential to reduce poverty in Nigeria are pulses, goats and sheep, poultry and eggs, fish and aquaculture, cattle and dairy, and traditional cash crops**

BASELINE OR TARGETED SECTOR WITHIN AGRICULTURE	ESTIMATED SEMI-PGE (SECTORAL RANK IN PARENTHESES)	
	NATIONAL POVERTY HEADCOUNT	RURAL POVERTY HEADCOUNT
Baseline	**−0.09**	**−0.12**
Maize	0.15 (14)	0.24 (14)
Sorghum and millet	0.16 (15)	0.25 (15)
Rice	0.01 (13)	0.17 (13)
Pulses	−1.80 (1)	−2.62 (2)
Edible oil seeds	−0.06 (10)	0.00 (11)
Cassava	−0.04 (11)	−0.06 (10)
Yams	0.00 (12)	0.00 (11)
Vegetables	−0.19 (8)	−0.12 (8)
Bananas	−0.18 (9)	−0.09 (9)
Fruits	−0.35 (7)	−0.34 (7)
Cash crops	−0.94 (6)	−1.36 (4)
Cattle and dairy	−1.03 (5)	−0.77 (6)
Poultry and eggs	−1.64 (3)	−1.72 (3)
Goats and sheep	−1.78 (2)	−2.65 (1)
Fish and aquaculture	−1.52 (4)	−1.21 (5)

Source: Original calculations for this book using the International Food Policy Research Institute's Rural Investment and Policy Analysis (RIAPA) model and social accounting matrix (SAM).
Note: Semi-PGE (poverty growth elasticity) is the percentage point change in the poverty rate per 1 percent increase in GDP per capita driven by GDP growth originating from within the targeted value chain group.

VALUE CHAINS WITH THE MOST POTENTIAL TO IMPROVE NUTRITION

Because poor people face challenges in accessing nutritious foods, it is important to examine which value chain groups have more potential to improve their nutrition outcomes. The assessment of the potential of value chain groups to improve nutrition relies on estimates of dietary diversity growth elasticity, which measures the percentage change in the dietary diversity score of poor households divided by the per capita GDP growth rate. The dietary diversity score is calculated for household groups using food expenditure shares. Diversity is estimated using a generalized entropy measure across six food categories: cereals and roots; vegetables; fruits; meat, fish, and eggs; milk and dairy; and pulses and oil seeds. A more diverse diet is associated with better nutrition outcomes. Food groups that dominate production and consumption (main staples) perform poorly in the dietary diversity score, primarily because such foods already occupy a large share of the consumption basket and productivity growth makes them more available and cheaper, which further reduces the diversity of diets and leads to poor nutrition outcomes. Sorghum and millet have the worst dietary diversity growth elasticity, followed by yams, cassava, maize, bananas, rice, and edible oil seeds. Furthermore, the scores for maize, rice, and sorghum and millet are lower for rural households (relative to urban households) and worse among

TABLE 3.5 Food groups with the highest potential to improve nutrition outcomes in Nigeria are cattle and dairy, fruits, poultry and eggs, goats and sheep, fish and aquaculture, and vegetables

TARGETED SUBSECTOR WITHIN AGRICULTURE	ESTIMATED DDGE (SECTORAL RANK IN PARENTHESES)		
	ALL HOUSEHOLDS	RURAL HOUSEHOLDS	POOR RURAL HOUSEHOLDS
Maize	−2.25 (12)	−2.61 (13)	−3.73 (14)
Sorghum and millet	−2.58 (15)	−3.08 (14)	−6.98 (15)
Rice	−1.78 (10)	−2.01 (11)	−2.08 (13)
Pulses	0.20 (7)	0.20 (7)	0.97 (7)
Edible oil seeds	−0.70 (9)	−0.79 (9)	−0.50 (9)
Cassava	−2.38 (13)	−3.12 (15)	−1.97 (12)
Yams	−2.38 (14)	−2.24 (12)	−1.88 (11)
Vegetables	1.40 (6)	1.31 (6)	1.02 (6)
Bananas	−2.04 (11)	−1.72 (10)	−0.60 (10)
Fruits	5.15 (2)	4.28 (3)	2.86 (4)
Cash crops	0.19 (8)	0.16 (8)	0.12 (8)
Cattle and dairy	6.88 (1)	6.34 (1)	9.51 (1)
Poultry and eggs	4.90 (3)	4.24 (4)	3.58 (3)
Goats and sheep	4.39 (4)	5.73 (2)	5.62 (2)
Fish and aquaculture	4.07 (5)	1.74 (5)	2.62 (5)

Source: Original calculations for this book using the International Food Policy Research Institute's Rural Investment and Policy Analysis (RIAPA) model and social accounting matrix (SAM).
Note: Dietary diversity score (DDS) measures the unevenness of the real value of consumption across major food groups (that is, negative entropy distance from equality). Dietary diversity growth elasticity (DDGE) is the percentage change in the DDS per 1 percent increase in GDP per capita driven by GDP growth originating within the targeted value chain group.

poor rural households. Food groups with the highest scores are cattle and dairy, fruits, poultry and eggs, goats and sheep, fish and aquaculture, and vegetables—in that order (table 3.5). These findings lead to the conclusion that livestock food groups and fruits and vegetables are the most effective at improving nutrition outcomes among not only poor rural households but also other rural and urban households.

CONCLUSIONS

This chapter addressed two interrelated questions—first, the amount of growth that is required for the agribusiness sector to meet the sectoral jobs targets set in government policy and, second, the value chains with the most potential to create jobs, reduce poverty, and improve nutrition outcomes to support human capital development.

With regard to the first question, the simulations from base year 2018 show that the agribusiness sector in Nigeria needs to grow by about 5.4 percent annually to create 6 million jobs between 2019 and 2024. Although the required growth rate is higher than what the sector achieved in 2018 by about 2 percentage points, there are many examples of low-income and lower-middle-income countries where the agribusiness sector grew by more than 5 percent between 2013 and 2018. The examples include Ethiopia, Mali, Niger, and Senegal. A major conclusion from the results is that jobs would be created faster when primary agriculture and off-farm agribusinesses grow in tandem and that any jobs target will become harder to achieve if either segment stagnates. These findings reinforce the need for coordinated investments between on-farm and off-farm segments as part of a "whole-of-agribusiness" growth strategy.

The value chain groups with most potential to create jobs are traditional cash crops, edible oil seeds, pulses, rice, and cassava. The jobs are derived from both on-farm and off-farm segments of these value chains. However, the data show that the value chain groups with most potential to create jobs tend to have relatively more of their GDP generated from the off-farm segment, which is consistent with the findings in chapter 2 showing that future jobs will increasingly be generated in the off-farm segments. In particular, the traditional cash crops and pulses and oil seeds have relatively higher shares of GDP from the off-farm segment. Productivity growth in these value chains groups would significantly reduce costs and increase supply of raw materials to downstream processing segments, thus generating demand for complementary inputs and trade and transportation services and ultimately creating more jobs in the economy.

The value chain groups with most potential to reduce poverty are pulses, goats and sheep, poultry and eggs, fish and aquaculture, cattle and dairy, and traditional cash crops. The list is dominated by livestock value chains, except for pulses and traditional cash crops. These findings provide important insights to address the regional dimensions of poverty. Poverty in Nigeria is concentrated in the North: the poverty rate in most northern states is more than 61 percent compared to less than 20 percent in most southern states. Because livestock is a relatively more important activity in the North than the South (except for the poultry sector), targeting the livestock value chain groups would inherently target the region with the highest prevalence of poverty and enable the country to progress faster toward the goal of pulling 100 million out of poverty within a decade.

The value chains with most potential to improve nutrition are cattle and dairy, fruits, poultry and eggs, goats and sheep, fish and aquaculture, and vegetables. These findings lead to the conclusion that fruits and vegetables and livestock food groups are the most effective at improving nutrition outcomes among not only poor rural households but also other rural and urban households.

The performance of any value chain depends not only on investments in its various segments but also on productivity-enhancing infrastructure, especially transport and energy, and the agribusiness-enabling environment. These issues will be taken up in more detail in the next chapter. It's important to note that there are major gaps in roads and energy infrastructures across the country, especially in rural areas, and that these gaps increase the cost of inputs such as seeds and fertilizers and lower farm gate prices offered to farmers by downstream agribusinesses. The infrastructure gaps directly contribute to making Nigeria a costly producer for many agricultural commodities and reduce competitiveness of domestic value chains, even in the domestic market. The high levels of food waste and loss in the country are directly related to infrastructure gaps and weak coordination between on-farm and off-farm segments. For example, it is estimated that more than 50 percent of loss and waste in tomato value chains occurs during transport, handling, and storage (World Bank 2020). This means that the productivity-enhancing investments assessed in this chapter should be accompanied by provision of critical infrastructure and policy reforms to improve the agribusiness-enabling environment.

The overarching conclusion from this chapter is that the value chains with most potential to create jobs are not necessarily the most effective at reducing poverty and improving nutrition, clearly calling for a deliberate selection of value chains depending on the policy objective. However, a number of value chains can address multiple objectives. Traditional cash crops and pulses concurrently address the jobs creation and poverty reduction goals. Similarly, the following livestock value chains help reduce poverty and improve nutritional outcomes: cattle and dairy, fruits, poultry and eggs, goats and sheep, and fish and aquaculture.

NOTE

1. The choice to target a 1 percent increase in agricultural GDP is somewhat arbitrary because results are largely unaffected by the magnitude of the target growth acceleration.

REFERENCES

Benfica, Rui, and James Thurlow. 2017. "Identifying Investment Priorities for Malawian Agriculture." Presentation to the Ministry of Agriculture, Irrigation, and Water Development, Lilongwe, February 8.

ESC (Economic Sustainability Committee, Nigeria). 2020. "Bouncing Back: Nigeria Economic Sustainability Plan." Budget Office of the Federation, Abuja.

Ivanic, Marcos, and Will Martin. 2018. "Sectoral Productivity Growth and Poverty Reduction: National and Global Impact." *World Development* 109 (September): 429–39.

Ligon, Ethan, and Elisabeth Sadoulet. 2018. "Estimating the Relative Benefits of Agricultural Growth on the Distribution of Expenditures." *World Development* 109 (September): 417–28.

World Bank. 2020. "Nigeria: Food Smart Country Diagnostic." World Bank, Washington, DC.

4 Major Challenges in Primary Agriculture and Off-Farm Agribusiness

The preceding chapter identified the agricultural value chains with the most potential to create jobs, reduce poverty, and improve nutrition outcomes. The extent to which those value chains could do so is mediated through a complex set of foundational and competitiveness factors that ultimately determine productivity, competitiveness, and other outcomes. Foundational factors relate to the macroeconomic environment, trade policies, sector development policies, and institutions (World Bank 2019). These factors determine the incentive structure for farmers and agribusinesses to invest and compete in domestic and external markets. They also determine the approaches used by actors to organize investments and transactions. The various segments of the agribusiness sector—inputs suppliers, farmers, processors, food services, and so on—rely on public institutions to deliver the necessary amounts of public goods and services to catalyze private investments. Competitiveness factors operate within the foundational factors to ultimately determine productivity and competitiveness. Competitiveness factors include access to improved technology of production, finance, skills of workers, and markets.

This chapter takes a deep dive to assess both types of factors constraining primary agriculture and off-farm agribusinesses from attaining their potential, and it explores the opportunities for mitigating those challenges. First, the analysis considers the problem of low-productivity growth in primary agriculture by taking advantage of recent country-level data from the United States Department of Agriculture's Economic Research Service to compare total factor productivity (TFP) in Nigeria's agriculture sector with that in comparator countries. A discussion of factors that contribute to low TFP helps to identify approaches that may help to increase broad-based productivity growth, including opportunities to operationalize key policy reforms on seed development, plant variety protection, and fertilizer quality control as well as investments in research and development (R&D) and extension and advisory services.

Next, the chapter explores major challenges faced by off-farm agribusiness small and medium enterprises (SMEs) in the food sector. It compares the performance of off-farm agribusiness segments in Nigeria with that of structural peers across the world and of regional peers in Sub-Saharan Africa, building on results from chapter 2. Those results show that the structure of Nigeria's agribusiness sector is comparable to that of middle-income peers such as Pakistan and Vietnam and regional peers such as Ghana and Kenya. Data for the analysis come primarily from responses to the most recent World Bank Enterprise Surveys. Agribusinesses identifiable in the data are firms in the food sector, including those engaged in processing, marketing, and exporting. Agribusinesses in the nonfood sector were lumped together with other sectors (for example, transport and trading) and are not identifiable in the data. However, the book will use the terminology of agribusiness to discuss the findings even though the analysis captures only the food segment and excludes the nonfood segment.

FRAGMENTATION OF AGRICULTURAL VALUE CHAINS

One of the foremost challenges constraining growth of agribusiness value chains in Nigeria is the fragmentation and lack of coordination between inputs supply, primary agriculture, and downstream off-farm agribusinesses. Survey data continue to confirm farmers' limited use of improved inputs, including improved seeds and fertilizers, primarily because these inputs are not readily available to farmers and are often of poor quality. The lack of coordination has persisted because of weak incentives for the private sector to invest in seed development and multiplication. However, recent reforms of seed and fertilizer policies[1] have the potential to, among other things, create an enabling framework for private sector investments in seed segments, support the recognition and protection of intellectual property rights in breeding, enforce seed quality standards and appropriate labeling, and enable imports and commercialization of seeds certified outside the country.

Downstream off-farm segments such as processors and exporters face significant difficulty in building and organizing supply chains, primarily because off-farm agribusinesses have to work with smallholder farmers. Working with smallholder farmers presents several challenges to agribusinesses. The main challenges, at least from the perspective of downstream agribusinesses, include (1) variable quality of production and low productivity due to weak access to improved technology of production and quality inputs; (2) weak access to credit and risk-sharing services, especially by smallholder farmers, which has led to investments in assets with poor returns; (3) high ex post transaction costs for contract enforcement; and (4) ineffective farmer organizations that cannot effectively monitor disparate smallholders or enforce their adherence to obligations under vertical coordination arrangements. The ineffectiveness of farmer organizations persists despite a long history of development projects organizing smallholder farmers into groups—mainly because such groups are formed primarily to pursue livelihoods objectives. It takes significant investments to transition the groups into growth-oriented organizations, such as cooperatives or producer companies, that can form long-term relationships with growth-oriented agribusinesses and incentivize member farmers to invest in appropriate technology to produce the quality desired by remunerative markets.

MAJOR CHALLENGES IN PRIMARY AGRICULTURE

Primary agriculture is dominated by smallholder farmers who rely on rain-fed production systems rather than on irrigation. Smallholder production systems dominate across all regions of the country, accounting for 88 percent of Nigeria's farming population (FAO 2018). The national average area cultivated per household in 2018–19 was 1.12 hectares, with female-headed households cultivating 0.45 hectares compared to 1.24 hectares cultivated by male-headed households. There are, however, some differences across the regions. Area cultivated is lowest in the South East and South South regions, where on average, households cultivated 0.30 hectares and 0.43 hectares, respectively (table 4.1). Farmers in the North East region cultivated the largest area (2.03 hectares) followed by North Central (1.95 hectares). On average only about 2.2 percent of plots operate under irrigation, and irrigation is lowest in the South West (0.6 percent of plots under irrigation) and highest in the North West (5.6 percent of plots under irrigation). The development of irrigation infrastructure coupled with extension services to improve water use efficiency will increase the production capacity of smallholder farmers.[2]

TFP in primary agriculture has not improved for decades. The principal interventions to improve TFP are research to develop and disseminate improved technologies (crop varieties, livestock breeds, management practices, and so on) that are more productive and resilient to agroclimatic changes. TFP captures differences in productivity that are due not to differences in the use of inputs but to factors such as technological progress and efficiency in the conversion of inputs to outputs. A comparison of TFP in agriculture with clusters of countries in Sub-Saharan Africa indicates that TFP in Nigeria has hardly changed since 2005, whereas other countries are making progress (see figure 4.1).

TFP is driven by technical change and technical efficiency change. Technical change is associated with release and application of new technology (farmers reaching a new production frontier), whereas technical efficiency change is about how well farmers use existing technologies (progress toward an existing production frontier). Nigeria's lack of progress on TFP is mainly explained by (1) the significant underinvestment in agriculture research that is required to generate high-yielding and climate-resilient crop varieties and livestock breeds, and (2) weak farmer extension and advisory services that are required to disseminate crop and livestock management practices to enable farmers to use existing technologies efficiently. Nigeria's investment in agricultural research as a share of agricultural gross domestic product (GDP) fell from an already low 0.39 percent in 2008 to 0.22 percent in 2017 (Beintema, Nasir, and Gao 2017). In comparison, the share in Ghana is 0.99 percent, and in South Africa it is 2.79 percent. In the

TABLE 4.1 **The average Nigerian farmer is a smallholder who relies on rain-fed agriculture with little irrigation**

REGION	NUMBER OF PLOTS	NUMBER OF CULTIVATED PLOTS	AVERAGE PLOT SIZE (HECTARES)	SHARE OF PLOTS IRRIGATED (%)	TOTAL LAND HOLDINGS (HECTARES)	TOTAL CULTIVATED AREA (HECTARES)
North Central	3.10	2.76	0.66	1.3	2.05	1.95
North East	2.81	2.08	0.83	1.1	2.31	2.03
North West	2.87	2.16	0.46	5.6	1.28	1.21
South East	3.04	2.08	0.17	1.1	0.52	0.30
South South	3.06	2.31	0.18	0.8	0.55	0.43
South West	1.96	1.41	0.63	0.6	1.24	0.99
Nigeria average	2.85	2.16	0.45	2.2	1.28	1.12

Source: Nigeria General Household Survey, Panel 2018–19, Wave 4.

FIGURE 4.1

Total factor productivity in Nigeria's agriculture sector has barely improved in decades

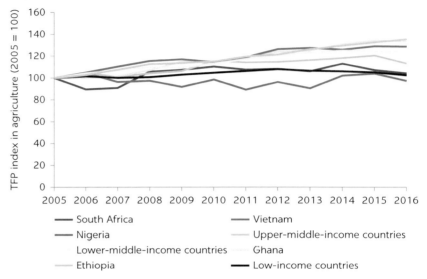

Source: International Agricultural Productivity database (United States Department of Agriculture Economic Research Service) accessed December 2020, https://www.ers.usda .gov/data-products/international-agricultural-productivity/.
Note: TFP = total factor productivity.

face of changing climate and an increasingly fragile natural resource base, targeted agricultural R&D and effective advisory and extension services are critical to deliver the triple wins of improved productivity, enhanced resilience and adaptation, and reduction of greenhouse gas emissions.

A regionally differentiated approach to raising TFP in Nigeria makes sense given the major differences in attained agricultural efficiency across the country and the vast differences in agricultural potential. On the one hand, in states or regions with high or very high agricultural efficiency, agricultural TFP can be increased by shifting to a new production frontier through research to generate and disseminate new varieties, innovations, and management practices that are more productive and resilient. On the other hand, in states or regions with low or moderate efficiency, the priority is for farmers to move toward the existing production frontier, which calls for effective agricultural extension and education to ensure that farmers are able to efficiently apply existing technologies, innovations, and management practices. A combination of measures to shift to a new production frontier and move toward existing frontier would be required in states or regions with medium efficiency. The regionally differentiated approach would need to be supported by measures to address the broader challenges facing farmers, including insufficient availability of improved inputs and technologies, limited private investment in developing improved seeds and fertilizers, and weak access to finance for agriculture (World Bank 2019).

Only farmers in North Central appear to have balanced use of fertilizer and improved seeds. The imbalanced use of these inputs suggests technical inefficiency in most parts of the country and is perhaps due to limited availability of inputs and poor design of fertilizer subsidy programs. Significantly more farmers use inorganic fertilizers than improved seeds in the North West and South East, whereas more farmers use improved seeds than inorganic fertilizers in North East, and South (table 4.2). Overall, less than 10 percent of farmers used improved seeds and inorganic fertilizers together in 2018–19, which is quite low compared to Ethiopia and Kenya where about 40 and 30 percent of farmers, respectively, used improved seed and inorganic fertilizer together (Sheahan and Barrett 2017). The overall proportion of farmers using inorganic fertilizers is higher (35.4 percent) compared to farmers using improved seed (10.1) percent (table 4.2). That disparity points to technical inefficiency in the use of inputs because inorganic fertilizers should be combined with improved seeds, not traditional seeds. It would be important to understand what is driving the poor combination of inputs. Farmers are unlikely to purchase fertilizer at cost only to combine it with traditional seeds; however, if farmers can access fertilizers through subsidy programs at less than full cost, and if such programs don't provide the fertilizers as a package with improved seeds, farmers would quite likely end up using inorganic fertilizers on traditional seeds. Recent estimates suggest that the supply of open pollinated varieties and hybrid seeds from the formal sector was 47 percent of potential demand in Nigeria (Setimela et al. 2017).

Efficiency in the use of inorganic fertilizers and improved seeds can be raised by incentivizing production and distribution of the inputs and adopting the principles of smart subsidies in public fertilizer supply programs. The two key principles of smart subsidies are (1) targeting farmers who need to learn about the proper use of fertilizers or those who could use them but are limited by working capital constraints and (2) delivering subsidies through the private sector by adopting voucher systems mandating that farmers purchase package of fertilizers and improved seeds together. Smart subsidies need to be accompanied with effective extension and service delivery so that farmers can learn about such things as nutrient deficiencies in their plots, nutrient requirements for different crops, crop water requirements, and critical irrigation periods. Access to extension is limited because less than 10 percent of farmers in Nigeria reported receiving advice on new seeds, pest control, and fertilizers (Sheahan and Barrett 2017).

TABLE 4.2 Imbalanced use of improved seeds and inorganic fertilizers suggests technical inefficiency among many farmers in Nigeria

REGION	SHARE USING INORGANIC FERTILIZER (%)	SHARE USING ORGANIC FERTILIZER (%)	SHARE USING PESTICIDE (%)	SHARE USING HERBICIDES (%)	SHARE USING IMPROVED SEEDS (%)	SHARE USING ANIMAL TRACTION (%)	SHARE USING HOUSEHOLD LABOR (%)	SHARE USING HIRED LABOR (%)	SHARE USING EXCHANGE LABOR (%)
North Central	31.6	10.9	9.2	69.3	32	16.3	97.9	70.0	42.2
North East	45.2	23.3	24.3	57.1	72	41.5	99.3	70.4	47.1
North West	69.1	59.8	21.4	23.4	9.7	43.7	98.2	81.8	38.7
South East	29.5	14.7	4.7	12.4	9./	0.0	99.0	78.8	21.3
South South	5.6	2.1	1.0	20.0	21.0	0.0	99.1	58.2	27.8
South West	1.8	0.4	23.9	29.7	8.3	0.0	98.5	76.6	20.1
Nigeria average	35.4	23.1	13.1	34.7	10.1	19.5	98.6	72.8	34.2

Source: Nigeria General Household Survey, Panel 2018–19, Wave 4.

Smallholder farmers have weak access to credit for various reasons. The commercial lending sector tends to consider smallholder agriculture too risky, primarily because lenders face challenges in distinguishing between good and bad borrowers. Furthermore, lenders incur significant costs in processing a large number of relatively small loans to smallholder farmers. Smallholders have weak land rights and face difficulties using land as collateral for commercial credit. They are less likely than medium- and large-scale farmers to have their lands formally registered, primarily because most smallholders acquire land through inheritance, and it is often subdivided among siblings without passage of full rights. In addition, smallholders tend to demand small and high-frequency loans that don't match the financial products available. Agribusiness SMEs also struggle to access credit and to invest in productive assets, capacities, and technologies that increase competitiveness and growth.

The federal government has implemented various schemes to de-risk the sector, but much unfinished business remains. The federal government has taken various measures to help reduce the risks to the financial sector when it lends to agricultural enterprises. A major government initiative was to establish the Nigeria Incentive-Based Risk-Sharing System for Agricultural Lending (NIRSAL)[3] to facilitate lending to agriculture. Other approaches to increase access to financing include the Commercial Agriculture Credit Scheme and the Anchor Borrowers Program. Although these programs may have improved farmers' access to finance,[4] the sector has not been de-risked sufficiently from the perspective of the financial sector, and access to credit is still a big concern among farmers and off-farm agribusinesses that work to establish supply chains. In addition, there is enormous scope for disruption in the financial sector through financial technology (fintech), mobile money, and innovations that deepen financial inclusion, generate information on creditworthiness of entrepreneurs, and improve return on investments in specific value chains. Recent advances in fintech and mobile money (for example, M-PESA in Kenya) have enabled smallholders and informal enterprisers across sectors to access small and high-frequency loans with repayment terms that match their cashflow profiles. In addition, fintech and mobile money applications have proven effective in generating credit records for smallholders, and this information can be harnessed by traditional banks to identify good risks among smallholder farmers.

Governments can support digital agriculture through various type of foundational public investments and policy and regulatory reforms. Technology firms are working around the clock to develop and introduce new digital technologies, platforms, and products in Africa; however, these innovations will benefit only those economies that embrace digitization, invest in the required infrastructure, and introduce an enabling regulatory framework. The main areas for public interventions include policies that lay the foundations for innovation and scaling out of digital technologies, expansion of supporting rural broadband and supporting infrastructure, and collection and digitization of plot-level data on farmers (figure 4.2). Nigeria is already among the leading adopters of digital technologies in agriculture, ranking third behind Kenya and South Africa in 2018 in terms of the number of scalable, disruptive agri-tech hubs (Kim et al. 2020), and second behind South Africa in 2018 in terms of the number of technology incubators and accelerators (Bayen 2018).

FIGURE 4.2

Public investments to support expansion of digital technologies in agriculture

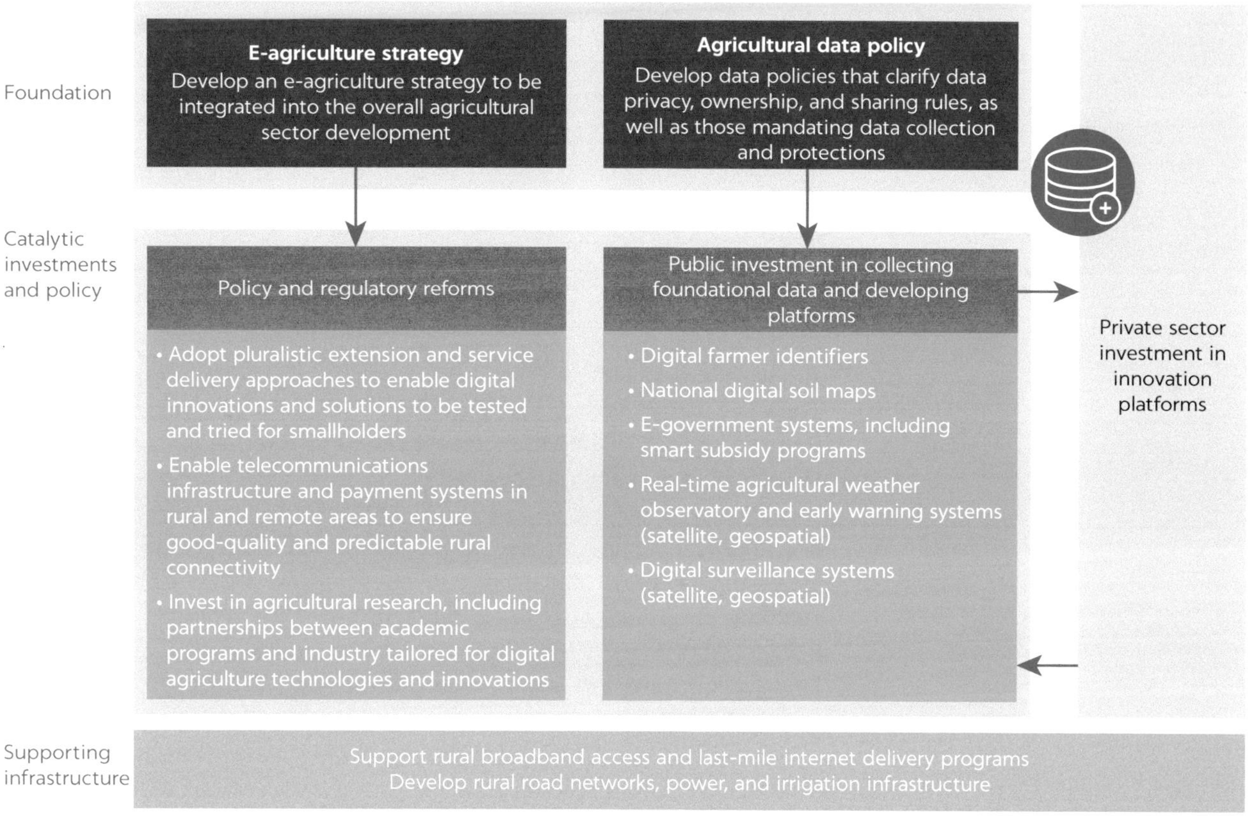

Source: Kim et. al. 2020.

Digital technologies have great potential to catalyze productivity growth in primary agriculture and off-farm agribusiness. Digital tools for monitoring climate risks can help identify the onset of climatic shocks before they happen, thus facilitating responses for building resilience and supporting decision-making at the farm level. They can also increase efficiency in the use of resources for agricultural production, for example by using automated irrigation systems, soil sensors, and drones. Access to finance can be increased when service provision is organized using digital tools, including through platforms for accessing credit, inputs, and crowdfunding capital—for example, Farmcrowdy[5] in Nigeria. With regard to delivery of extension and advisory services, digital tools can be used to diagnose agronomic problems faced by farmers, relay extension advice in real time to address the challenges, enable high-frequency soil testing using digital portable soil testers, and provide farmers with the necessary education and skills to adopt climate-smart management practices and innovations. Digitally enabled tractor-hiring services are improving access to mechanization (for example, Hello Tractor[6]). Agricultural value chains can be strengthened in various ways through digital tools. For example, e-commerce platforms can integrate smaller farmers into value chains and help farmers eliminate the transaction costs of locating demand and determining prices. Food use and food safety can be improved when digital tools are employed for traceability and monitoring of food hazards.

AGRIBUSINESS-ENABLING ENVIRONMENT

The business environment plays an important role in influencing private sector development in a country. An enabling business environment lays the foundation for firms to innovate and invest, which in turn increases productivity, creates employment, and generates taxes and public revenues to support public investments such as infrastructure and security. By contrast, a weak business environment creates obstacles to entrepreneurship and ingenuity of the private sector, leading to lack of innovation and productivity, weak private sector development, and lack of competitiveness in national, regional, and global markets. Trade facilitation services are a key aspect of the enabling environment for accessing regional and global markets. The services include enforcement of global quality standards and improvements in customs procedures and facilities. Trade facilitation services can help reduce transaction costs and improve firm competitiveness, leading to increased access to external markets (Djankov, Freund, and Pham 2010; Iwanow and Kirkpatrick 2009; Rodriguez and Rodrik 2000; Rodrik, Subramanian, and Trebbi 2004). The benefits of economic openness in generating high income and growth are well documented and evidence increasingly suggests that these outcomes increase with a better business-enabling environment (Chang, Kaltani, and Loayza 2009; Freund and Bolaky 2008). In particular, regulatory quality, customs efficiency, quality of infrastructure, and access to finance are among the drivers of export performance (Seker 2011).

Nigeria has made significant improvements in the overall business-enabling environment and agriculture sector policies. It is imperative that recent policy reforms are fully operationalized to generate results and maintain momentum to address the remaining gaps. The overall climate for doing business is improving in Nigeria; it ranked 131 out of 190 economies in the World Bank ease of doing business survey 2020,[7] a major improvement from previous years but still behind the top performers in Sub-Saharan Africa—Rwanda and Kenya at 38 and 56, respectively. The most recent business-enabling environment reforms include the Companies and Allied Matters Act 2020, which provides for improved company registration procedures (including e-signatures for registration), improved insolvency process, enhanced protection of minority investors, and so on. The National Agricultural Seeds Council Act 2019, the National Fertilizer Quality (Control) Act 2019, the Plant Variety Protection Bill, and the legal and regulatory framework for warehouse receipts have significantly improved Nigeria's agribusiness-enabling environment; but they have not been fully operationalized and need to be translated into action plans for implementation. The specific issues in the enabling environment are discussed in the following subsections, focusing on seed development and quality control, fertilizer quality control, warehouse receipt systems, and responsible and inclusive land administration.

Seed development and quality control

Plant breeding. The development of new varieties is critical to ensure that farmers have a steady stream of plants that continue to raise yields while building resilience to effects of climate change, such as new diseases and pests, heat stress, and so on. Plant breeding allows the development of new varieties to adapt to such challenges; therefore, an effective legal and regulatory framework for plant breeding directly affects agricultural productivity. A key aspect of the legal and regulatory environment is the extent to which it grants intellectual property rights over plant materials, which is vital for encouraging private sector investments in the seed sector. Specific regulatory issues include granting and protecting breeder's rights, the duration of the protections granted, nondiscrimination between national and foreign breeders seeking protection, the availability of a list of protected varieties, and the right to license protected varieties. In addition, the private sector needs to be able to access materials essential for innovative breeding, such as early generation seed (breeder seed) developed by the public sector, germplasm stored in publicly managed gene banks, and genetic material imported for research purposes.

Seed quality control. The ultimate objective of the entire formal seed system is to assure that seeds coming to market are of high quality and properly labeled and that low-quality seeds are not sold to farmers. For example, registered or certified seed is produced according to standards set by government regulations and through a process that allows traceability. By contrast, quality declared seed does not meet the standards of registered or certified seed but is considered by relevant authorities to be of sufficiently high quality. Seed quality control systems include tests for specific quality parameters, recordkeeping to ensure traceability of breeding materials through labeling, and provisions for third-party accreditation or self-accreditation to allow the private sector to complement the government process.

The legal and regulatory framework for seed development and quality control has improved tremendously with the passage of the National Agricultural Seeds Council Act 2019, but that act still needs to be operationalized. Among the major reforms embedded in the act is that it empowers the council to encourage the establishment of private seed companies to carry out research, production, processing, and marketing of seed. It also recognizes plant breeders' rights. Although it contains no specific measures to protect those rights, the act empowers the council to approve and implement programs and measures to protect the rights. Private companies can now access early generation seed if their registration allows handling of the seed. Varieties already registered in another country are not automatically approved for commercialization, but the act empowers the Minister of Agriculture and Rural Development to, on the advice of the Seed Registration and Release Subcommittee, waive the testing requirements if an imported variety is already registered under a regional variety release system. For foreign varieties not registered under a regional release system, the subcommittee is empowered to determine the required "limited multi-locational verification trial" according to its rules and procedures. The new act does not require varieties for export or varieties to produce commodities for exports to be subject to variety release or registration requirements unless required by the importing country. However, the related legislation on phytosanitary and bio-safety controls legislation applies. Operationalization of the act will help remove poor quality seeds from the market. The act clarifies the functions of seed inspectors and provides them sufficient powers to take samples of any seeds of any variety from any person or entity marketing or purchasing seed, carry out seed testing, search premises handling seed, and carry out field inspection necessary to monitor seed production and certification.

Fertilizer quality control

Fertilizer production is energy intensive, and the industry benefits from economies of scale as well as low costs of raw materials. It is no surprise, therefore, that the world's production capacity is concentrated in a few countries. With just five countries producing half or more of the global supply of the most common types of fertilizer, simple and uncomplicated import procedures are essential to fertilizer access in countries around the world. In most countries, fertilizer cannot be imported, manufactured, distributed, sold, or used unless it has been registered with the designated authority in the country. Registration of fertilizer products ensures the safe entry of new products into the market because governments can provide market oversight through a registration scheme and test the fertilizer's impact on soil, human health, and the environment. Moreover, product registration gives farmers confidence in the products they use. This is important because the damage caused by adulterated fertilizer is typically not apparent until months after application. Such damage undermines trust in fertilizer quality and discourages farmers from using fertilizer. Quality control and inspection methods, as well as punishments for breaking laws, vary significantly across the world; however, a minimum set of standards to increase fertilizer quality control can be applied in all countries and across regions and income groups.

The National Fertilizer Quality (Control) Act 2019 sets the framework for effective quality control of fertilizers, and its full operationalization is critical. Under the old policy regime, the permit to import and distribute fertilizer was valid for only one year and the process to obtain it took three months. These factors were major disincentives for private sector participation in fertilizer importation and distribution. With the new act, the time for processing the permits for fertilizer imports, trade, and distribution is reduced from three months to 30 days. Furthermore, the duration of the permit has increased from one year to three years—and the owner of a permit need not apply afresh after three years but instead pays a renewal fee. This provision creates stable expectations among the private sector and has the potential to catalyze more investments in the fertilizer business. The act also provides elaborate procedures and timelines for conflict resolution when a permit or certificate of registration is canceled. In addition, the act sets a framework for effective quality control of fertilizers. It provides a detailed account of prohibited activities, offenses, and penalties in fertilizer handling and trade—including operating without registration, selling fertilizers that contain destructive ingredients or properties that are harmful to the plant group, repurposing of fertilizers to other uses, and obstruction of duly authorized officers from carrying out their enforcement and regulatory functions. The inspection and enforcement actions are specified in the new law, including the power to enter and inspect, taking of official samples for analysis, and the power of the Minister of Agriculture and Rural Development to issue orders that stop the sale or disposal of fertilizers whenever there is a reasonable cause. Labeling requirements are stipulated, including the maximum allowable quantity deviations between the label and the physical samples.

Warehouse receipt system

A warehouse receipt system (WRS) enables farmers and traders to access finance by liquidating part of the value of their nonperishable commodities while searching for better prices. The system is composed of the following parties: depositors of commodities—mainly farmers, farmer organizations, and traders; warehousing facilities and collateral management services; banks and financial institutions; and buyers of commodities and warehouse receipts, including traders, millers, exporters, and so on. The basic system works as follows. First, the owner of a commodity deposits the goods in a certified warehouse. The owner could be an individual farmer, an organization of farmers (for example, a cooperative) or a trader. The collateral management firm verifies quality on delivery at the warehouse and issues a warehouse receipt to the depositor who takes the receipt to a participating bank and receives credit up to a certain value of the commodity deposited. The credit is normally below full value, however full value is assessed. The transaction normally happens around harvest time when market prices are low. As market prices improve, the depositor looks for buyers, reaches agreement on purchase price, and informs the bank holding the warehouse receipt. The buyer pays the agreed purchase price to the bank in exchange for the warehouse receipt. The bank deducts the loan repayment amount, pays collateral manager and warehousing costs, and credits the balance to the depositor's account. Finally, the buyer takes delivery of the commodity from the collateral manager.

The completion of the legal and regulatory framework for a WRS is imperative to enable operationalization of various warehouse receipts initiatives (box 4.1). Various stakeholders have made enormous efforts in the past few years to develop a WRS, including investments in warehouses and farmer training programs. On the legal and regulatory front, a warehouse receipt bill was duly passed by parliament and other organs of government and presented for presidential assent in 2019. The bill did not receive presidential assent, however, primarily because a major financial regulatory agency thought the bill was consistent with broader laws defining negotiable instruments, passage of title for goods, use of assets as collateral, bankruptcy laws, contract laws, and so on. The legal and regulatory vacuum means that any warehouse receipts issued are not negotiable instruments and cannot be used as collateral in the commercial banking sector.

In addition to the legal and regulatory frameworks, various physical investments and institutions are required to facilitate a functioning WRS. The required physical investments, institutions, and services relate to warehousing infrastructure, collateral management, registration of warehouse receipts in the collateral registry, grading system for commodities in storage, banking and financial services, and capacity-building services, especially for farmers and their organizations.

Warehousing infrastructure. Certification of warehouses is a critical part of the system because not all storage facilities can preserve the quality of commodities. Certification must be credible and independently executed by reliable evaluators of assets and systems without any interference. Certification is typically carried out by private agencies on behalf of the WRS regulator (government agency or self-regulation by industry). Furthermore, warehouses must have adequate capacity and connection to transport and infrastructure, and be located close enough to production zones. In countries where the government owns warehouses that can be used for WRSs, the normal practice is to offer concessions to the private sector to upgrade, use, and maintain the facilities well before they are assessed by a certification agent. Concessions avoid conflicts of interest that can potentially erode trust in the system. Warehouses should be equipped with appropriate technology for verifying grades and quality of commodities

Box 4.1

Key elements of an effective legal and regulatory framework for a warehouse receipt system

The key elements of an effective legal and regulatory framework for a warehouse receipt system provide for the following:

- It defines the rights and obligations of all the parties.
- It specifically recognizes a warehouse receipt instrument as collateral that is different from general "goods in storage."
- It allows subsequent potential creditors of a warehouse receipt to determine whether there are any preexisting claims or encumbrances on the warehouse receipts themselves or assets that underlie the warehouse receipt.
- In the case of a default by the debtor, the law must clarify that the party holding a warehouse receipt has first priority to recover the underlying assets or their proceeds.
- It allows warehouse receipts to be transferred and clearly defines that the transfer of ware-

house receipt is the equivalent of transferring the underlying assets.

- It has an adequate insurance regulatory framework to cover the property in warehouses for damages.
- It legally establishes a body for certifying and supervising warehouses—either a government agency or a body that allows for self-regulation by the industry.
- It recognizes the grading systems for verifying the quantity and quality of the commodities stored.
- A dependable court system exists to settle commercial disputes. The courts should understand the warehouse receipt system and its enabling legal and regulatory framework and apply the law appropriately in cases of default.
- It includes institutionalized participatory processes for reviewing and updating the legal and regulatory framework to ensure parties are comfortable with the system.

upon delivery, including properly calibrated weighting scales and facilities to test for grain moisture content, size, and physical defects.

Collateral management. The proper management of goods in storage requires implementation of standard operating procedures for fumigation, packaging, labeling, and rotating commodities in storage. Because traceability is crucial for exportable commodities, part of collateral management involves tracing the practices, methods, and processes used in production. For example, food regulations in the European Union and the United States require that commodities are traced along the agricultural value chains and that data are available on specific health, safety, and agricultural practices. Part of collateral management will include installing an electronic traceability system in which bags are tagged with geo-referencing to area of production, aggregation points, washing and hulling stations, and so on.

Collateral registry. A warehouse receipt is a financial instrument that must be registered in a designated, reliable, easy-to-register, and easy-to-search registry that is designated by law. The registry should be searchable by all parties. Modern warehouse receipts are electronic and backed by an electronic collateral registry system, although paper-based instruments are still in use.

Grading system for commodities. Not all agricultural commodities can be accommodated in a WRS. A core requirement is that a commodity is not perishable and can be stored for a substantial amount of time. A WRS therefore tends to cater to grain commodities; however, recent innovations for perishables operate like a WRS using cold storage facilities.[8] In addition to nonperishability, commodities that benefit from a WRS tend to have the following characteristics: high volumes of production and marketing, prices set by the market instead of by the government, enough price movement to offset costs of storage and loans, and a formal and simple grading system that can be commonly understood by various parties, verifiable with simple technology, and founded on desirable attributes that are rewarded by the market. A formal grading system allows parties to engage on the basis of the commodity's description and without the need for physical inspection. WRSs operate at national or regional levels, and the grading systems used should be consistent with the reference market. In practical terms, however, a WRS could begin with national standards and evolve toward regional standards as market coverage expands.

Banking and financial services. The main role of banking and financial services is to assure WRS parties that warehouse receipts will be honored as valid negotiable instruments. As part of their due diligence, banks might be willing to trade the receipt only if the goods in storage are insured, hence the need for an active insurance sector that can cover insurable risks for goods in storage to indemnify banks in case of losses.

Capacity building. The main capacity building needs relate to enabling farmers to understand how to use the warehouse receipt instruments and their rights and obligations. Critical training needs often include grades and standards, proper postharvest handling, technology of aggregation, and marketing. When production is mostly small-scale, farmers benefit more if organized into effective farmer organizations with the capacity to aggregate commodities, ensure proper grading, and engage with large buyers. Without functioning farmer organizations, depositors will mainly be traders, and the small-scale farmers will lose the opportunity to use the WRS as a means for increasing access to finance.

Responsible and inclusive land administration

Land administration across Nigerian states operates under an ambiguous and nonuniform framework that lacks sufficient protections for the large number of agricultural households deriving livelihoods directly from the land. The requirements for land transfers are not standardized, and property rights are uncertain, contributing to thin land markets and weakened incentives for long-term investments by landholders. The legal framework for land administration consists of the Land Use Act of 1978 and the Urban and Regional Planning Act, Decree No. 88, of 1992. State governments control land administration within their state boundaries through executive governors who have legal authority to make any decisions on land administration in their states. In addition to the acts and the authority vested with the executive governors, legitimate customary and religious practices and norms often have the force of law. The ambiguous framework for land administration has encouraged informal land transfers that don't afford enough protections to the parties and don't create stable expectations that would enhance investments on land. It is estimated that nearly 70 percent of land transactions are informal (Butler 2012), and only 3 percent of land is formally registered.[9] Even private sector companies face enormous challenges when allocated land by state governments because in many cases the land is encumbered with competing claims. For example, out of about 140,406 hectares of land allocated to the private sector by the Ogun State government, investors have been able to occupy only 30 percent;[10] the remaining 70 percent is contested by the communities.

The adoption and implementation of the Framework for Responsible and Inclusive Land Intensive Agricultural Investments (FRILIA) is critical to addressing challenges in land administration for agricultural (and nonagricultural) purposes. Currently, only Ogun and Kaduna states have embarked on the process of adopting FRILIA[11] through the support of World Bank–financed projects.[12] The scaling-out of FRILIA to more states will afford enormous economies of scale and provide communities, investors, and other stakeholders with a modern framework to guide responsible land-based agricultural investments. In particular, the adoption of FRILIA would enable state governments to enhance regulatory, institutional, and operational systems and provisions for land administration to attract private sector investments while protecting existing land-based agricultural livelihoods, thus addressing competing claims on land without leaving any claimants worse off and mitigating social and environmental impacts related to land acquisition, resettlement of claimants, and new investments.

FRILIA comprises 33 principles organized into the following: overarching principles, principles on recognizing and protecting land rights, principles on state land acquisition and resettlement, and principles related to environmental and social sustainability. The principles are derived from two internationally negotiated agreements on responsible land-based investments: (1) the Voluntary Guidelines on the Responsible Governance of Tenure of Land, Fisheries, and Forests in the Context of National Food Security and (2) the United Nations Committee on World Food Security's Principles for Responsible Investment in Agriculture and Food Systems. FRILIA's overarching principles are the following:

- Investments in (agricultural) lands should occur transparently.
- Investments should be consistent with the objectives of social and economic growth and sustainable human development.
- Responsible investment should protect against dispossession of legitimate, including derivative, tenure rights holders.
- Responsible investment should protect against environmental damage.
- Investments should contribute to policy objectives, including but not limited to poverty reduction, food security, sustainable land use, employment creation, and socioeconomic support to local communities.
- Where possible, a range of production and investment models such as joint ventures, outgrower schemes, and other inclusive models that encourage partnerships with legitimate tenure holders should be considered as alternatives to the large-scale transfer of land.
- Investment models should seek to ensure that affected communities have the opportunity and responsibility to decide, based on informed choices, whether or not to make nonstate land available for investments; receive secure sustained and well-defined benefits; receive fair compensation for the land (including common areas) and natural resources (excluding subsurface resources) that they make available to investment; engage in partnerships with investors and government; be able to hold investors accountable to their commitments; and respect and abide by their own commitments.

- Investment should include consultation with affected people and communities, including those that are disadvantaged or vulnerable; they should be informed of their rights and assisted by government or others to develop their capacity to engage in consultations and negotiations.
- Large-scale investments should be preceded by independent assessments of potential positive and negative impacts on tenure rights, food security, livelihoods, and the environment.
- All existing legitimate rights, including customary and informal rights and rights to common property resources, should be systematically and impartially identified.
- Investments should be monitored and grievance redress mechanisms provided for aggrieved parties.

The specific FRILIA principles on land acquisition and resettlement are the following:

- Land acquisition and related adverse impacts should as much as possible be minimized or avoided.
- Economic and social impacts caused by land acquisition or loss of access to natural resources (excluding subsurface resources) shall be identified and addressed, including those affecting people who may lack legal rights to assets or resources they use or occupy.
- Compensation will be provided sufficient to purchase replacement assets of equivalent value and to meet any necessary transitional expenses, paid before taking of land or restricting access.
- Supplemental livelihood improvement or restoration measures will be provided if taking of land causes loss of income-generating opportunity (for example, loss of crop production or employment).
- Public infrastructure and community services that may be adversely affected will be replaced or restored.
- Where livelihoods of displaced persons are land-based, or where land is collectively owned, displaced persons should be offered an option for replacement land, unless equivalent land is not available.
- Economically displaced people with legal rights or claims should receive replacement property (for example, agricultural or commercial sites) of equal or greater value, or, where appropriate, cash compensation, at replacement cost.
- If it is demonstrated that replacement land or resources are unavailable, economically displaced people should be provided with options for alternative income-earning opportunities, such as credit facilities, skills training, business start-up assistance, employment opportunities, or cash assistance additional to the compensation.
- Transitional support will be provided as necessary to all economically displaced persons, based on a reasonable estimate of the time required to restore their income-earning capacity, production levels, and standards of living.
- Displaced persons need to be engaged about their options and rights pertaining to involuntary resettlement, including processes on involuntary resettlement; and livelihood restoration should include options and alternatives from which project-affected persons may choose. Disclosure of relevant information and meaningful consultation should take place throughout the design and implementation phases of the resettlement process.
- Compensation standards for categories of land and fixed assets need to be disclosed and applied consistently. Compensation rates may be subject to

upward adjustment when negotiations strategies are employed. In all cases, a clear basis for calculation of compensation will be documented and compensation distributed in accordance with transparent procedures.

- Particular attention should be paid to the engagement and needs of vulnerable groups among those displaced, especially those below the poverty line, the landless, elderly, women and children, people with disabilities, or other displaced persons who may not be protected through national land compensation legislation.

- Grievance redress mechanisms need to be established to provide accessible and affordable procedures for third-party settlement of disputes arising from displacement or resettlement; these mechanisms should consider the availability of judicial recourse and community and traditional dispute mechanisms.

- Any action related to the displacement of people must comply with federal and state laws and be conducted in a manner consistent with basic principles of due process (including provision of adequate advance notice, meaningful opportunities to lodge grievances and appeals, and avoidance of the use of unnecessary, disproportionate, or excessive force).

The specific FRILIA principles on environmental and social sustainability are the following:

- Investments should incorporate recognized elements of environmental and social assessment good practice, including early screening of potential effects; consideration of strategic, technical, and site alternatives (including the "no action" alternative); explicit assessment of potential induced, cumulative, and transboundary impacts; identification of measures to mitigate adverse environmental or social impacts that cannot be otherwise avoided or minimized; and responsiveness and accountability through stakeholder consultation, timely dissemination of program information, and responsive grievance redress measures.

- Investments should incorporate due consideration for social risks and impacts, including threats to human security through the escalation of personal, communal, or interstate conflict; crime or violence; risks that project impacts fall disproportionately on individuals or groups who may be disadvantaged or vulnerable; any prejudice or discrimination toward individuals or groups in providing access to investment benefits, particularly in the case of those who may be disadvantaged or vulnerable; and any risks related to conflict or contestation over land and natural resources.

- Investments should include appropriate measures for early identification and screening of potentially important biodiversity and cultural resource areas.

- Investments should support and promote the conservation, maintenance, and rehabilitation of natural habitats; avoid the significant conversion or degradation of critical natural habitats, including legally protected forest reserve; and, if avoiding the significant conversion of natural habitats is not technically feasible, include measures to mitigate or offset impacts of program activities.

- Investments should consider potential adverse impacts on physical cultural property and, as warranted, provide adequate measures to preserve such property and avoid, minimize, or mitigate such adverse impacts.

- Investments should promote community, individual, and worker safety through the safe design, construction, operation, and maintenance of physical infrastructure, industrial, and agricultural facilities; or, in carrying out activities that may be dependent on such infrastructure and facilities, with safety measures, inspections, or remedial works incorporated as needed.

- Investments should promote the use of recognized good practice in the production, management, storage, transport, and disposal of hazardous materials generated through program construction or operations; promote the use of integrated pest management practices to manage or reduce pests or disease vectors; and provide training for workers involved in the production, procurement, storage, transport, use, and disposal of hazardous chemicals in accordance with international guidelines and conventions.
- Investments should promote fair treatment, nondiscrimination, and equal opportunity of workers and prevent the use of all forms of forced labor and child labor in accordance with national and state laws.
- Investments should include measures to avoid, minimize, or mitigate community, individual, and worker risks when program activities are located within areas prone to natural hazards such as floods, hurricanes, earthquakes, or other severe weather or climate events.

MAJOR CHALLENGES IN OFF-FARM AGRIBUSINESS SMALL AND MEDIUM ENTERPRISES

Access to skills and quality certification

Agribusinesses in Nigeria scored average on workforce skills development and tend to have relatively inexperienced managers. As with other private enterprises, growth of off-farm agribusiness depends on the abilities of its workforce, including entrepreneurial skills, technical knowledge, and managerial capacity (Rao 2012; World Bank 2013; Yumkella et al. 2011). With respect to workforce development, Nigerian agribusinesses scored average in terms of offering formal training, with only 36 percent of Nigerian agribusinesses doing so (figure 4.3). In addition to private sector initiatives for skills development, there is need for private-public partnerships with government to develop technical college curriculums that enable students to learn critical skills demanded for transformation of the food industry. For example, the World Bank–financed Ogun State Economic Transformation Project integrates support for agricultural value chains with skills development and improvement in the business-enabling environment. Investments that augment skills include adoption of quality standards and processes. About 43.8 percent agribusiness in Kenya and Pakistan possessed an internationally recognized quality certification, compared to 11.4 percent and 16.7 percent in Nigeria and Ghana, respectively (figure 4.4).

Access to finance

In countries where businesses struggle, particularly across Sub-Saharan Africa, financial institutions (FIs) have difficulty lending to business that cannot provide sufficient evidence of past performance or clearly convey their ongoing financial viability. Agricultural SMEs may go out of business frequently, change their main activity, or evolve in unplanned ways. Financing discrete projects by obscure entrepreneurs who may disappear, or against whom FIs have little legal recourse, is riskier than financing an established agribusiness. In these situations, businesses may be able to get small amounts of financing, but it is rare for

FIGURE 4.3

Nigerian agribusinesses score average in terms of offering formal training

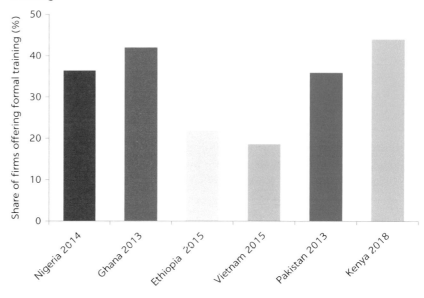

Source: World Bank Enterprise Surveys data.

FIGURE 4.4

Relatively few Nigerian agribusinesses have international certification

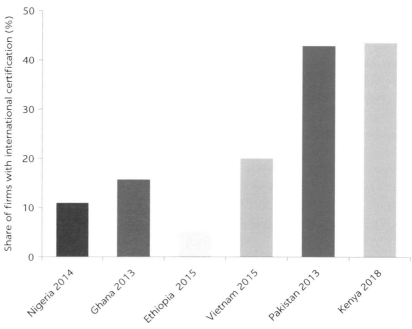

Source: World Bank Enterprise Surveys data.

them to obtain sufficient capital to grow. FIs require large guarantees from these borrowers, and interest rates are high. Agribusinesses and FIs have difficulty reconciling their respective needs, and a dynamic may emerge in which agribusinesses feel that FIs do not provide sufficient investment and working capital financing for profitable projects, while FIs feel that agribusinesses do not take measures to share sufficiently the considerable downside investment risks of the projects presented for financing.

Off-farm agribusinesses in Nigeria have difficulty accessing investment and working capital financing from banks. Access to finance is a common problem faced by agribusinesses across all comparator countries (figure 4.5), such that firms rely more on internal financing for most of their investment needs and less on financing from banks. The problem appears to be more severe in Nigeria: only 6.7 percent of Nigerian agribusinesses have a credit or loan from a bank compared to more than 40 percent in Ethiopia, Kenya, and Vietnam (figure 4.6). Furthermore, access to bank financing for working capital is lowest among Nigerian agribusinesses, with only 1.7 percent of working capital financed by banks compared to about 27 percent in Vietnam, 18 percent in Ethiopia and Kenya, and 7 percent in Ghana (figure 4.7). Faced with difficulties in obtaining working capital from banks, Nigeria agribusinesses rely more on credit from suppliers and customers to meet about 41 percent of their working capital needs (figure 4.8). The use of supplier- and customer-financed working capital in Nigeria is comparable to Kenya and higher than in Ethiopia, Pakistan, and Vietnam. Such financing arrangements are used extensively in developing countries to lower repayments risks, and are promoted widely through public programs, private business to business efforts and by nongovernmental organizations.

Coordinated value chain financing arrangements can concurrently address the financing needs faced by farmers and off-farm agribusinesses while removing fragmentation of agricultural chains. The factors contributing to weak access to credit by agribusinesses are varied and include foundational and structural issues in the financial services sector, weak competitiveness of agribusinesses in domestic and export markets, high risk of failure and stunted growth, lack of financing instruments such as WRSs, and the structure of primary agriculture, which is dominated by smallholders whom banks perceive as bad risks. These challenges require a multipronged approach that includes reforming the financial services sector, improving the agribusiness-enabling environment, and disruption of the financial services sector with fintech products that meet the needs of agribusiness SMEs and smallholders while generating information on creditworthiness of the farmers and riskiness of specific agricultural enterprises. In addition to these reforms, there is evidence that coordinated value chain financing arrangements can be very successful in Nigeria because they take a "whole-of-agribusiness" approach to address financing needs across multiple actors in the value chains. The Babban Gona model provides important lessons on interventions that can effectively link smallholder farmers to input suppliers and output markets while providing financial services and building capacity of farmer organizations (box 4.2). The model operates in northern parts of Nigeria and could be scaled out to other value chains around the country.

Without value chain financing, SMEs that face relatively more severe financial constraints cannot invest in innovative technologies and risk being

FIGURE 4.5

In Nigeria, less than 10 percent of investment is financed by banks

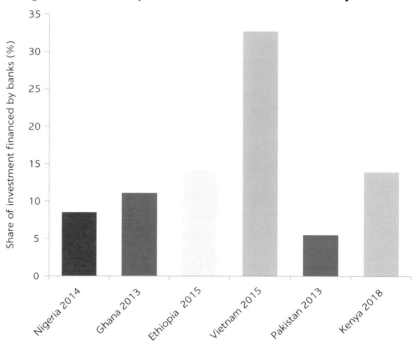

Source: World Bank Enterprise Surveys data.

FIGURE 4.6

Nigeria has the lowest proportion of agribusinesses accessing finance

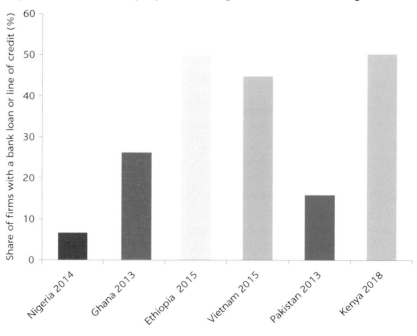

Source: World Bank Enterprise Surveys data.

FIGURE 4.7

Less than 2 percent of working capital for agribusinesses in Nigeria is financed by banks

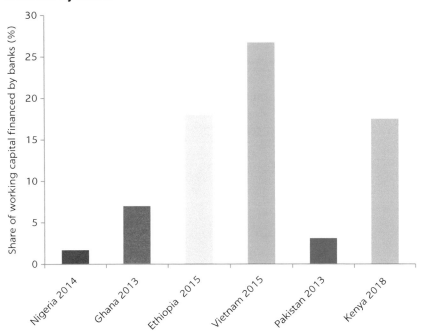

Source: World Bank Enterprise Surveys data.

FIGURE 4.8

Nigeria agribusinesses rely more on suppliers and customers for working capital

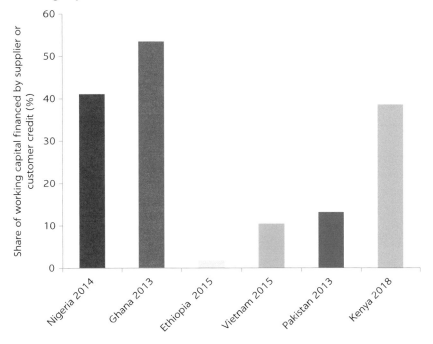

Source: World Bank Enterprise Surveys data.

Box 4.2

The Babban Gona model

Babban Gona works with growth-oriented small-holder farmers and provides them a private sector channel for cost-effective delivery of enhanced agricultural technologies and end-to-end services that optimize yields and labor productivity, while simultaneously improving market access. In particular, the model provides member smallholder farmers the following services: (1) financial services—de-risking members of farmer groups to access cost-effective financing; (2) agricultural input services—timely provision of quality inputs at competitive prices to increase productivity and product quality, while minimizing impacts on the environment; (3) training and development—strengthening farmer organizations; and (4) market access—access to market services, good warehousing practices, and increased profits. Among other goals, Babban Gona aims to reach 1 million farmers by 2025 and increase their incomes fourfold.

Source: Based on Babban Gona's Our Model web page, https://babbangona.com/our-model/.

eliminated from value chains. A case study of the soybean value chain in Kaduna, Nigeria, illustrates the gradual elimination of SMEs that cannot access finance to invest in solvent process technologies (box 4.3).

Informality

Informality is widespread among business in Nigeria and is evident through various characteristics of firms. Firms may possess aspects of informality but still behave like formal businesses. For example, some firms may register their businesses with the authorities but then operate without obtaining necessary licenses or fail to maintain financial statements or a system of accounting. Others may be registered and obtain all legally required licenses, yet they hire employees without using formal employment contracts, or fail to withhold income taxes, or fail to make legally mandated payments into the national social security system on behalf of their employees.

Nigerian agribusinesses perceive less competition from unregistered or informal firms, but this is likely because they tend to possess more characteristics of informality themselves. Nearly 48 percent of agribusinesses in Nigeria compete with unregistered, informal sector firms, which is lower than Ghana (71 percent) and Kenya (60 percent) (figure 4.9). However, less than 15 percent of Nigeria's agribusinesses consider the practices of the informal sector as a major constraint, compared to 32.3 percent and 48.0 percent in Ghana and Kenya, respectively (figure 4.10). Nigerian agribusinesses may perceive less competition from unregistered or informal firms than their counterparts in Ghana and Kenya because Nigerian agribusinesses tend to possess more characteristics of informality themselves. It is also possible that operating as a formal agribusiness business in Ghana and Kenya has costs that put agribusinesses in these countries at a relatively greater cost disadvantage with respect to informal and unregistered agribusinesses. These assumptions are worth exploring through a more rigorous analysis of informality.

Box 4.3

Lack of coordinated value chain financing is eliminating soybean small and medium enterprises that carry out primary processing

Small and medium enterprises (SMEs) in soybean oil processing operate in the middle segment of the value chain, receiving soybeans from farmers and carrying out primary processing to produce oil. Soybean yields have not increased appreciably over the years, but demand and prices for the commodity are rising. Most of the value chain is organized through spot markets such that processors make deals with farmers at the point of harvest. Contract farming is uncommon.

Incentives for processors to develop vertical coordination arrangements are weak because of the poor environment for contract enforcement and the risk that competitors can buy the commodity from farmers under contract without any recourse. The organization of the value chain is such that SMEs carry out primary processing and sell the oil to large enterprises for final processing. However, the technology gap in processing between large enterprises and SMEs keeps widening. Large enterprises are increasingly investing in solvent extraction, but SMEs face more severe constraints on access to capital and continue to rely on mechanical extraction technologies. Mechanical extraction is increasingly inefficient, and the increasingly unfavorable cost structure of SMEs means that large enterprises with more efficient technology can increase margins by avoiding SMEs and integrating backward into primary processing.

More SMEs are competing with the large enterprises they used to work with, and these large enterprises can offer better prices to farmers because their extraction technology is more efficient and their costs are lower. Coordinated value chain financing would enable SMEs to upgrade processing technology from mechanical to solvent and develop new and quality by-products such as oil cakes for the feed industry. The arrangement could also benefit other value chain actors—for example, by enabling research institutions to develop high-yield varieties and farmers to adopt those high-yield varieties and use complementary inputs.

Innovation and technology

An innovation system encompasses

> a network of organizations, enterprises and individuals focused on bringing new products, new processes and new forms of organization into economic use, together with the institutions and policies that affect their behavior and performance. The innovation concept embraces not only the science suppliers, but the totality and interaction of actors involved in innovation. It extends beyond knowledge creation to encompass factors that affect demand for and use of knowledge in novel and useful ways. (World Bank 2007)

The development and adoption of innovations depend on knowledge and education (the supply side), business and enterprise (the demand side), and bridging institutions that facilitate knowledge transfer between the supply and demand side (Arnold and Bell 2001). Agribusinesses are increasingly using innovations to improve efficiency in various parts of the food system, including inputs delivery, primary production, trading, processing, and food services. More recently, innovations in digital technologies have been transforming various aspects of primary agriculture in African countries that offer a more conducive environment, especially in Kenya and South Africa (Kim et al. 2020).

FIGURE 4.9

Many agribusinesses in Nigeria compete with the informal sector

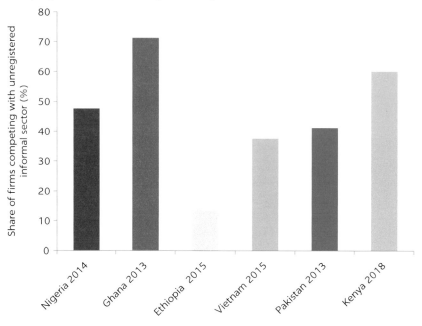

Source: World Bank Enterprise Surveys data.

FIGURE 4.10

Less than 15 percent of agribusinesses in Nigeria find practices of the informal sector a major issue

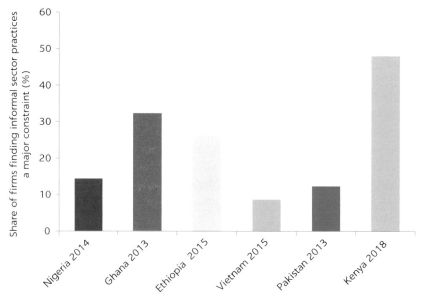

Source: World Bank Enterprise Surveys data.

Lagging innovation and technology adoption in Nigeria's agribusinesses are constraining competitiveness. Only 6.4 percent of Nigerian agribusinesses reported using technology licensed from foreign companies, and 13.3 percent reported spending on R&D. Both these indicators are higher in Ghana, Kenya, and Vietnam (figure 4.11 and figure 4.12); however, Nigeria agribusinesses lead the comparator countries in terms of introducing new products and services and process innovation (figure 4.13 and figure 4.14). The relatively higher rates of introducing new processes (70 percent) may indicate that Nigerian agribusinesses are catching up with peers whose rates are much lower (about 38 percent in Ethiopia and Vietnam and less than 26 percent in Kenya and Pakistan). At the same time, Nigerian agribusinesses compare unfavorably with respect to internet usage: only 19.7 percent of firms reported having a website.

Access to infrastructure

Access to various types of infrastructure is a major problem across countries. In Nigeria, access to electricity is a bigger problem than access to transportation and water services. About 48 percent of agribusinesses in Nigeria consider access to electricity a major constraint, whereas transportation and water are considered major constraints by 18 percent and 15 percent, respectively. Electrical outages are quite rampant; across all comparator countries (except Vietnam) more than 75 percent of agribusinesses reported experiencing electrical outages (figure 4.15). Figures are highest in Nigeria (93 percent) and Kenya (96 percent). On average, Nigerian agribusinesses reported 24.5 outages per month (nearly every weekday) with each lasting about 15 hours, which is considerably higher than the rest of the countries except Pakistan (figure 4.16). Each power outage lasts more than half a day in Nigeria (figure 4.17), and the outages resulted in an

FIGURE 4.11

Relatively few agribusinesses in Nigeria use foreign-licensed technology

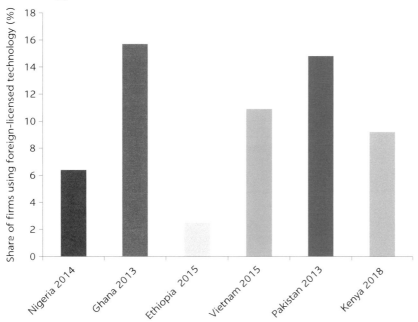

Source: World Bank Enterprise Surveys data.

FIGURE 4.12

Nigeria's agribusinesses spend relatively less on research and development

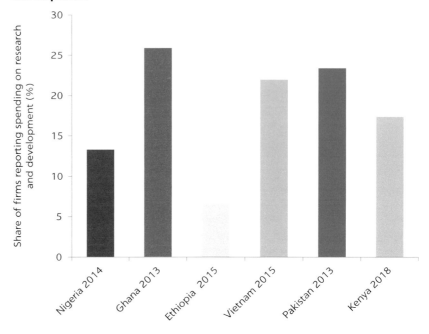

Source: World Bank Enterprise Surveys data.

FIGURE 4.13

Nigeria has highest share of agribusinesses introducing a new product or service

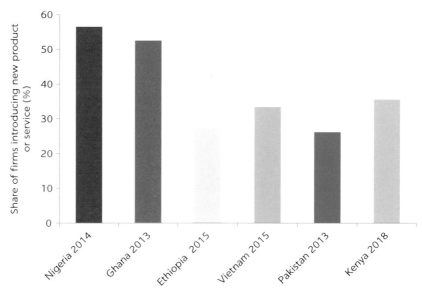

Source: World Bank Enterprise Surveys data.

FIGURE 4.14

Nigeria has higher share of agribusinesses introducing process innovation

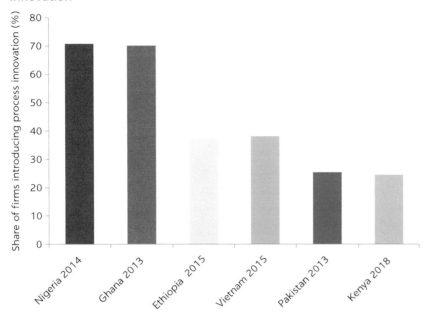

Source: World Bank Enterprise Surveys data.

FIGURE 4.15

Electrical outages are a common problem faced by agribusinesses, Nigeria and comparator countries

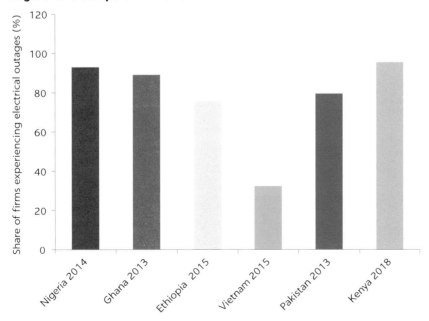

Source: World Bank Enterprise Surveys data.

FIGURE 4.16

Nigerian agribusinesses experience electrical outages nearly every weekday

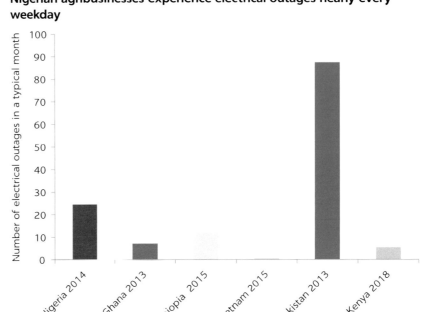

Source: World Bank Enterprise Surveys data.

FIGURE 4.17

Each power outage lasts more than half a day in Nigeria

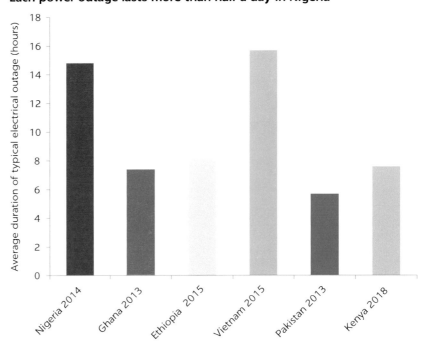

Source: World Bank Enterprise Surveys data.

FIGURE 4.18

Electrical outages cause significant loss of sales and spoilage of products in Nigeria

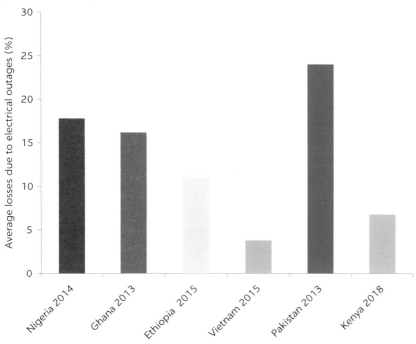

Source: World Bank Enterprise Surveys data.

estimated loss of 17.8 percent of sales (figure 4.18), higher than the average of the comparator countries. Transportation problems were cited as major constraints by 18 percent of Nigerian agribusinesses, which is lower than in Ghana, Kenya, and Pakistan.

CONCLUSIONS

This chapter examined the major issues determining whether on-farm and off-farm agribusinesses can attain sufficient productivity growth to achieve their potential in creating jobs, reducing poverty, and improving nutrition outcomes. Perhaps the most salient feature of the on-farm segment is that it is dominated by smallholder farmers who rely on rain-fed production systems, rather than irrigated agriculture, and are slow to adopt improved technology of production. These characteristics of smallholder farmers impose significant challenges to agribusinesses that are involved in downstream postharvest management activities. The poor adoption of improved technology of production means that production from smallholder farmers tends to be of variable quality, making it hard for agribusinesses to provide consistent quality of products to their forward markets. In cases where the products are inputs to another production process, the weak adoption of technology at the farm level can trap an entire agribusiness segment in a low-productivity equilibrium. Smallholders can be organized into farmer organizations (for example, cooperatives) that operate at sufficient scale to agglomerate production and meet the quantities demanded by agribusinesses. However, farmer organizations are often unable to effectively monitor disparate smallholders to adhere to their obligations under vertical coordination arrangements with agribusinesses, despite a long history of development projects organizing smallholder farmers into groups. The main constraint is that many farmer organizations tend to pursue livelihoods objectives. It takes significant investments to create growth-oriented farmer organizations, such as cooperatives or producer companies, that can incentivize member farmers to invest in appropriate technology of production and produce the quality desired by growth-oriented downstream agribusinesses.

Agricultural TFP in Nigeria has not improved for decades. The lack of progress is attributed to weak technical change at the farm level, which in turn is explained by inability of farmers to access improved technologies of production and suboptimal application of the technologies by the farmers who have access. Weak access to improved technologies is mainly due to underinvestment in agricultural R&D—a prerequisite to generate innovative agricultural management practices and high yielding and climate-resilient crop varieties and livestock breeds. Suboptimal use of available technologies is mainly due to weak extension and advisory systems that fail to build farmers' capacity to correctly apply existing technologies. For example, the data show that most farmers use fertilizers inefficiently, either applying them in fields that are not planted with improved seeds or vice versa. A well-functioning farmer extension and advisory system would improve efficiency in the technical allocation of these inputs. Furthermore, the suboptimal use of these costly inputs (seeds and fertilizers) suggests that farmers may not be paying the full price and are relying on poorly designed subsidy programs that don't provide the inputs as a package. Input use efficiency can be improved through reforms that increase the supply of quality inputs to farmers and retooling of input subsidy programs according to the principles of smart subsidies. The principles entail (1) targeting farmers who need to learn about proper use of fertilizers or those who could use it profitably but are not able to do so because of working capital constraints and (2) delivering the subsidy through the private sector by adopting voucher systems that require farmers to purchase a package of fertilizers and improved seeds together.

Although the agribusiness-enabling environment has improved significantly in recent years, significant gaps remain, and this continues to hold back the agribusiness sector from achieving its potential. The passage of the National Fertilizer Quality (Control) Act 2019 and National Agricultural Seeds Council Act 2019 has tremendously improved the legal and regulatory frameworks for fertilizer quality control and seed development and quality control. However, important elements of the reforms in these acts are yet to be operationalized. The implementation of these laws will improve availability of the quality of these inputs, create incentives for adoption by farmers, and ultimately contribute to improved TFP. Some of the major gaps in the agribusiness environment relate to an incomplete legal and regulatory environment for warehouse receipts and slow progress on land reforms. The framework for land administration in Nigeria is ambiguous and nonuniform across states. There are not enough protections for the large number of agricultural households that derive livelihoods directly from land. Furthermore, the requirements for land transfers are not standardized, and property rights are uncertain, contributing to thin land markets and weakening incentives for long-term investments by landholders. Kaduna and Ogun states have made important steps to adopt and implement FRILIA, and scaling it out to other states would provide a unified approach to responsible land administration and enable Nigeria to maximize the role of land in development while effectively mitigating the risks of land-based investments.

Access to finance is a major problem faced by various actors in agribusiness value chains. The factors contributing to weak access to credit are varied and include foundational and structural issues in the financial services sector, weak competitiveness of agribusinesses in domestic and export markets, high risk of failure and stunted growth, lack of financing instruments such as WRSs, and the structure of primary agriculture, which is dominated by smallholders who are perceived as bad risks by banks. Experience from other countries suggest that there is enormous scope for disruption of the financial sector through reforms to enable fintech, mobile money, and innovations that deepen financial inclusion. In addition to these reforms, there is evidence that coordinated "value chain financing" arrangements can be very successful in Nigeria as they take a "whole-of-agribusiness" approach to concurrently address financing needs across multiple actors in the value chains.

NOTES

1. For example, the National Agricultural Seeds Council Act 2019, National Fertilizer Quality (Control) Act 2019, and Plant Variety Protection Bill 2019.
2. Given that climate change is estimated to reduce crop yields by 50 percent, access to water and irrigation will be an important determinant of the stability of yields and the adaptation to the effects of climate change.
3. NIRSAL is a nonbanking financial entity wholly owned by the Central Bank of Nigeria. It was established in collaboration with the Federal Ministry of Agriculture and Rural Development and the Nigerian Bankers' Committee in 2013 to redefine, measure, reprice, and share agribusiness-related credit risk in Nigeria and was financed with US$500 million. NIRSAL's mandate is to augment the flow of affordable finance and investments into the agricultural sector by de-risking the agribusiness finance value chain, fixing agricultural value chains, building long-term capacity, and institutionalizing incentives for agricultural lending.
4. The study could not obtain data on the performance of these programs.
5. For more information on Farmcrowdy, see https://www.farmcrowdy.com/.
6. For more information on Hello Tractor, see https://hellotractor.com/.
7. Data from the Doing Business data set (World Bank, Washington, DC), https://www.doingbusiness.org/en/data/exploreeconomies/Nigeria.
8. For example, in the Indian state of West Bengal, farmers can receive warehouse receipts on potatoes stored under cold storage and use the receipts to obtain loans from the commercial banking sector. The receipts are guaranteed by the cold store owner operator, who also provides storage and collateral management services.
9. Doing Business data set.
10. Data provided by Ogun State government during consultations on the World Bank financed Ogun State Economic Transformation Project.
11. The state of Jigawa has adopted the Land Acquisition and Resettlement Framework (LARF).
12. Those projects are the Kaduna State Economic Transformation Program for Results and the Ogun State Economic Transformation Project.

REFERENCES

Arnold, Erik, and Martin Bell. 2001. "Some New Ideas about Research for Development." In partnership at the leading edge: A Danish vision for knowledge, R&D. Danish Ministry of Foreign Affairs.

Bayen, Maxime. 2018. "Africa: A Look at the 442 Active Tech Hubs of the Continent." *GSMA: Mobile for Development* (blog), March 22, 2018. https://www.gsma.com /mobilefordevelopment/programme/ecosystem-accelerator/africa-a-look-at-the-442 -active-tech-hubs-of-the-continent/.

Beintema, Nienke, Abdullahi M. Nasir, and Lang Gao. 2017. "Agricultural R&D Indicators Factsheet: Nigeria." International Food Policy Research Institute and Agricultural Research Council of Nigeria.

Butler, S. 2012. "Nigerian Land Markets and the Land Use Law of 1978." Focus on Land in Africa, Gates Open Research. https://gatesopenresearch.org/documents/3-1414.

Chang, Roberto, Linda Kaltani, and Norman V. Loayza. 2009. "Openness Can Be Good for Growth: The Role of Policy Complementarities." *Journal of Development Economics* 90 (1): 33–49.

Djankov, Simeon, Caroline Freund, and Cong S. Pham. 2010. "Trading on Time." *Review of Economics and Statistics* 92 (1): 166–73.

FAO (Food and Agriculture Organization of the United Nations). 2018. "Small Family Farms Country Factsheet: Nigeria." FAO. http://www.fao.org/3/I9930EN/i9930en.pdf.

Freund, Caroline, and Bineswaree Bolaky. 2008. "Trade, Regulations, and Income." *Journal of Development Economics* 87 (2): 309–21.

Iwanow, Thomasz, and Colin Kirkpatrick. 2009. "Trade Facilitation and Manufactured Exports: Is Africa Different?" *World Development* 37 (6): 1039–50.

Kim, Jeehye, Parmesh Shah, Joanne Catherine Gaskell, Ashesh Prasann, and Akanksha Luthra. 2020. *Scaling Up Disruptive Agricultural Technologies in Africa*. International Development in Focus. Washington, DC: World Bank.

Rao, B. S. Sudarshan 2012. "Human Capital Development for the Management of Food and Agribusiness in India." *International Food and Agribusiness Management Review* 15 (A): 1–4.

Rodriguez, Francisco, and Dani Rodrik. 2000. "Trade Policy and Economic Growth: A Skeptic's Guide to the Cross-National Evidence." In *NBER Macroeconomics Annual*, Vol. 15, edited by Ben S. Bernanke and Kenneth Rogoff, 261–338. MIT Press.

Rodrik, Dani, Arvind Subramanian, and Francesco Trebbi. 2004. "Institutional Rule: The Primacy of Institutions over Geography and Integration in Economic Development." *Journal of Economic Growth* 9 (2): 131–65.

Seker, Murat. 2011. "Importing, Exporting, and Innovation in Developing Countries." Policy Research Working Paper 5156, World Bank, Washington, DC.

Setimela, P. S., C. Magorokosho, R. Lunduka, E. Gasura, D. Makumbi, A. Tarekegne, J. E. Cairns, T. Ndhlela, O. Erenstein, and W. Mwangi. 2017. "On-Farm Yield Gains with Stress-Tolerant Maize in Eastern and Southern Africa." *Agronomy Journal* 109 (2):406–17.

Sheahan, Megan and Christopher B. Barrett. 2017. "Ten Striking Facts about Agricultural Input Use in Sub-Saharan Africa." *Food Policy* 67: 12–25.

World Bank. 2007. "Enhancing Agricultural Innovation: How to Go Beyond the Strengthening of Research Systems." World Bank, Washington, DC.

World Bank. 2013. "Growing Africa: Unlocking the Potential of Agribusiness." World Bank, Washington, DC.

World Bank. 2019. "Nigeria on the Move: A Journey to Inclusive Growth." Nigeria Systematic Country Diagnostic, June 2019. World Bank, Washington, DC.

Yumkella, Kandeh K., Patrick M. Kormawa, Torben M. Roepstorff, and Anthony M. Hawkins, eds. 2011. *Agribusiness for Africa's Prosperity*. Vienna: United Nations Industrial Development Organization.

5 Competitiveness and Policy Priorities in the Cashew Nut Value Chain

The three main conclusions from chapter 3 are that (1) traditional cash crops, cassava, rice, oil seeds, and pulses have the most potential to create jobs; (2) pulses, livestock value chains, and traditional cash crops have the most potential to reduce poverty; and (3) livestock value chains and vegetables are key to improving nutritional outcomes. The next four chapters dive deeper to identify opportunities for increasing the competitiveness of specific value chains with the most potential to create jobs, reduce poverty, and improve nutrition. In particular, each of the next four chapters considers a specific value chain—cashew nuts (representing traditional cash crops), rice, cassava, and poultry (representing livestock value chains). Clearly, productivity growth in those value chains needs to increase significantly to contribute to jobs creation and poverty reduction. Increasing productivity growth calls for strategic and coordinated investments between on-farm and off-farm segments and improvements in the agribusiness-enabling environment. With the aim of identifying sources of competitiveness and policy priorities in Nigeria, the analysis benchmarks yields, costs, prices, and other aspects of competitiveness with similar value chains in Vietnam. The analysis also draws lessons on policy and regulatory actions that can increase productivity and competitiveness in domestic and export markets. Conclusions are presented at the end of each chapter.

WHY COMPARE NIGERIA WITH VIETNAM?

Vietnam has emerged as a global leader in agribusiness and a top exporter in several commodities and products that are important in Nigeria's agribusiness sector. In 2019, Vietnam generated export earnings of at least US$3 billion from each of the following commodities—cashew nuts, rice, cassava, fish, coffee, tea, black pepper, and rubber (figure 5.1)—resulting in total agricultural export revenue of US$40 billion (World Bank 2020). Those eight value chains have experienced strong export growth, founded on productivity growth in on-farm and off-farm segments and improved coordination of investments across the value chains. Access to remunerative export markets has generated broad-based gains

FIGURE 5.1

Vietnam agricultural exports in selected commodities doubled in the past decade

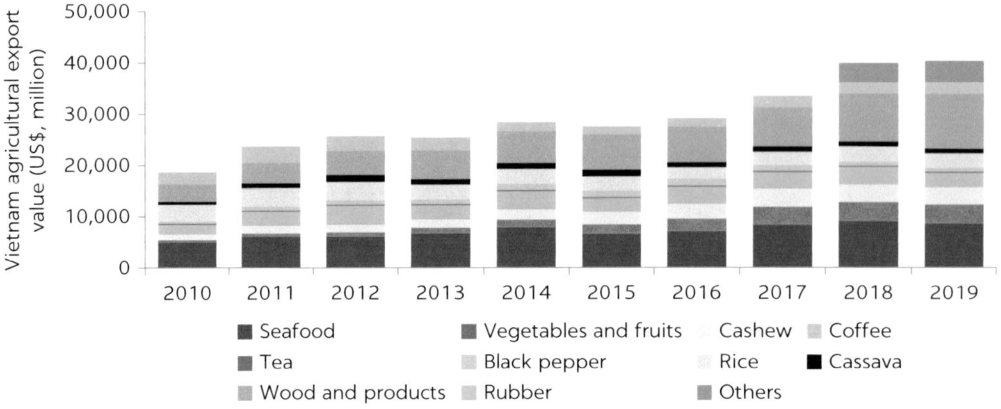

Source: World Bank 2020.

in the incomes of farmers and higher returns for agribusinesses, thus increasing foreign exchange earnings and public revenues.

The strong performance of the agribusiness sector in Vietnam has ushered in a model of structural transformation that could serve Nigeria very well. The growth of agricultural value chains in Vietnam has been driven by increased productivity in primary production and improved coordination with downstream value addition. Agricultural wage rates and farmer incomes increased rapidly between 2010 and 2018, contributing to about 75 percent of the poverty reduction in rural areas (World Bank 2019). The strong performance of agricultural value chains has spurred the rural economy because farm incomes have been invested in rural sectors and created job opportunities outside farming. Perhaps the most interesting feature of Vietnam's model of structural transformation is that labor released from farming has been productively absorbed in the rural nonfarm sector, which differs from the usual pattern in which labor migrates to urban sectors, leaving rural sectors without skills and demand for the services and goods necessary to catalyze rural development. Although about 80 percent of rural households in Vietnam continue to engage in agriculture, many of those households are increasingly involved in the rural nonfarm sector, and the diversification of income sources has not only raised those households' incomes but also increased their resilience to economic shocks.

CASHEW NUTS

Nigeria was a leading cashew nut producer in the early 2000s. Since then, Nigeria has lost its position and now ranks 13th in the world and 8th in Africa. Nigeria currently produces about 240 thousand tons of cashew nuts annually, which is about 7.5 percent of global cashew nut production (table 5.1). The cashew nut subsector contributes about 0.65 percent to agriculture gross domestic product (GDP), with a gross production value of US$15 million in 2018, which is a fraction of Vietnam's gross production value of US$4.2 billion. Since 2002, Vietnam has ranked as the world's leading cashew nut producer, with production quantity of 2.7 million tons in 2018, accounting for 45 percent of world

TABLE 5.1 Importance of cashew nuts in Nigeria and Vietnam, 2018

INDICATOR	YEAR	NIGERIA	VIETNAM
GDP (current US$, billion)	2018	397.30	245.2
Cashew nut production value (tons)	2018	240,000	2,663,885
Share of world's production (%)	2018	7.50	45.0
Gross production value (current US$, million)	2018	15.0	4211.8
Share of agriculture GDP (%)	2018	0.65	13.0
Cropland (hectares, million)	2018	40.50	11.5
Harvested area (% of cropland)	2018	0.15	2.5

Source: GDP data from World Development Indicators, World Bank; cashew nut production value, gross production value, and cropland data from FAOSTAT (Statistics Division, Food and Agriculture Organization of the United Nations).

cashew nut production. Cashew nut production in Vietnam achieved an average annual growth rate of 16.1 percent between 2001 and 2018—and contributed about 13 percent to agriculture GDP. Cashew is grown in most of the tropical countries around the world, and India has traditionally been the largest producer. However, production growth increased rapidly in West Africa beginning in 2003, driven mostly by Côte d'Ivoire, such that West Africa has become the leading region in commercial cashew production—accounting for 45 percent of global production. The five major producers of cashew nuts are Vietnam, India, Côte d'Ivoire, Benin, and the Philippines.

The production of cashew nuts requires specific agroclimatic conditions and is sensitive to temperature and rainfall conditions. In Nigeria and Vietnam, production is concentrated in areas where the temperatures range from 20°C to 30°C, annual precipitation is 1,000 mm to 2,000 mm, and a well-defined dry season covers at least four months. In Nigeria, production occurs in 27 out of 36 states, clustered around the South West "cashew belt." Cashew is the main crop in the major producing states such as Kwara where the crop occupies more than 20,000 hectares (ha). Although Kwara leads other states in terms of production volumes, the best quality originates from Oyo State (Große-Rüschkamp, Topper, and Grenzebach 2010). Most of the export-quality cashew nuts are produced in the South West region, especially Oyo and Osun states (Gbenga-Ogu 2017). Vietnam's cashew belt transverses the Southeast Region, and production is centered in Binh Phuoc province.

TECHNOLOGY OF PRODUCTION

A major reason Nigeria lost its leading position in cashew nut production is that old orchards were not optimally replaced with new and higher-yielding varieties. In particular, production in Nigeria dropped rapidly by 87 percent between 2010 and 2014 and then stabilized at a very low level of about 98,000 tons in 2018 (figure 5.2). The rapid decline in production was driven by a 67 percent contraction in area harvested (figure 5.3) and 62 percent decline in yields (figure 5.4), although yields rebounded to some extent and are now higher than in India and West African neighbors, including Côte d'Ivoire. Considering that cashews are a perennial tree crop, such a rapid contraction in area harvested suggests

FIGURE 5.2

Cashew nut production in Nigeria decreased rapidly from 2000 to 2018

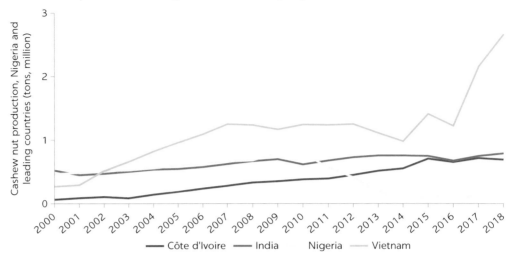

Source: FAOSTAT (Statistics Division, Food and Agriculture Organization of the United Nations).

FIGURE 5.3

Area harvested contracted in Nigeria between 2010 and 2014, contributing to declining production

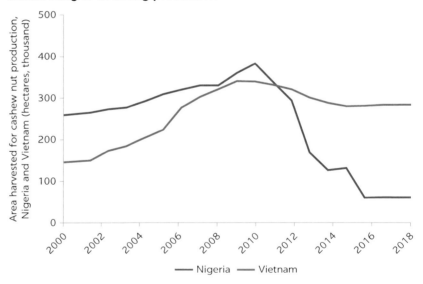

Source: FAOSTAT (Statistics Division, Food and Agriculture Organization of the United Nations).

widespread aging of trees without replacement. In general, cashew trees attain commercial levels of production after 4 years at about 300 kg/ha, but peak yields are attained after 10 years at about 1,800 kg/ha—and last for another 10 years. Yields decline about 25 years after planting, and the trees lose commercial value after year 30. Production in Nigeria is expected to increase in the coming years, primarily because estimates of the age distribution of cashew trees indicate that at least 40 percent of the trees were planted within the last 10 years and have not reached peak production.

FIGURE 5.4

Yields in Nigeria declined between 2010 and 2014, but rebounded quickly and are now higher than major producers in West Africa

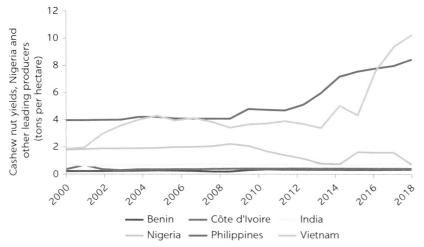

Source: FAOSTAT (Statistics Division, Food and Agriculture Organization of the United Nations).

In contrast with Nigeria, production in Vietnam followed what could be described as the expected trend for cultivation of perennial tree crops: old trees are continuously replaced with new and higher-yielding varieties. Production increased rapidly for 6 years (2000–07) as new trees reached maturity and then stabilized as some of the old orchards were replaced (2007–14). Production has increased rapidly again since 2014 as newer orchards have reached maturity. In the past decade, production growth in Vietnam was driven solely by yields, reflecting a strong push by the government to develop and disseminate high-yielding and early-maturing varieties. The government of Vietnam has been at the forefront in ensuring that farmers have access to new and high-yielding varieties, including varieties that mature early and begin to produce nuts about 24 months after planting and dwarf varieties that allow higher-density planting of up to 500 trees/ha compared to the normal density of 200 trees/ha. More recently, the Binh Phuoc Department of Agriculture has aggressively supported replanting with higher-yielding varieties and is also promoting more intensive production systems, with higher fertilization rates and irrigation. However, processors have warned that variety selection should focus more on kernel outturn rate (KOR) because some of the newer varieties tend to have a higher percentage of empty shells. Vietnam's Ministry of Agriculture and Rural Development recommends the following varieties—PN1, MH4, and MH5—and local varieties such as PL18, DP41, DP27 and DC44 (MARD 2019).

TRADE COMPETITIVENESS

Nigeria is the fourth-largest exporter of cashew nuts in Africa, exporting about 64 percent of the national production in the form of raw cashew nuts (RCN) and earning about US$0.1 billion in 2018. In contrast, Vietnam—the world's largest exporter—earned US$2.6 billion from cashew nuts exports in 2018 (figure 5.5). Exports have soared in Vietnam by more than 1,200 percent in the past two decades; however, Vietnam is also a large importer of RCN sourced from around the world, including from Nigeria, and it processes imported RCN into various products for exports. Net exports of cashew nuts in Vietnam are estimated at US$1.4 billion in 2018. RCN importation, processing, and export have soared since 2011 (figure 5.6) and contributed enormously to net foreign earnings in the country. Processed cashew nuts occupy 99 percent of export share in Vietnam, with RCN accounting for only 1 percent of exports. In contrast, 93 percent of exports from Nigeria are RCN and only 7 percent is value added. Imports to Nigeria are 98 percent processed cashew nuts with only a small share of RCN.

Nigeria formally exports RCN and processed cashew nuts to more than 30 countries, but Vietnam and India are the major export destinations. Between 2017 and 2019, exports to Vietnam accounted for 62 percent of all exports of

FIGURE 5.5

Vietnam has achieved tremendous export growth, whereas export growth in Nigeria has been fleeting, 2000–18

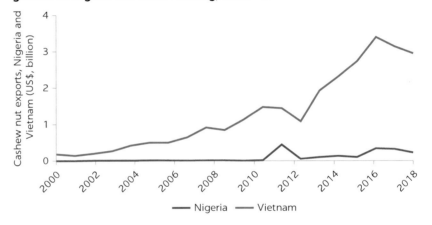

Source: FAOSTAT (Statistics Division, Food and Agriculture Organization of the United Nations).

FIGURE 5.6

The tremendous export growth in Vietnam is driven by imports of raw cashew nuts that are processed and exported, 2000–18

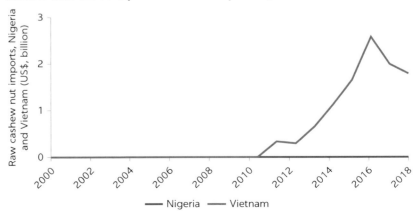

Source: FAOSTAT (Statistics Division, Food and Agriculture Organization of the United Nations).

processed cashew nuts and 43 percent of exports of RCN (figure 5.7). Exports to India accounted for 25 percent and 6 percent of processed cashew nuts and RCN, respectively. The rest of Nigeria's cashew nut exports go to China, Malaysia, Senegal, Tanzania, and the United Arab Emirates. In turn, Vietnam exports processed cashew nuts to more than 40 countries; the main destinations are the United States and China, respectively accounting for 34 percent and 15 percent of exports in 2017–19 (figure 5.8).

Olam International is the largest processor of cashew nuts in Nigeria. Within the last four years, the company has installed processing capacity of 33,000 tons. Capacity utilization is low, however, and there are indications that Olam has increasingly exported RCN to Vietnam. Olam's exports of RCN to Vietnam might be a more profitable business venture because it has significant shares in the largest processing company in Vietnam—Long Son.

The quality of RCN from Nigeria is lower than RCN from Vietnam and far lower than RCN from Guinea-Bissau, the world's leading producer of cashew nuts in terms of quality. The quality of cashew nuts is measured using KOR and nut count (small nuts). The KOR for Nigeria is 45–48 lbs/bag, comparable to Benin, Côte d'Ivoire, and Ghana (ACA 2019a), and lower than Vietnam (KOR of 48–52) and Guinea-Bissau (KOR of 50–54). A low KOR is partly caused by a high nut count (relatively small nuts), a high percentage of empty shells, and difficulty of peeling. Both KOR and nut count are functions of a combination of variety, climatic conditions, soil characteristics, and crop husbandry practices. Furthermore, KOR tends to be higher at the start of the harvesting season and lower at the end. Some regions such as Oyo State are known for larger nuts, whereas others like Nasarawa reportedly have smaller nuts (SAPcashewconcept 2016). RCN from Nigeria tend to have high moisture content because nuts are not properly dried, resulting in price discount and in some cases outright rejection of consignments. On average, RCN from Nigeria attract a price discount of 14 percent compared to RCN from Benin

FIGURE 5.7

Nigeria's raw cashew nut exports have increased significantly since 2012, and Vietnam has become a major destination

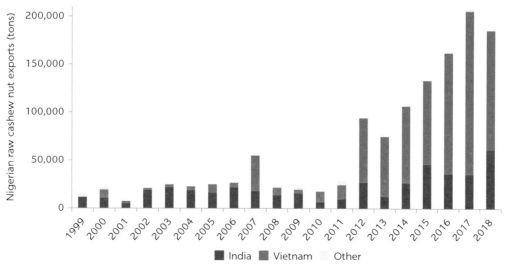

Source: United Nations Comtrade Database 2020 (as reported by importing countries) and Government Statistics Office of Vietnam.

FIGURE 5.8

Vietnam exports processed cashew nuts mainly to the United States, China, and the Netherlands

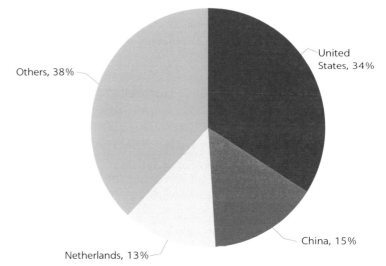

Source: United Nations Comtrade Database 2020.

(ACA 2019a, 2019b). There have also been multiple cases of rejections—for example, about 37,000 tons exported to Vietnam were rejected on arrival in 2018 (Economic Confidential 2020). Table 5.2 illustrates data from processors in Vietnam showing how RCN quality parameters (KOR and nut quality) affected the quality of the processed kernels in 2019, comparing RCN from Cambodia, Côte d'Ivoire, Ghana, Nigeria, and Vietnam.

Nigeria saves its best quality RCN for domestic processing, and its exported kernels generally sell for better prices than Vietnam's. However, the volume of processed kernels exported from Nigeria is a fraction of Vietnam's (export value of US$0.1 billion from Nigeria compared to US$2.6 billion from Vietnam). A comparison of prices of processed kernels exported to the United States in 2019 shows that kernels from Nigeria fetched a better price than those for competitors for a good part of the year (figure 5.9). In particular, kernels from Nigeria fetched the highest prices between March and June 2019, outperforming the world's largest exporters—Brazil, Côte d'Ivoire, India, and Vietnam. The higher prices fetched by kernels from Nigeria show potential to add value to RCN within the country.

Going forward, the cashew nut trade is expected to focus more on quality as prices have dampened because global supplies have caught up with demand. A price analysis shows that the Free on Board price of processed kernels more than doubled between 2001 and 2017, driven by demand in high-income countries. Prices have decelerated significantly from the 2017–18 peak, however, reducing margins for processors that had already purchased the 2019 crop. The price drops relate to reduced demand for kernels and the oversupply of almond markets in the United States—a substitute for kernels. The future price outlook for RCN and processed kernels is uncertain because of the COVID-19 (coronavirus) pandemic's effect on global markets, which is partly due to reduction of processing activity in India (CashewInfo.com 2020) and reduced availability of working capital credit to exporters in West Africa (Fages 2020).

TABLE 5.2 **Relationship between quality of raw cashew nuts and quality and prices of processed kernels, by country of origin**

COUNTRY OF ORIGIN		VIETNAM AND CAMBODIA	CÔTE D'IVOIRE AND GHANA	NIGERIA	SALES PRICE (US$/KG)
Raw cashew nuts	KOR (lb/bag)	51.2	48	48	
	KOR (%)	29	27	27	
	Nut count	155	202	190	
Processed kernels	WW240 and larger (%)	32	11	10	8.5
	WW320 and smaller (%)	40	51	45	7.3
	Lightly blemished whites (%)	8	13	3	7.0
	White splits (%)	11	10	15	4.5
	Large pieces (%)	5	8	5	3.0
	Other (%)	5	9	22	4.0
Weighted average price (US$/kg)		7.0	6.5	6.0	

Source: Institute for Policy and Strategy for Agriculture and Rural Development, Vietnam, 2020.
Note: KOR = kernel outturn rate; WW240 = white whole kernels of 220–240 nuts per pound; WW320 = white whole kernels of 300–320 nuts per pound.

FIGURE 5.9

Processed kernels from Nigeria fetched a higher price than those from competitors for a good part of 2019

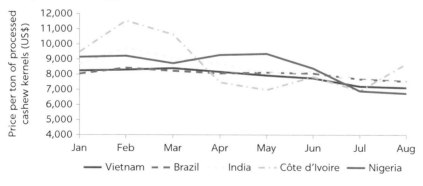

Source: CashewInfo.com 2019.

A strategy for developing Nigeria's cashew nuts subsector should consider providing incentives for importation of RCN from neighboring West African countries to be processed in Nigeria for export markets. This approach has been successfully adopted and executed by Vietnam. A large share of the US$2.6 billion value of kernels processed in Vietnam consists of RCN imported from West Africa (figure 5.10). Nigeria enjoys stronger economic relations with the major cashew nut producers in West Africa than India or Vietnam does, and it can harness the apparatus of the Economic Community of West African States (ECOWAS) to establish partnerships among actors in those countries. However, deliberate efforts are needed to encourage RCN imports from West Africa.

FIGURE 5.10

West African countries are a major source of imports of raw cashew nuts processed in Vietnam

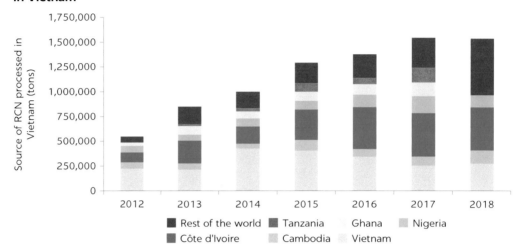

Source: United Nations Comtrade data (as reported by Vietnam); domestic production figures obtained from the Vietnam Cashew Association and Government Statistics Office of Vietnam; INC production data converted from kernel basis to RCN at KOR of 28 percent.
Note: KOR = kernel outturn rate; RCN = raw cashew nuts.

The current tariff regime—in which RCN imports face the same import duties (20 percent) as processed kernel imports—needs to be reconsidered to provide incentives for expanding processing in the country, including by ensuring that import duties are lower for RCN.

In addition, installed processing capacity for cashew nuts in Nigeria operates below optimum levels. Recent estimates suggest that the installed capacity for cashew nut processing in Nigeria was about 48,000 tons[1] in 2015; however, only 30 percent of the capacity is utilized (Fitzpatrick 2017; Ricau 2019; Vanguard 2015). Nigeria could draw lessons from some of the approaches it has been using to increase processing capacity for other agricultural commodities. For example, it has implemented preferential tariff quota systems so that millers can import rice and wheat with the aim of expanding processing capacity and establishing backward linkages with farmers through outgrower schemes. Olam International—a major player in the cashew nuts subsector in Nigeria—has previously benefited from these arrangements. Nigeria also has opportunities to expand its domestic consumer market because per capita consumption of cashew nuts is quite low—only 0.004 kg annually compared to 0.23 kg in Vietnam (IndexBox 2020).

CHARACTERIZATION OF CASHEW NUT VALUE CHAINS

The organization of cashew nuts value chains in Nigeria and Vietnam depends on whether the end product is RCN or processed kernels. The main actors in the RCN export value chains in Nigeria are producers/farmers, licensed buying agents, and RCN exporters. In the value chain for processed kernels, the RCN exporter is replaced by a processor that also plays the role of exporter. In Vietnam, the main actors in the value chain that rely on domestic production are producers/farmers, local traders, and processors/kernel exporters.

The processors also import RCN from the other producers (see figure 5.10). In both countries, a licensed buying agent (LBA) or local trader intermediates between farmers and processors/RCN exporters to provide the important functions of aggregation and transport to the processing/export facility, often as a commission agent of the processor/exporter. Some LBAs in Nigeria work through subbuyers strictly as commission agents of the LBAs. The high competition for RCN in the LBA/trader part of the value chains, especially in Nigeria, often leads to farmers facing pressure to harvest immature nuts—in turn, leading to poor quality RCN. The problem is compounded by a delay in drying the nuts once harvested, often leading to poor peeling quality (CashewInfo.com 2015). The storage and drying of nuts mainly occurs at the processor/RCN exporter level, and neither farmers nor LBAs/traders invest in storage capacity. The competition for nuts has been tempered in Vietnam since 2018; processors no longer buy future harvests in import countries and have increasingly preferred spot transactions.

Processors in both countries convert RCN to intermediate kernels for bulk exports. The final processing and packaging are carried out in the countries where the kernels are consumed. The intermediate processing for bulk exports includes roasting and shelling, peeling of the skin covering the kernel, cleaning, sorting, grading, and bulk packaging.[2] The final processing is mostly done in Europe and the United States, and it includes roasting, salting, spicing, mixing with other nuts, and packaging. The technology of intermediate processing has evolved significantly in Vietnam over the years, transitioning from the use of manual labor in shelling and peeling to the development of a competitive range of equipment for all stages of processing. Despite increased mechanization, the cashew processing industry in Vietnam is a major employer with each facility employing about 2,000–3,000 people on average and the largest facilities employing about 12,000 people.[3] The scale of processing is much lower in Nigeria. In addition to industrial processing in Nigeria for export markets, there is a cottage industry of low-volume processing for the domestic market by so-called backyard processors. These processors undertake all operations themselves, or they procure low-grade (broken, small, or scorched) kernels from exporters and sell them in local shops.

Vertical coordination is weak in both countries, despite the existence of national industry-level associations that bring together farmers/producers, processors, exporters, and other actors. Contract farming arrangements and outgrower schemes are rare in both Nigeria and Vietnam. However, Olam International—and probably other companies—supports farmers with seedlings of high-yielding varieties and training. Farmer organizations in Nigeria tend to be weak, and even cooperatives tend to pursue short-term needs rather than growth-oriented investments in productive assets, enforcement of quality standards, and establishment of long-term relationships with buyers and suppliers. The National Cashew Association of Nigeria (NCAN), which brings together farmers, exporters, processors, and other stakeholders, is recognized as the national umbrella organization representing the sector. In Vietnam, the Vietnam Cashew Association (VINACAS) is an important multistakeholder platform representing the industry, but farmers are underrepresented in it.

The processing capacity in Vietnam was built when global demand for kernels was soaring and without much competition from other parts of the world. Processors enjoy first-mover advantages and scale economies. The main competitive advantage of Vietnamese processors is the sheer scale of installed capacity, which enables efficient processing and shipping of one grade per container. Emerging processors in West Africa are entering the global market at a time when global kernel prices are falling (supply has just caught up with demand), and they must face competition from established processors in Vietnam. Given that the processors in Vietnam produce intermediate kernels that undergo final processing in the final consumption markets, the emerging processors in West Africa have an option to "move up the value chain" and deliver final processed kernels to final consumers in Europe and the United States. Furthermore, it is likely that final processing costs are lower in West Africa than in Europe or the United States, suggesting that various business models could be considered, such as franchising and joint ventures. Perhaps a more rewarding option would be to develop niche, branded, and differentiated cashew nut products for direct selling to supermarkets in western countries, including organic and fair-trade labelled products. These strategies call for strong public-private partnerships to improve the business-enabling environment, reform policies that discourage importation of RCN from neighboring countries, develop infrastructure (especially roads and energy) in clusters where processing can cost efficiently occur, and so on.

Nigeria's enabling environment needs to improve significantly to support growth of the cashew nut subsector, and there are important lessons to learn from Vietnam (see box 5.1). Although the Nigerian Export Promotion Council (NEPC) subsidizes the export of cashew nuts, the process to obtain the subsidy is very bureaucratic, resulting in high administrative costs that may exceed the value of the subsidy. In addition, the payment of the subsidy is often

Box 5.1

Policy lessons from Vietnam for developing the cashew value chain in Nigeria

Major policy milestones in the Vietnam cashew nut sector provide important lessons for Nigeria.

- Vietnam has developed a sector-specific policy strategy. The strategy is outlined in Decision No. 579/QD-BNN-TT of February 13, 2015, General Development Planning for Viet Nam Cashew Industry to 2020 and Orientation to 2030. The policy aims to guide all aspects of development of the cashew nut industry. Production support to farmers has centered on provision of high-yielding and early maturing varieties to replace aging trees. The national ministry responsible for agriculture and provincial authorities are implementing long-term plans that have involved the distribution of 522,000 seedlings to farmers, including 2,153 distributed in Binh Phuoc alone in 2019 to farmers through farmers associations.

- The Vietnam Cashew Association (VINACAS) has developed into an influential multi-takeholder platform that provides effective coordination and stewardship to the industry. VINACAS was established in 1990 under Decision No. 346 NN-TCCB/QD of the former Ministry of Agriculture and Food Industry. Today, VINACAS members are researchers, farmers, processors, and exporters.

- The government provides incentives for private sector investments in agriculture and agribusiness, including schemes to improve access to finance for agricultural production. In particular, Decree 57 of 2018 put forward several investment incentives and instruments aimed at increasing the private sector investments in agriculture and supporting agribusiness enterprise development, including investment

continued

Box 5.1, *Continued*

subsidies, reduced land and water surface rents, preferential interest rates, marketing, and training. Furthermore, a series of decrees in 2010, 2015, and 2018 (Decree 41/2010/ND-CP, Decree 55/2015/ND-CP, and Decree 116/2018/ND-CP) helped to remove difficulties in accessing capital and credit for agricultural production, including setting specific loan amounts that farmers could obtain without collateral under risk-sharing arrangements that involve the government.

- The Vietnam cashew industry has developed standards for trading of raw cashew nuts (RCN). In January 2019, the Vietnamese Ministry of Science and Technology published a national standard for RCN imports: TCVN:2018. The standard was developed by the Ministry of Agriculture in collaboration with VINACAS and is the world's first specialized standard for raw cashew nuts. It serves as a basis for grading and quality inspection to support trading and

handling disputes of RCN. It is intended to help the Vietnamese cashew industry adapt to market demand by enhancing the quality and safety management of RCN imports (VINACAS 2019).

- The trade tariff regime aims to encourage imports of RCN and discourage imports of processed kernels to create incentives for the domestic processing industry. Since 2010, the import duty for RCN has been 5 percent or lower for most origin countries (most favored nation [MFN] rate) and 0 percent for members of the Association of Southeast Asian Nations (Cambodia and Indonesia), which is much lower than import duties for coconuts and Brazil nuts (30 percent) in the same harmonized system 0801 group. The import tax on cashew kernels is significantly higher at 25 percent (MFN). For comparison, the import duties for RCN and processed kernels are both 20 percent in Nigeria.

delayed—sometimes for up to three years (JMSF Agribusiness 2020). The Nigeria Export Levy (NXP) and the Nigeria Export Supervision Scheme (NESS) both charge a fee on exports, leading to claims of "double taxation." At the state level, the promotion and monitoring of cashew production is part of the mandate of the Tree Crops Development Units (TCDUs) of the states' ministries responsible for agriculture. However, the TCDU at the federal level lacks information about the cashew nuts subsector and has no readily available data on production areas or volume of processing or exporting (JMSF Agribusiness 2020). Furthermore, there is no specific policy developed for cashew production, and no strategy exists for promoting the commodity. Several local markets in the states have laws prohibiting the street selling of cashew kernels by vendors to control theft of cashew nuts.

COSTS AND MARGINS OF VALUE CHAIN ACTORS

This section compares costs and margins for the actors of cashew nut value chains. Figure 5.11, panels a and b, provides a summary of the costs, selling prices, and margins for each actor along the value chain in Nigeria and Vietnam, respectively. Cashew is a perennial crop with economic useful life of about 30 years. Producer costs in any particular year are just a snapshot, and the costs in figure 5.11 reflect a mature crop and exclude establishment costs. Prices are in

US$/kg of kernel, meaning that the prices and costs for producers correspond to the amount of RCN needed to produce 1 kg of kernel (3.61 kg in Vietnam and 4.00 kg in Nigeria). The cost buildup relies on data from primary surveys carried out in Nigeria and Vietnam, corroborated by secondary sources of data. In particular, the data for Nigeria were collected from Kwara, Ogun, and Oyo states in 2020[4] and corroborated with additional data collected in 2019 for the baseline of the Agro-Processing, Agricultural Productivity Enhancement and Livelihood Improvement Support (APPEALS) Project. Production-level data from Vietnam were collected in 2019,[5] and processing-level data were collected in 2020.[6]

The comparison of costs and margins shows that cashew nut production is more profitable in Nigeria than in Vietnam, despite the higher yields in Vietnam. This is primarily because the costs of production are significantly lower in Nigeria, even without considering the opportunity cost of land, which is certainly higher in Vietnam because farmers there have more alternative value chains that compete with cashew nuts for land. Assuming average yields for both countries and excluding planting costs, the estimated cost of production is US$4.476/kg of RCN in Vietnam and US$0.6/kg to US$1.96/kg in Nigeria, depending on the location of production (table 5.3). The main cost advantages arise from lower hired labor costs and low use of variable inputs, especially fertilizers and other agrochemicals. Hired labor costs are at least four times higher in Vietnam than in Nigeria, accounting for 43 percent of total costs in Vietnam and 13 percent to 21 percent of labor costs in Nigeria. The revenues illustrated in table 5.3 do not include the value of cashew apple—the other product of the cashew tree.

Investing in cashew plantations generates a positive internal rate of return for farmers in both countries, with higher returns in Nigeria. Assuming a plantation of 1 ha and cash flows over a 25-year period, the cost-benefit analysis for cashew

FIGURE 5.11

Cost buildup for the cashew nut value chain, Nigeria and Vietnam

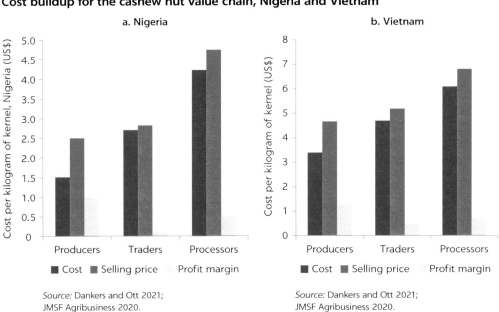

Source: Dankers and Ott 2021; JMSF Agribusiness 2020.

TABLE 5.3 Cost of production per kilogram of raw cashew nuts based on average farm size and yields on mature trees in Nigeria and Vietnam

	NIGERIA (ENUGU)[a]	NIGERIA (KWARA, OGUN AND OYO)[b]	VIETNAM (BINH PHUOC)[c]
Fertilizer	0.176 (8%)	0.068 (3%)	1.282 (27%)
Transportation	0.040 (2%)	—	0.256 (5%)
Labor	0.300 (13%)	0.564 (21%)	2.531 (31%)
Agrochemical cost	0.088 (4%)	0.040 (1%)	0.412 (9%)
Mechanization	—	1.021 (38%)	—
Other	—	0.280 (11%)	—
Total costs	**0.60**	**1.960**	**4.476**
Gross margins	1.724	0.712	0.191
Total revenues	**2.328**	**2.672**	**4.668**
Yield (kg/ha)	786	417	1,215

Source: Dankers and Ott 2021; JMSF Agribusiness 2020.
Note: Costs are US dollars. ha = hectare; kg = kilogram; — = either not applicable or too few data points to analyze.
a. Agricultural Productivity Enhancement and Livelihood Improvement Support Project project data from 2019.
b. Data from 2020 collected for this study.
c. Based on 2019 data collected for the Rural Investment Plan prepared by Cora Dankers, Food and Agriculture Organization of the United Nations Investment Centre.

nuts production shows a positive net present value (NPV) of cash flows (table 5.4). The investment costs occur in the first year and include the costs of seedlings, which varied from US$600/ha to US$1,100/ha in Nigeria depending on variety and location. Seedling costs are about 10 times lower in Vietnam—US$69/ha. The estimated NPV in Nigeria is US$647 in the states of Kwara, Ogun, and Oyo, and US$886 in Enugu, corresponding to an internal rate of return of 15 percent in the first three states and 16 percent in Enugu. The NPV in Vietnam is US$883, which corresponds to an internal rate of return of 12 percent. Those calculations do not include income from cashew apples or streams of cash flows from the crops cultivated in cashew fields, which could be significant because cashew is usually intercropped in both countries. In the same vein, the calculations do not include the opportunity costs of land, which is certainly higher in Vietnam than in Nigeria.

Although cashew nut processing costs are lower in Nigeria than in Vietnam, processors in Vietnam earn better margins because their selling price for processed kernels is higher (table 5.5). The kernels processed in Vietnam fetch higher prices because the quality is better and the conversion rate from RCN to kernels is relatively higher—28 percent in Vietnam compared to 25 percent in Nigeria. But processors in Vietnam face higher costs because RCN are cheaper in Nigeria, costing US$2.83/kg of kernel equivalent compared to US$4.86 in Vietnam. The RCN price differences reflect Nigeria's comparative advantage in production relative to Vietnam (table 5.5) and the Costs, Insurance, and Freight (CIF) of importing RCN from West African countries with a similar production cost profile as Nigeria. However, the variable costs of processing are remarkably higher in Nigeria, including higher costs of transport, energy, labor, and operating costs. Weak transportation and energy infrastructure diminish the competitiveness of processors in Nigeria. For example, the cost of energy in Nigeria is nearly twice that of Vietnam because the lack of regular supplies of electricity pushes the industry in Nigeria to also use generators. Transport costs are four times higher in Nigeria, reflecting a weak roads network and long distances.

TABLE 5.4 **Cost-benefit analysis of cashew investments in Nigeria and Vietnam**

		YEAR 1	YEARS 2–4	YEARS 5–8	YEARS 9–25
Nigeria (Enugu)	Investment costs	854.1	0	0	0
	Recurrent costs	118	118	118	118
	Yield	0	100	550	871
	Farm gate price	0.58	0.58	0.58	0.58
	Revenues	0	58	320	506
	Gross margin	−972	−60	202	388
	NPV @10%, US$	886			
	IRR (%)	16			
Nigeria (Kwara, Ogun, and Oyo)	Investment costs	572.1	0	0	0
	Recurrent costs	204	205	205	205
	Yield	0	100	475	943
	Farm gate price	0.67	0.67	0.67	0.67
	Revenues	0	67	317	630
	Gross margin	−777	−138	113	426
	NPV @10%, US$	651			
	IRR (%)	15			
Vietnam (Binh Phuoc)	Investment costs	745.7	0	0	0
	Recurrent costs	703	832	988	1191
	Yield	0	100	700	1743
	Farm gate price	1.29	1.29	1.29	1.29
	Revenues	0	129	905	2254
	Gross margin	−1,448	−703	−83	1,063
	NPV @10%, US$	883			
	IRR (%)	12			

Source: Dankers and Ott 2021; JMSF Agribusiness 2020.
Note: All costs, revenues, prices, and margins are US dollars per hectare, and yield is kilogram per hectare. IRR = internal rate of return; NPV = net present value.

TABLE 5.5 **Cashew nut processing costs in Nigeria and Vietnam**

	NIGERIA	VIETNAM
Raw cashew nuts	2.83 (60%)	4.86 (73%)
Labor	0.44 (9%)	0.24 (4%)
Transport	0.18 (4%)	0.04 (1%)
Electricity	0.03 (1%)	0.05 (1%)
Generators	0.04 (1%)	0 (0%)
Operating costs	0.71 (15%)	0.58 (9%)
Total Costs	4.24	5.76
Margin	0.52	0.91
Revenues	4.75	6.67

Source: Dankers and Ott 2021; JMSF Agribusiness 2020.
Note: All costs, revenues, and margins are US dollars per kilogram of kernel equivalent. The % in parentheses reflects the share of cost elements in revenues.

CONCLUSIONS

Nigeria can draw important lessons from Vietnam on policy reforms and investments to increase the competitiveness of its cashew nuts subsector. On the one hand, Vietnam has emerged as the world's leading exporter of not only cashew nuts but also several other commodities and products that are important in Nigeria's agribusiness sector. In 2019, Vietnam generated export earnings of more than US$3 billion from cashew nuts alone. On the other hand, Nigeria has over the past two decades lost its position as one of the leading countries in cashew nuts production, and it now ranks 13th in the world and 8th in Africa. The relatively weak performance of the cashew nuts subsector in Nigeria is driven by several reasons. Perhaps the foremost challenge relates to lack of improvement to the technology of on-farm production, leading to rapid decline of yields as orchards have aged and to contraction of area under cultivation. In contrast, yields have been growing rapidly in Vietnam since 2014 because of a strong push by the government to develop and disseminate high-yielding and early maturing varieties, including dwarf varieties that allow higher-density planting of up to 500 trees/ha compared to normal density of 200 trees/ha. Going forward, production is expected to increase in Nigeria because the age distribution of cashew trees indicates that at least 40 percent of the trees were planted within the last 10 years and have not yet reached peak production.

A strategy for developing the cashew nuts subsector in Nigeria could consider providing incentives for importation of RCN from neighboring West African countries to be processed in Nigeria for export markets. This approach has been successfully adopted and executed by Vietnam. A large share of the US$2.6 billion value of kernels processed in Vietnam consists of RCN imported from West African countries. Nigeria enjoys stronger economic relations with the major cashew nuts producers in West Africa than India or Vietnam and can harness the apparatus of ECOWAS to establish partnerships among actors in these countries. However, deliberate efforts are needed to encourage RCN imports from West Africa into Nigeria. Currently, RCN imports to Nigeria attract import duties of 20 percent—the same as imports of processed kernels. This tariff regime needs to be reconsidered to provide incentives for expanding processing in the country, including by ensuring that import duties are lower for RCN and higher for processed kernels. Emerging processors in Nigeria would be entering the global market at a time when global kernel prices are falling (supply has just caught up with demand) and must face competition from established processors in Vietnam.

New investors in cashew nut processing could aim to "move up the value chain" and develop niche, branded, and differentiated cashew nut products for direct selling to supermarkets in western countries, including organic and fair-trade labeled products. The business model of processors in Vietnam centers on intermediate processing for bulk shipments to consumption markets in Europe and the United States. The final processing occurs in Europe and the United States. The emerging processors in West Africa could aim to deliver final processed kernels to final consumers in Europe and the United States if final processing costs are competitive in West Africa relative to those markets. Various business models could be considered, such as franchising and joint ventures. Perhaps a more rewarding option would be to develop niche, branded, and differentiated cashew nut products for direct selling to supermarkets in the western countries, including organic and fair-trade-labeled products. These strategies call for strong public-private partnerships to improve the business-enabling environment, reform policies that discourage importation of RCN from neighboring countries, develop infrastructure (especially roads and energy) in clusters where processing can efficiently occur, and so on.

A key lesson emerging from Vietnam is that Nigeria needs to improve the enabling environment for the cashew nuts subsector. Currently, there is no specific sector policy for cashew nuts to coordinate actions among the various stakeholders. Vietnam has not only prepared a sector-specific policy strategy to guide all aspects of development of the cashew nut industry, but also developed standards for trading of RCN. The standard was developed by the Ministry of Agriculture in collaboration with VINACAS and is the world's first specialized standard for RCN. It serves as a basis for grading and quality inspection to support trading and handling disputes of RCN. It is intended to help the Vietnamese cashew industry adapt to market demand by enhancing the quality and safety management of RCN imports. In addition, the tariff regime aims to encourage imports of RCN and discourage imports of processed kernels to create incentives for the domestic processing industry. Since 2010, the import duty for RCN has been 5 percent or lower for most origin countries (most favored nation rate) and 0 percent for members of the Association of Southeast Asian Nations (Cambodia and Indonesia), whereas the import tax on cashew kernels is significantly higher at 25 percent (MFN).

NOTES

1. Most of that industrial capacity is with one company—Olam International.
2. The main processors in Nigeria include Olam Edible Nuts (Olam International, the biggest processor, whose facility is located in Ilorin, Kwara State), Oxley, Farmforte, Lion Ltd, Foodpro, Abod Success, KD Foods, Valency, Esteema Diamonds Global Inv. Ltd (EDGIL), and ACET Nigeria Ltd.
3. According to discussions with the Vietnam Cashew Association.
4. JMSF Agribusiness collected data for this book.
5. The original data supported the Rural Investment Plan prepared by Cora Dankers, Food and Agriculture Organization of the United Nations (FAO) Investment Centre.
6. Data were collected by the Institute for Policy and Strategy for Agriculture and Rural Development, Vietnam, for this book.

REFERENCES

ACA (African Cashew Alliance). 2019a. "AfriCashew Splits." Week 15: April 8–14, 2019, No. 10, ACA, Accra. http://www.africancashewalliance.com/sites/default/files/documents /africashewsplits_week_15_market_report_16042019.pdf.

ACA (African Cashew Alliance). 2019b. "AfriCashew Splits." Week 21: May 20–26, No. 16. ACA, Accra. http://www.africancashewalliance.com/sites/default/files/documents/africashew splits_week_21_market_report_29052019.pdf.

CashewInfo.com. 2015. Proceedings of the World Cashew Convention. Dubai, February 5–6.

CashewInfo.com. 2020. "Cashew Exports Are Still Rising Despite the Great Spread of the COVID-19 Pandemic Worldwide." https://www.linkedin.com/pulse/cashew-exports -rise-despite-covid-19-pandemic-spread-worldwide-khong.

Dankers, C., and A. Ott. 2021. "Nigeria–Viet Nam Value Chain Benchmarking Cashew Nut Synthesis Report." Background paper for this book. Unpublished.

Economic Confidential. 2020. "Nigeria Can Generate N71bn From Cashew Export Yearly." *Economic Confidential*, January 31, 2020. https://economicconfidential.com/2020/01/nigeria-n71bn-cashew-export/.

Fages, Claire. 2020. "La Noix de Cajou Ouest-Africaine en Mal de Financements Bancaires." Podcast, Radio France Internationale, May 25, 2020. http://www.rfi.fr/fr/podcasts/20200525-la-noix-cajou-ouest-africaine-en-mal-financements-bancaires.

Fitzpatrick, J. 2017. "Outlook and Opportunity World Cashew Market." Presentation at the Mozambican Cashew Industry Conference, Maputo, December 7–8.

Gbenga-Ogu, Yejide. 2017. "Cashew Seed Exportation: Here Lies the Goldmine." *Nigerian Tribune*, May 16, 2017. https://tribuneonlineng.com/cashew-seed-exportation-lies-goldmine/.

Große-Rüschkamp, A., C. Topper, and E. Grenzebach E. 2010. "Analysis of the Cashew Value Chain in Nigeria and Analysis of a Cashew Country Study for Nigeria." African Cashew Initiative, African Cashew Development Project, GIZ.

IndexBox. 2020. "Featuring the Strong Processing Industry, Vietnam and India Dominate Global Raw Cashew Nut Market." *Global Trade*, October 30, 2020. https://www.globaltrademag.com/featuring-the-strong-processing-industry-vietnam-and-india-dominate-global-raw-cashew-nut-market/.

JMSF Agribusiness. 2020. "The Cashew Value Chain Report." Background paper for this book. Unpublished.

MARD (Ministry of Agriculture and Rural Development, Vietnam). 2019. "Overview of Cashew, Pepper, and Fruit." Unpublished working report for project preparation.

Ricau, Pierre. 2019. "The West African Cashew Sector in 2018: General Trends and Country Profiles." Nitidæ. https://www.nitidae.org/files/41dc7432/wa_cashew_sector_review_2019_nitidae.pdf.

SAPcashewconcept. 2016. "I Need 2 Know." SAPcashewconcept (blog), March 29, 2016. http://sapcashewconcept.mozello.it/page/params/post/819118/i-need-2-know.

Vanguard. 2015. "Nigerian Cashew Processors Operating below Installed Capacity." Vanguard, September 7, 2015. https://www.vanguardngr.com/2015/09/nigerian-cashew-processors-operating-below-installed-capacity/.

VINACAS (Vietnam Cashew Association). 2019. "The 11th VINACAS Golden Cashew Rendezvous." Hue City, Vietnam, March 1–3.

World Bank. 2019. "Better Opportunities for All: Vietnam Poverty and Shared Prosperity Update." World Bank, Washington, DC.

World Bank. 2020. "Improving Agricultural Interventions under the New National Target Programs in Vietnam." World Bank, Washington, DC.

6 Competitiveness and Policy Priorities in the Rice Value Chain

Rice is a strategic crop in both Nigeria and Vietnam, but for different reasons. In Nigeria, rice provides the single largest source of income to farmers. Nigerian diets are shifting strongly in favor of rice, with consumption per capita increasing rapidly. The increasing importance of rice has elevated the crop to the cornerstone of food price policy in Nigeria. In Vietnam, rice is the main staple food and a major source of export earnings, generating revenues of nearly US$3 billion in 2019 alone. Vietnam has a comparative advantage in producing rice for the domestic, regional, and international markets; and it competes in the global markets with leading exporters like Thailand and India. The domestic market in Vietnam is larger than in many countries with a similar population size. For example, per capita consumption of rice in Vietnam is nearly three times that in Nigeria; therefore, Vietnam's domestic market is relatively larger, despite Vietnam being a smaller country. In 2018, per capita consumption in Vietnam stood at about 97 kg/year compared to 34 kg/year in Nigeria.

Even with the relatively low per capita consumption, however, Nigeria leads other African countries in aggregate consumption and was one of the world's largest rice importers until 2013. Nigeria also ranks first in rice production in Africa. Farmers in Nigeria sell about 80 percent of their total production to domestic consumers and use the remaining 20 percent as food. The rice sector contributes about 3.2 percent of total annual agriculture production value in Nigeria and occupies 8 percent of total cultivated crop land (table 6.1). About 1.4 million farmers are directly employed in rice production, and the rice milling industry employs another 0.3 million.[1] These employment figures pale in comparison with those in Vietnam where the rice value chain employs over 21 million people, including about 8.5 million in rice cultivation and 13 million in various segments of the rice value chain. In Vietnam, rice contributes 28.5 percent of the total annual agriculture production value and occupies 36 percent of total cultivated cropland.

TABLE 6.1 Contribution of rice to the economies of Nigeria and Vietnam

	NIGERIA	VIETNAM
Agriculture gross production value (US$, million)	30,998	43,312
Paddy production value (US$, million)	981	12,324
Share of GDP (%)	0.24	6.00
Number employed in primary production (million)	1.4	8.5
Number employed in downstream value addition (million)	0.3	13
Share of agriculture production value (%)	3.2	28.5
Harvested area (hectares)	3,745,134	7,737,100

Sources: Based on data from the World Bank; data on paddy production value and harvested area are from FAOSTAT (Statistics Division, Food and Agriculture Organization of the United Nations); data on harvested area in Vietnam are from Vietnam's General Statistical Office.
Note: For harvested area, 17 percent of irrigated land is double cropped, so double cropped land is counted twice.

TECHNOLOGY OF PRODUCTION

In the 1960s, rice consumption in Nigeria was limited to special occasions and events. Since then, consumption demand has increased faster than in any other West African country, driven by urbanization and economic growth. Demand for rice is concentrated in urban centers as higher-income consumers increasingly demand foods that are easy to prepare or ready to eat. In addition, rice is preferred because it has much shorter cooking times compared to traditional cereals like millet, sorghum, fresh cassava, and yam roots. The rising demand led to sharp rises in rice imports and prompted both import restrictions and a supply-side push by the government to increase domestic production.

Whereas the growth of Nigeria's rice sector has been driven by consumer demand, the dramatic growth of yields in Vietnam has been largely driven by supply-side interventions by the government for self-sufficiency and exports. The first modern varieties were introduced in Vietnam at the end of the 1960s, and by the 1970s rice yields in Vietnam reached the average yields in Nigeria today. Achieving rice self-sufficiency and export surplus was the main goal of agricultural production planning and investments in irrigation in Vietnam. However, following the liberalization of the economy and increased population growth, demand for rice increased rapidly providing further impetus to growth.

Average rice yields in Nigeria are nearly three times lower than yields in Vietnam. In Nigeria, yields are estimated to be about 2.1 tons per hectare (ha) compared to 5.8 ton/ha in Vietnam. It is important to note that rice production volume and yields in Nigeria and Vietnam grew at the same pace until the early 1980s (figure 6.1). Since then, however, yields dramatically increased in Vietnam but remained relatively flat in Nigeria (figure 6.2). The only source of production growth in Nigeria is increased area under cultivation, mainly in rain-fed lowlands or drylands; irrigated rice area has hardly changed in the last two decades. In Vietnam, production growth is driven by both yields and increased cultivated area. Although average rice yields are 2.1 ton/ha in Nigeria (JMSF Agribusiness 2020) and 5.8 ton/ha in Vietnam (Tran Cong Thang 2020), the highest yield reported in both countries (the observed yield frontier) is about 6.5 ton/ha—which means that the average farmer in Vietnam operates closer to the observed

FIGURE 6.1

Rice production in Nigeria and Vietnam grew at similar rates until the early 1980s

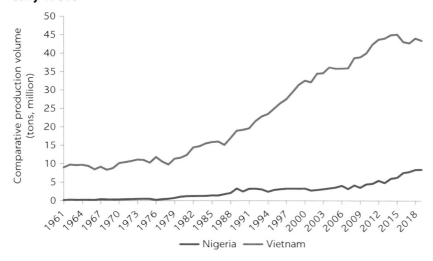

Source: FAOSTAT (Statistics Division, Food and Agriculture Organization of the United Nations).

FIGURE 6.2

Rice yields in Vietnam have increased rapidly since the 1980s but declined in Nigeria in most of the 1990s

Source: FAOSTAT (Statistics Division, Food and Agriculture Organization of the United Nations).

national frontier than the average farmer in Nigeria. This is not surprising because the agroecological zones and production environment are relatively more homogeneous in Vietnam, where rice is grown either on irrigated plains around the Mekong River Delta (MRD) and the Red River Delta or in rice terraces in the mountainous North. In contrast, the production environment varies greatly in Nigeria—from the mangroves of the Niger Delta to the dry Sahel zones—and the country likely has multiple production frontiers depending on agroecological zone and technology of production. Overall, farms are relatively larger in Nigeria and average 2.2 ha compared to 0.35 ha in Vietnam, but the averages mask wide differences across the various regions in both countries (table 6.2).

The widely varying yields in Nigeria result from differences in the varieties cultivated, quality of seeds, technology of water management, and agroecological zones. The main rice systems in Nigeria are irrigated land, rain-fed lowlands (*Fadamas*[2]), and rain-fed uplands (or drylands). Overall, yields are higher in irrigated rice fields than under rain-fed conditions, although *Fadamas* with improved water control and management can achieve yields comparable to those in irrigated fields.[3] A survey conducted by the International Food Policy Research Institute in six states found the lowest yields in Enugu (average of 2.0 ton/ha) and the highest in Kano (average of 3.7 ton/ha; IFPRI 2019). Another survey from the same year reported even lower average yields of 1.5 ton/ha in Benue and Nasarawa (Ayedun and Adeniyi 2019). Going forward, climate change could have a major impact on rice yields in Nigeria; recent estimates suggest that yields could decrease by 5.7 percent by 2030 (IFAD 2017).

Technology of production differs greatly between Nigeria and Vietnam. Only 17 percent of rice area is irrigated in Nigeria compared to about 80 percent in Vietnam. Furthermore, the use of improved seeds and fertilizers is considerably lower in Nigeria. About 80 percent of irrigated fields in Vietnam can cultivate two to three crops per year, whereas in Nigeria only two crops per year are possible in irrigated fields and improved *Fadamas*. The use of chemical fertilizers differs greatly between the two countries. In Nigeria, farmers on average use 40 kg to 77 kg of nitrogen per ha compared to an average 195 kg of nitrogen per ha in Vietnam. Fertilizer application rates in Nigeria vary greatly depending on the agroecological zones and the use of irrigation. For example, very low application rates of less than 9.4 kg of nitrogen per ha were reported in Niger and Taraba (Erhabor and Ahmadu 2013), average rates of 40 kg of nitrogen per ha were reported in Ebonyi state (Chidiebere-Mark 2018), and higher rates of about 86 kg of nitrogen per ha were reported in Abuja (Julius and Chukwumah 2014). Although high use of fertilizers has contributed to high yields in Vietnam,

TABLE 6.2 Summary of the characteristics of rice production in Nigeria and Vietnam

	VIETNAM	NIGERIA
Avg. rice area per household (ha)	0.35	2.2
Small-scale farmers	< 0.2 (54%)	< 2.5
Medium-scale farmers	0.2–2.0 (43%)	2.5 to 5.0 < 5.0 (90%)
Large-scale farmers	> 2.0 (3%)	> 5.0 (10%)
Farm employment	3.7 million people, from 8.5 million households	Estimated 1.43 million rice farmers in total
Irrigation (ha)	2.8 million (70% of total rice area)	293,117, if most double cropped (17% of total area harvested)
Share of area double cropped (%)	Est. 80	Est. 28 (irrigated and part of *Fadama*)
Average yield (ton/ha)	5.81	2.17
Yield potential (ton/ha)	6.5 (reached by large-scale farms in MRD with low-grade IR50404)	Irrigated: 6.5 (large-scale farm in Kano)

Sources: For Nigeria, average rice area per household from Ayedun and Adeniyi 2019; small- and medium-scale farmers from Bamba et al. 2010; farm employment from Obi 2019; irrigation from World Bank 2014; yield potential from JMSF Agribusiness 2020. For Vietnam, information from Tran 2020, using 2017 data from Institute of Policy and Strategy for Agriculture and Rural Development.
Note: ha = hectare; MRD = Mekong River Delta.

application rates are considerably above recommended levels and have led to suboptimal returns in farm profitability and high environmental costs.

Part of the reason driving excessive fertilizer use in Vietnam is the lack of soil testing and the small size of plots. Without soil testing, farmers cannot know the combination of nutrients needed to optimize productivity. Excessive fertilizer use, together with inadequate water management practices, means that a large proportion of fertilizer either runs off into streams and groundwater or is emitted as nitrous oxide (World Bank 2016). Farmers in Vietnam would use about 30–35 percent less fertilizers and pesticides if they were to apply good agricultural practices (GAPs). Vietnam's Ministry of Agriculture and extension system are now making efforts to extend the use of GAPs, including integrated pest management, and these efforts are beginning to show some results in terms of reduced use of fertilizers.

Another difference between the two countries is their use of improved seeds. In Nigeria, in addition to having low fertilizer application rates, farmers lack access to improved varieties and good quality seed. Instead, they rely on seed from previous seasons. The use of improved seed varies greatly in Nigeria, and recent surveys suggest it is relatively higher in Kebbi where farmers use purchased seed every 3 years and retain seed from previous harvests in between (Osawe 2018). In Vietnam about 65–70 percent of paddy area is grown with certified quality seeds every year (Giong Ca Mau 2019).

TRADE COMPETITIVENESS

Vietnam ranks among the top three rice exporters in the world, with most exports originating from a relatively small percentage of rice farmers in the MRD. Beginning in 2009, Vietnam has exported more than 4 million tons of rice per year with an average annual value of US$3 billion (figure 6.3)—a major contribution to foreign exchange earnings. However, the MRD produces 55 percent of Vietnam's rice by volume and accounts for 90 percent of total national export, most of which originates in three provinces (Kien Giang, An Giang, and Dong Thap). Those three provinces form "the core rice belt" (Tran Cong Thang 2020). Rice is cultivated by about 1.4 million households, but two-thirds of the net surplus is produced by the top 20 percent of growers—the commercial farmers with larger landholdings (World Bank 2016). For example, in An Giang province rice area under cultivation ranges from 3 ha to 20 ha per household, compared to the national average of 0.35 ha. The price of Vietnam's rice exports generally follows Thailand's export price trends (figure 6.4). The average Free On Board export price of 5 percent broken rice reached US$418/ton in 2018, which was higher than exports from India (US$401/ton) and Pakistan (US$402/ton), and nearly the same as exports from Thailand (US$419/ton).

Until 2013, Nigeria was for many years one of the world's largest rice importers. Rice imports have decreased dramatically in recent years because of import restrictions and increased domestic production. Even with increased domestic production, local rice has not been able to meet domestic demand in terms of quality and taste. Growth in rice imports to Nigeria started to increase rapidly in 1995, and this prompted trade policy responses to reduce the import bill, beginning with the introduction of import tariffs in 1995. Those tariffs have been revised several times over the years. For example, import tariffs increased from 50 percent to 100 percent between 1995 and 2005, were reduced to 30–50 percent

FIGURE 6.3

Since 2009, Vietnam has exported more than 4 million tons of rice per year at a value of about US$3 billion

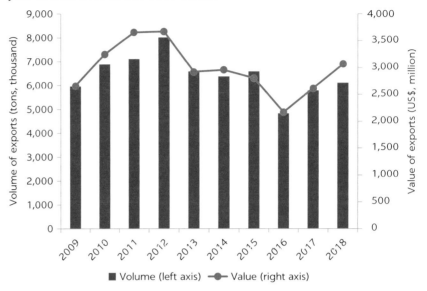

Source: General Department of Customs, Vietnam.

FIGURE 6.4

The price of Vietnam's rice exports generally follows Thailand's export price trends

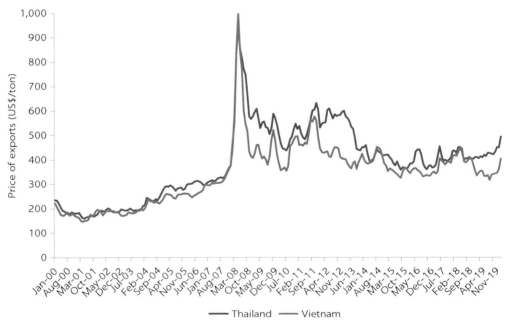

Source: Food Price Monitoring and Analysis Tool, Food and Agriculture Organization of the United Nations.

between 2008 and 2012, and then were raised again to 110 percent in 2013. A major shift in import policy occurred in 2016 when the government banned rice imports through land borders, in addition to the 110 percent import tariff (Abbas, Agada, and Kolade 2018). Rice trade policy milestones are illustrated in box 6.1.

Rice import volumes responded to the varying import tariff regime, with imports rapidly expanding after relaxation of tariffs in 2008 and then falling rapidly after 2013 following the higher tariffs (figure 6.5). Although the rapid decline in rice imports that started in 2013 has continued, imports into neighboring

Box 6.1

Rice trade policy milestones in Nigeria

1995:	Import tariff set at 100% (Munonye 2016 for most data before 2012)	**2012:**	Import quota, outside quota tariff at 72% (Dorosh and Malek 2016)
1996–2000:	Import tariff revised to 50%	**2013:**	Import quota, outside quota tariff at 110% (Dorosh and Malek 2016)
2001:	Import tariff revised to 85%		
2002:	Import tariff revised to 100%	**2014:**	Import quota, of which 70% of
2003:	Import tariff revised to 50%		volume at 30% tariff, and 30% of
2005:	Import tariff revised to 100%, but		volume at 70% tariff
	preferential tariff of 50% to two	**2016:**	Ban of imports through land borders
	companies	**October 2016:**	Increase in the import tariff from 10%
2006:	Duty suspended		to 60% (The Economist 2018)
2008:	Duty reintroduced, at 30% (Abbas, Agada, and Kolade 2018)	**2017:**	Import tariff of 70%, and de facto ban on rice imports through monetary
2009:	Import tariff revised to 5% to 30% tariff		measures (USDA 2018, 2019)
2010:	Import tariff revised to 30% to 50% tariff	**2018–19:**	Import tariff of 70% (10% and a 60% levy) (USDA 2018, 2019)
2011:	Import tariff revised to 50%	**August 2019:**	Closure of land borders to prevent the imports of rice through Benin

FIGURE 6.5

Rice imports to neighboring countries (especially Benin) increased because a large share of those imports was destined for Nigeria

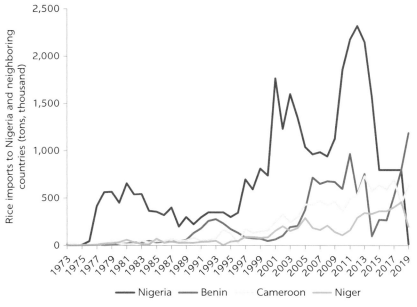

Source: FAOSTAT (Statistics Division, Food and Agriculture Organization of the United Nations).

countries (especially Benin) have increased rapidly. Most of the incremental imports into neighboring countries were reexported unofficially to Nigeria through porous borders, with recent estimates suggesting that about 80 percent of rice imports to Benin are generally destined for the Nigeria market.[4] The ban on rice imports in 2016 did not stop imports, and in 2017 the Central Bank of Nigeria introduced monetary measures to bar importers from using formal and informal sources of foreign exchange for rice imports. In 2019 the government decided to close borders with neighboring countries to eliminate smuggling of agricultural commodities such as rice into the country. Despite these measures, rice import tariffs did not have an impact on domestic prices until after 2015 (figure 6.6), perhaps because more rice was smuggled through the borders. Along with import tariffs, the ban, and border closures, the government during various periods issued import quotas for paddy and brown rice at preferential tariff rates. The quota volumes were based on the supply gap between domestic production and consumption, and eligibility was linked to importers' investments in rice mills and outgrower schemes.

Prices for imported and local rice vary greatly across Nigeria. Most of that variation is explained by the distance from production areas (local rice) or port of entry and the grade (imported rice). Most imported rice enters the country in the South, whereas most local rice is produced in the North and transported to large urban consumption markets in the South. Imported rice tends to be cheaper in southern markets and more expensive further North; local rice tends to be cheaper in the North and relatively more expensive in the South. Other factors causing differences in rice prices are the retail channels in which the rice is sold and the quality of rice. Traditional retail channels include street vendors and small shops that sell produce that is often not packaged. Consumers use traditional retailers because those retailers are cheaper and close to where they live. However, in recent years there has been an increase in sales of packaged rice in

FIGURE 6.6

Before 2015, rice import tariffs had no impact on domestic prices mainly because of rice smuggled through borders

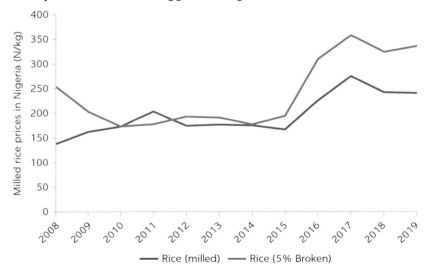

Source: 2020 data from FEWS NET, average of all markets for which data were available.
Note: N = Nigerian naira.

urban centers through supermarkets and branded products identifying the processing company, weight, and grade. Rice is increasingly being substituted for traditional staples as urban consumers seek foods that are easy to prepare and store. Higher-income urban consumers show a distinct preference for higher-priced imported aromatic rice and are willing to pay a premium for such attributes.

CHARACTERIZATION OF RICE VALUE CHAINS

Rice value chains in both Nigeria and Vietnam are characterized by spot market transactions and weak vertical coordination. The main actors in the rice value chains are farmers, input dealers, traders (small and large), millers, exporters (Vietnam), wholesalers, and retailers. Most of the rice in both countries is marketed through value chains that rely on spot markets, even when the actors have engaged repeatedly. However, some millers in both countries contract farmers to produce rice, and these relationships typically involve millers providing farmers with inputs on credit, including seeds, fertilizers, agrochemicals, and technical advice. About 275,000 ha of rice in Nigeria is cultivated on outgrower schemes, with contracted tenants and independent farmers supplying to mills. This amount represents about 7.3 percent of total rice acreage. When contract farming arrangements exist, the relationships are fraught with several challenges such as high transaction costs in Vietnam and side selling in Nigeria. The main approach millers take to limit side selling is threshing the rice for the farmer and then taking delivery on the spot.

Contract farming in Nigeria works better when farmer organizations are strong and modeled as producer companies with growth objectives, rather than as livelihood-oriented farmer organizations. In Nigeria, large-scale industrial millers such as Olam and Vetee have well-structured outgrower systems to source high-quality local rice that can compete with imported rice for the same consumer segment. Contracts with small-scale farmers are usually organized through their cooperatives, but the contract performance of such farmer organizations is mixed, depending primarily on whether they are pursuing a relationship to enable their medium-term growth or to achieve short-term profits. Rice exporters in Vietnam prefer operating contracts with large farmers because of the high transaction costs involved in monitoring many small farmers, especially when the commodity is destined to export markets that demand higher quality. Monitoring aspects include the use of a specific certified variety, good practice in application of agrochemicals, and consistent quality of grain. In the case of the Loc Troi Group, company technicians supervise farmers, and the company buys rice only from farmers who strictly follow technical guidelines. Medium-size mills that contract farmers as outgrowers tend to also integrate backward and produce their own paddies.

More than three-quarters of rice produced in Nigeria is processed by small-scale millers with processing capacity of less than 3,000 tons per year (table 6.3), whereas in Vietnam millers of this size hardly exist. More than 60 percent of millers in Vietnam have capacity of more than 10,000 tons per year; in Nigeria only 23 percent of millers have this capacity. The large-scale milling capacity in Nigeria is mostly located in the states of Kebbi and Kano, which mill about 36 percent of the rice in Nigeria (figure 6.7 and figure 6.8).

TABLE 6.3 **Milling segment of rice value chains, Nigeria and Vietnam**

	NIGERIA	VIETNAM
Small scale	<3,000 ton/year (77% of rice milled)	<10,000 ton/year (38.5% of mills)
Medium scale	3–10,000 ton/year (3% of rice milled)	10–100,000 ton/year (58.5% of mills)
Large scale	> 10,000 ton/year (20% of rice milled)	> 100,000 ton/year (3% of mills)
Conversion factor	Average: 63% to 66%	70%
	Kebbi: 70% (paddy to parboiled milled)	
	Kano: 60% (paddy to milled rice)	

Sources: Vietnam data from Tran Cong Thang 2020. Nigeria data from JMSF Agribusiness 2020; Johnson and Masias 2016; Udemeze 2013.

FIGURE 6.7

At least 60 percent of the rice milling capacity in Nigeria is in the North West region

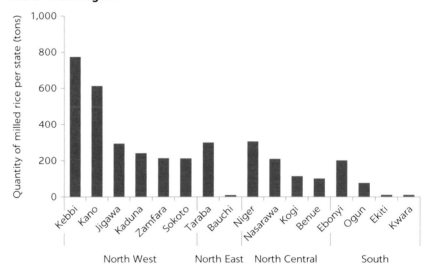

Source: Obi 2019.

FIGURE 6.8

The state of Kebbi accounts for 20 percent of milled rice in Nigeria

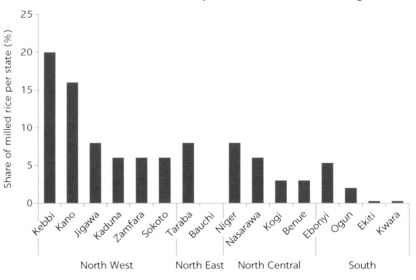

Source: Obi 2019.

The relatively small size of millers in Nigeria is partly due to the lack of a consistent, reliable supply of high-grade paddy to the mills (PwC 2018). Establishing a large viable mill requires investment in developing a reliable supply, either through vertical integration toward farming or vertical coordination with farmers. However, the milling segment in Nigeria has integrated forward into parboiling, with 90 percent of local rice parboiled. This forward integration has not happened in the milling segment in Vietnam. The technology employed by large-scale millers is quite advanced in both countries, but small-scale millers in Nigeria use old equipment and face challenges obtaining spare parts. The rice conversion factor of paddy to rice is higher in Vietnam (70 percent) relative to Nigeria (63–66 percent; Johnson and Masias 2016; USDA 2019). However, significant differences exist across Nigerian states. For example, Kebbi—a leader in many aspects of the rice sector, including yields and installed processing—has a conversation factor of 70 percent, and Kano's is 60 percent (JMSF Agribusiness 2020).

The technology farmers use for postharvest drying differs in Nigeria and Vietnam. Most farmers in Nigeria dry paddy on tarpaulin or concrete blocks, resulting in high foreign matter and high moisture content of the paddy (poor rice quality) as well as high postharvest losses. In contrast, farmers in Vietnam increasingly use combine harvesters that integrate threshing and winnowing in the harvest process, and about 50 percent of the rice is machine dried. Vietnam's government policy encourages farmers to combine small plots that are managed as one large field, allowing for mechanization even in small pieces of land. It is estimated that the rate of mechanization is 93 percent in land preparation, 75 percent in pesticide applications, and 50 percent in harvesting operations. The policy has also encouraged vertical coordination arrangements between farmers and millers, although spot transactions still dominate the value chains. Farm-level postharvest losses in Nigeria during harvesting, threshing, and winnowing are estimated at 9.5 percent (Udemeze 2013) compared to 3.0 percent in Vietnam (Đoàn 2012). Overall, the loss and waste in Nigeria are estimated at nearly 25 percent compared to 14 percent in Vietnam.

Farmers have less bargaining power in setting market prices compared to all other actors in the value chains. Traders in Nigeria aggregate paddy purchased from many small-scale farmers and deliver to the mills. Prices are largely set by the traders after considering their costs of aggregating and delivering to the mills. Similarly, traders in Vietnam have more bargaining power relative to the farmers. The price is in many cases negotiated with farmers while the crop is still in the field and is based on a trader's assessment of expected quality of paddy and prevailing market prices.

COSTS AND MARGINS OF VALUE CHAIN ACTORS

This section compares costs and margins for the actors of rice value chains in Nigeria and Vietnam. Figure 6.9 provides a summary of the costs, selling prices, and margins for each actor along the value chain in Nigeria and Vietnam. Prices are in milled-rice equivalent, which means that costs and margins for paddy have been adjusted to correspond to the amount of paddy needed to make 1 kg of milled rice. The amounts of paddy needed to make 1 kg of milled rice (milled-rice equivalents) are 1.4 kg for Vietnam and 1.5 kg for Nigeria. The comparisons treat

FIGURE 6.9

Buildup of costs, prices, and margins for rice value chains, Nigeria and Vietnam

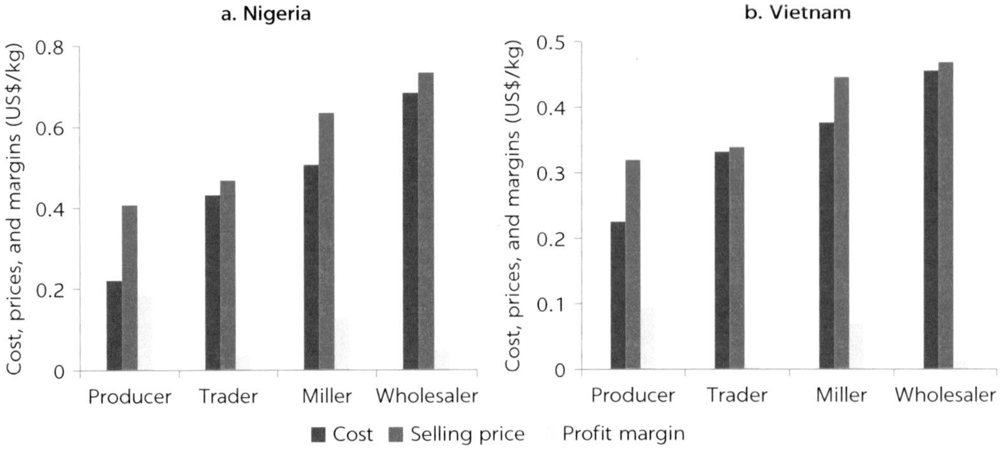

Sources: IFPRI 2019; Tran Cong Thang 2020; JMSF Agribusiness 2020; Johnson and Ajibola 2016.

rice as a homogeneous commodity and do not distinguish between variety or quality. On average, the rice produced and milled in Nigeria can be considered lower quality than rice from Vietnam, which exports about 70 percent of production. However, about 90 percent of the rice milled in Nigeria is parboiled, which increases the nutrition value. Rice from Vietnam is not parboiled. The margins correspond to the difference between the identified costs and the sales price at each level of the value chain, which means any other costs not identified are subsumed under the listed costs.

Data are drawn from farmers in Kano in Nigeria and the MRD in Vietnam. The costs at the producer (farm) level for both countries include costs incurred by farmers to purchase various inputs, including seeds, fertilizers, chemicals, irrigation water, land preparation, labor, and hiring a harvester. The share of most of these inputs in the cost of production is within the 5 percent difference range between Nigeria and Vietnam—except for the cost of labor, which contributes 23 percent to the cost of production in Nigeria[5] compared to 6 percent in Vietnam. Overall, production costs account for 6.9 percent of the retail sales price in Nigeria and 6.1 percent of that price in Vietnam. The margins are higher at the production level because farmers deal with relatively lower volumes compared to other actors in the chain. The costs for millers include asset depreciation costs because millers incur significant up-front investment to buy the machinery and start the mill. The margins for millers do not include sales of by-products because the cost buildup is focused on milled rice.

Although farmers in Nigeria have higher margins per kg of rice sold, their counterparts in Vietnam earn higher margins annually because of higher yields and an additional crop per year. The additional crop is due to access to irrigation, and the higher yields are driven by government policy of consistent investments in research to develop new and high-yielding varieties. A summary of selected rice sector policies in Vietnam is provided in box 6.2. The total value of margins from production to milling levels is nearly three times higher in Nigeria—US$0.35/kg compared to US$0.13/kg in Vietnam. However, the total costs at the same levels of the value chains (from production to milling) are quite

Lessons from policies and public investments that have supported growth in the rice sector in Vietnam

The government of Vietnam has set strategic policies and made investments that have contributed to the rapid growth of the country's rice sector. The nature of these investments provides important lessons that can be considered in Nigeria. Specific investments include the following:

- Publicly funded research to develop high-yielding varieties that meet consumer tastes and management practices to optimize productivity under local growing conditions. The improved varieties and management practices are disseminated through a professional technical system from the central to communal level, delivering effective extension to farmers.

- Institutional transformation of old cooperatives into new generation cooperatives modeled as producer companies. Cooperatives play an important role in organizing small farmers and facilitating public and private service delivery. Since 1997, successive laws have facilitated the transformation of old-style cooperatives into service cooperatives and the formation of new cooperatives. As a result, cooperatives play an important role in the rice sector, providing various services to their members, including input supply, irrigation management, extension management, and marketing.

- Vietnam's traditional policy of protecting rice land and restricting its conversion to other uses. This policy has prevented diversification and reduced farmers' earnings. Irrigation systems were specifically designed for rice crops (up to three crops a year), and rotation with other crops has proved difficult. The government policy has shifted recently to support diversification to more high-value crops, and rice acreage has been decreasing since 2013. Although rice cultivation has significantly benefited most stakeholders, research shows that earlier diversification into other sectors could have resulted in higher earnings for farmers and more efficient use of public funds (World Bank 2016).

similar—US$0.28/kg in Nigeria compared to US$0.27/kg in Vietnam. Actors in Nigeria, though, tend to work with much lower volumes per year, which leads to relatively lower annual margins even though margins per kg are higher. The differences in volumes begin at the production level. Most farmers in Vietnam's MRD (the study area) can grow between two and three crops per year, compared to two crops in Kano (the study area in Nigeria). Furthermore, the estimated yields from the value chain studies are higher in Vietnam (6,500 kg/ha) than in Nigeria (3,710 kg/ha; table 6.4). These field estimates are higher than respective national averages, which are 5,800 kg/ha in Vietnam and 2,100 kg/ha in Nigeria. Accounting for the higher yields but without the additional crop per year in Vietnam, the average farmer in Vietnam earns margins (revenue minus costs) annually that are 24 percent higher than the average farmer in Nigeria, that is, about US$2,570 in Vietnam compared to US$2,072 in Nigeria.

The volume advantages of Vietnam's actors go beyond farming and are especially higher in the milling segment where size really matters. In Vietnam about 60 percent of millers have capacity of more than 10,000 tons/year, whereas in Nigeria only 23 percent of millers have this capacity. The rest of the milling capacity in Nigeria (about 77 percent) is composed of small-scale millers with capacity of less than 3,000 tons/year—a size that rarely exists in Vietnam. The capacity of millers sampled in both Nigeria and Vietnam is lower than the

TABLE 6.4 Rice farmers in Nigeria have higher per kg margins, but farmers in Vietnam earn higher annual margins because of higher yields and an additional crop

	COST ELEMENTS	NIGERIA (KANO), PER YEAR	VIETNAM (MEKONG RIVER DELTA), PER YEAR
Farmers	Plot size (ha)	2.20	3.00
	Yield per season (kg/ha)	3,710	6,500
	Number of seasons	2	2
	Volume of milled equivalent (kg)	11,100	27,300
	Gross margin per kg of milled rice (US$)	0.19	0.09
	Total annual gross margin (US$)	2,072	2,570
	Revenue per kg of milled rice (US$)	0.41	0.32
	Total revenue (US$)	4,520	8,717
Millers	Volume of milled equivalent (kg)	1,278,000	4,200,000
	Gross margin per kg of milled rice (US$)	0.03	0.07
	Total annual gross margin (US$)	40,207	292,355
	Revenue per kg of milled rice (US$)	0.63	0.45
	Total revenue (US$)	802,080	1,872,143

Source: FEWS NET 2019 data; IFPRI 2019; IPSARD 2017; JMSF Agribusiness 2020; Johnson and Ajibola 2016.
Note: ha = hectare.

respective national averages. In Vietnam, the average milling capacity of the surveyed millers is 4,200 tons/year compared to the national median of more than 40,000 tons/year—and in Nigeria the field surveys sampled millers with average margins of 1,300 tons/year compared to the national median of more than 2,000 tons/year. Although the discrepancy is clearly higher in Vietnam than in Nigeria, the millers' margins are seven times higher in Vietnam compared to Nigeria (table 6.4). In both countries, millers have the second-largest share of the total margin (figure 6.10) but enjoy the largest volumes (table 6.4). The higher volumes enable millers to obtain the highest annual margins in the rice value chains. By contrast, farmers get the highest share of margins per kg, but their annual revenues are modest relative to millers because these small-scale farmers deal in small volumes.

Although Vietnam is not a traditional exporter of rice to Nigeria, its rice would be competitive in Nigeria's domestic markets in the absence of import tariffs. Vietnam is the world's third-largest exporter of rice after Thailand and India; however, the country does not have a history of exporting rice to Nigeria. Most official rice imports into Nigeria originate from Thailand and India, which respectively accounted for 51 percent and 35 percent of rice imported into Nigeria in 2014 (figure 6.11). In 2019, the export price of Vietnam's rice—which previously followed the price of rice from Thailand (see figure 6.4)—declined. This drop occurred because China,[6] Vietnam's main export market, dramatically reduced the quantities of rice imported from Vietnam.[7] As a result, the import parity price for rice from Vietnam is US$0.72/kg without tariff, comparable to local rice from Kano at the price of US$0.73/kg in Lagos.[8] However, the price of imported rice increases significantly with tariff—for example, a 70 percent tariff

FIGURE 6.10

Percentage of total profit margin by value chain actor, Nigeria and Vietnam

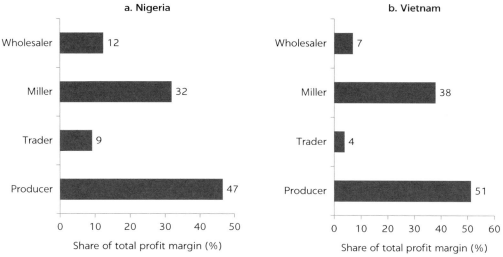

Source: FEWS NET 2019 data; IFPRI 2019; IPSARD 2017; JMSF Agribusiness 2020; Johnson and Ajibola 2016.

FIGURE 6.11

More than 80 percent of official rice imports in Nigeria originated from Thailand and India, 2014

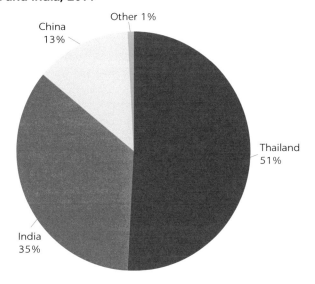

Source: United Nations Comtrade Database (as reported by Nigeria).

increases the price to US$1.07/kg, making imported rice uncompetitive (figure 6.12).[9] The ratio of imported rice without tariffs to imported rice with tariffs is 0.67; however, this ratio does not adequately reflect the economic trade-offs involved because it does not account for all the subsidies along the value chains in Nigeria and Vietnam, including the subsidies on inputs such as fertilizers and equipment.

FIGURE 6.12

Without tariffs, rice imports from Vietnam would be competitive in Nigeria's domestic market

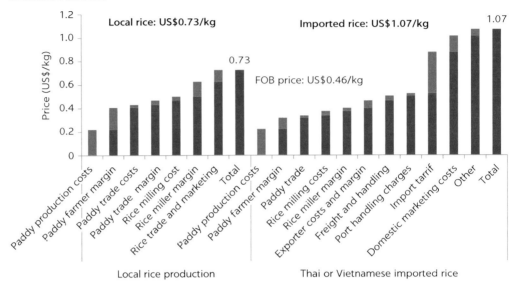

Sources: IFPRI 2019 for costs in Nigeria, with the exception of the traders' costs and margins that come from JMSF 2020; imported rice data from Tran Cong Thang 2020 adjusted for inflation; import tariffs computed using a tariff of 70 percent. Johnson and Ajibola 2016 for costs in Nigeria for imported rice, corresponding to 2012 data adjusted for inflation.
Note: FOB = Free on Board.

CONCLUSIONS

Rice provides the single largest source of income to farmers in Nigeria. For decades, consumer demand for rice has been growing faster than domestic production, leading to rising imports, especially between 1994 and 2013. The rising imports prompted the government to actively intervene through various policy measures that have elevated rice to the fore of food price policy in Nigeria. Trade policy measures have mainly involved import tariffs that were revised almost every year between 1995 and 2018. However, there is evidence that traders circumvented import tariffs by moving the commodity into Nigeria through the porous land borders. Since 2016, the trade policy measures transitioned from import tariffs to an import ban and eventually the closure of land borders. In particular, the government in 2019 closed borders with neighboring countries to eliminate smuggling of rice and other agricultural commodities. In addition to the trade policy measures, the government has been increasingly implementing supply-side interventions to increase domestic production.

The combination of trade policy and supply-side interventions has significantly increased domestic rice production; however, the supply response has waned in recent years, and it is becoming clear that these policies alone will not improve the competitiveness of the domestic rice subsector. Rice production grew steadily by more than 12 percent between 2010 and 2016, driven by expansion of area under cultivation, which increased by 6.74 percent in 2010–14 and by 10.63 percent in 2015–16. However, the expansion in area under cultivation could not be sustained because of negative growth of –5.23 percent in cultivated area in 2017–19. More important, the trade policies and current crop of supply-side interventions have not appreciably increased rice yields. The yields have remained persistently low relative to major producers in the world, and this continues to confine the domestic rice sector into a low-competitiveness trap.

The competitiveness of the rice subsector in Nigeria cannot increase without yield growth and improvement of rice quality. There is an imperative to invest in research and development to generate high-yielding varieties and improve quality attributes of local rice (taste, aroma, texture, and so on) under local growing conditions. Farmers need to have access to improved rice seed varieties at scale and through delivery systems that are sufficiently regulated to guarantee quality of seed. Other elements of the technology of production that need improvement include delivering farmer extension and advisory services, expanding access to irrigation and institutional improvements in irrigation water management, and increasing the supply and quality control of fertilizers. The effective operationalization of recent reforms in seed development and quality control (National Agricultural Seeds Council Act 2019) and fertilizer quality control (National Fertilizer Quality [Control] Act 2019) would make a huge contribution to increasing the competitiveness of rice and other crop sectors in Nigeria.

Effective vertical coordination of investments and operations between farmers and the milling industry is key to improving the competitiveness of rice value chains. Currently, outgrower schemes and contracting farming arrangements account for only 7.3 percent of rice area under cultivation in Nigeria. In contrast, the established milling capacity is mostly small-scale with processing capacity of less than 3,000 tons/year. The small millers handle more than three-quarters of rice produced in Nigeria. The millers use old equipment and face challenges obtaining spare parts, leading to a poor paddy–rice conversion factor of 63–66 percent compared to 70 percent in Vietnam. Establishing a large, viable mill requires investment in developing a reliable supply, which can be done through vertical coordination with farmers. This calls for coordinated investments to expand the milling capacity while providing farmers access to high-yielding varieties that have the attributes desired by consumers and other quality inputs. The farmers will also need to improve the technology for postharvest management. Currently, most farmers in Nigeria dry paddy on tarpaulin or concrete blocks, resulting in a paddy with high foreign matter, high moisture content, and high postharvest losses—estimated at nearly 25 percent compared to 14 percent in Vietnam.

Outgrower schemes and contract farming works better when farmer organizations are strong and modeled as producer companies with growth objectives, rather than as livelihood-oriented farmer organizations. This is one key lesson Nigeria can draw from Vietnam. The government of Vietnam has successfully implemented a deliberate policy of institutional transformation of old cooperatives into new generation cooperatives modeled as producer companies. The new generation cooperatives have been quite effective at taking a long-term investment approach to asset building and service provision in critical areas such as input supply, irrigation management, extension management, and marketing. Outgrower schemes and contract farming arrangements in Nigeria are usually organized through the cooperatives of small-scale farmers, but contract performance has been a problem, primarily because of side selling and high ex post transaction costs for contract enforcement.

NOTES

1. Data are not available on number of people employed in other off-farm segments of rice value chains (for example, trading and transportation).
2. In the Hausa language, *Fadama* means fertile or rich low-lying land. Flooding occurs during the rains, after which the water drains away. Where water remains easily accessible, it may be used to irrigate the rice late in the growth cycle of the crop or to irrigate a dry season crop through pumping water from an aquifer or use of canals for flood irrigation. Therefore, control over the water is very variable within the *Fadama* area. Improved *Fadamas* have increased control over the water table and are comparable to irrigated rice fields.
3. The draft Implementation Completion and Results Report for the World–Bank–funded Fadama project reports yield increases from 2.83 ton/ha to 4.93 ton/ha in the most improved and productive *Fadamas* (World Bank 2020).
4. Information from the web page "The World Bank in Benin" (https://www.worldbank.org /en/country/benin/overview).
5. Labor accounts for a higher cost of production in Cross River State, where it accounts for 45 percent of cost of production.
6. China accounted for 22 percent of rice exports from Vietnam in 2018.
7. In 2018, China imported 1.33 million tons of rice from Vietnam, but this amount reduced to 477,000 tons in 2019.
8. The reference market is Lagos; a different reference market could likely lead to different results because of transportation costs from Kano.
9. A similar analysis carried out by FEWS NET recorded prices estimated at an average of US$0.73/kg for local rice and US$0.87/kg for imported rice, and the difference was mainly due to lower costs of freight and handling.

REFERENCES

Abbas, A. M., I. G. Agada, and O. Kolade. 2018. "Impact of Rice Importation on Nigeria's Economy." *Journal of Scientific Agriculture* 2: 71–75.

Ayedun, B., and A. Adeniyi. 2019. "Determinants of Rice Production of Small-Scale Farmers in Mono-Cropping and Intercropping Systems in Nigeria." *Acta Scientific Nutritional Health* 3 (7): 75–85.

Bamba, I., A. Diagne, J. Manful, and O. Ajayi. 2010. "Historic Opportunities for Rice Growers in Nigeria." *Grain De Sel* No. 51, Special Report.

Chidiebera-Mark, N. 2018. *Analysis of Rice Value Chain in Ebonyi State, Nigeria.* Lambert Academic Publishing.

Đoàn Lập Vũ. 2012. Thất thoát lúa do thiếu máy gặt đập. Thanh Nien. https://thanhnien.vn /thoi-su/that-thoat-lua-do-thieu-may-gat-dap-490024.html.

Dorosh, P. A., and M. Malek, M. 2016. "Rice Imports, Prices, and Challenges for Trade Policy." In *The Nigeria Rice Economy*, edited by K. Gyimah-Brempong, M. Johnson, and H. Takeshima. Philadelphia: University of Pennsylvania Press.

Erhabor, P. O., and J. Ahmadu. 2013. "Technical Efficiency of Small-Scale Rice Farmers in Nigeria. Research and Reviews." *Journal of Agriculture and Allied Sciences* 2 (3).

Giong Ca Mau, 2019. Đề án: Phát triển sản xuất giống cây nông, lâm nghiệp, giống vật nuôi và giống thủy sản đến năm 2020. http://giongcamau.vn/Tin-tuc-giong-cay-trong/de-an-phat -trien-san-xuat-giong-cay-nong-lam-nghiep-giong-vat-nuoi-va-giong-thuy-san-den-nam -2020-117.html.

IFAD (International Fund for Agricultural Development). 2017. Commodity and Enterprise Analysis Survey of the Niger Delta of Nigeria (CEAS-ND).

IFPRI (International Food Policy Research Institute). 2019. "Agro-Processing Productivity Enhancement and Livelihood Improvement Support Project (APPEALS) Baseline Survey." Draft report, IFPRI, Washington, DC.

JMSF Agribusiness. 2020. "Sources of Growth in Agribusiness Small and Medium-Sized Enterprises (SMEs): Rice Report." Unpublished manuscript.

Johnson, M., and A. Ajibola. 2016. "Postharvest Processing Marketing and Competitiveness of Domestic Rice." In *The Nigeria Rice Economy,* edited by K. Gyimah-Brempong, M. Johnson, and H. Takeshima. Philadelphia: University of Pennsylvania Press.

Johnson, M., and I. Masias. 2016. "Assessing the State of the Rice Milling Sector in Nigeria." Working Paper 40, International Food Policy Research Institute, Washington, DC.

Julius, A., and A. F. Chukwumah. 2014. "Socio-economic Determinants of Small-Scale Rice Farmers' Output in Abuja, Nigeria." *Asian Journal of Rural Development* 4 (1): 16–24.

Munonye, Jane O. 2016. "Nigeria Rice Imports in the Last Three Decades under Different Trade and Fiscal Policies." *Unified Journal of Agriculture and Food Science* June: 2015–3351.

Obi, Goodluck. 2019. "Rice Industry Review." *KPMG Insights*, October 21, 2019. https://home .kpmg/ng/en/home/insights/2019/10/rice-industry-review.html.

Osawe, O. W. 2018. "Use of Modern Inputs and Complementary Farm Practices in the Nigeria Rice Value Chain: Implications for Policy." Policy Research Brief 74, Feed the Future Innovation Lab for Food Security Policy.

PwC (Pricewaterhouse Coopers) Nigeria. 2018. "Boosting Rice Production through Increased Mechanisation." Report. https://www.pwc.com/ng/en/assets/pdf/boosting-rice -production.pdf.

The Economist. 2018. "Grow Your Rice and Eat It: Nigeria Hopes High Tariffs Will Make It Grow More Rice." *The Economist*, March 15, 2018. https://www.economist.com/middle -east-and-africa/2018/03/15/nigeria-hopes-high-tariffs-will-make-it-grow-more-rice.

Tran Cong Thang. 2020. "Overview Rice Sector and Rice Value Chain in Viet Nam." Institute of Policy and Strategy for Agriculture and Rural Development, Ha Noi.

Udemeze, J. 2013. "Adoption of FARO 44 Rice Production and Processing Technologies by Farmers in Anambra State, Nigeria." MSc thesis, University of Nigeria, Nsukka.

USDA (United States Department of Agriculture). 2018. "Nigeria: Grain and Feed Annual, 2018." Global Agricultural Information Network Report, USDA Foreign Agricultural Service.

USDA (United States Department of Agriculture). 2019. "Nigeria: Grain and Feed Annual, 2019; Nigeria's Imports of Wheat and Rice to Rise." Global Agricultural Information Network Report NG-19002, USDA Foreign Agricultural Service.

World Bank. 2014. "Transforming Irrigation Management in Nigeria Project." Project Appraisal Document. World Bank, Washington, DC.

World Bank. 2016. "Transforming Vietnamese Agriculture: Gaining More from Less." Vietnam Development Report. World Bank, Washington, DC.

World Bank. 2020. "Third National Fadama Development Project (FADAMA III) (P096572), Implementation Status and Results Report." World Bank, Washington, DC.

7 Competitiveness and Policy Priorities in the Cassava Value Chain

Nigeria has been the world's highest cassava-producing country since 2005. Production reached 59.5 million tons in 2018, following a robust average annual growth rate of 3.5 percent between 2001 and 2018. As the world's leading producer of cassava, Nigeria accounts for 21.4 percent of world cassava production (table 7.1). Growth in the cassava subsector started around 1985 and was fueled by a rapidly increasing population, which created demand for the traditional food staple and supply of labor to cultivate the land (figure 7.1 and figure 7.2). During this period, the government provided several incentives that catalyzed growth, including the Presidential Cassava Initiative (2001–07) and more recently the Presidential Agricultural Transformation Agenda (2011–15). Cassava is cultivated by both men and women, for different purposes and in separate cassava fields. Whereas men produce cassava primarily for sale of fresh cassava roots to intermediaries (who then immediately process the crop), women produce cassava primarily for processing into pellets, flour, or garri for both household consumption and sales. In the South West region of Nigeria, women farmers commonly participate in cassava-processing groups, often paying a fee to use equipment owned by private individuals (Bentley et al. 2017; Forsythe, Posthumus, and Martin 2016). Overall, 90 percent of small-scale farmers grow cassava, and they do so on less than 1 hectare (ha) of land.

TABLE 7.1 Contributions of cassava to GDP and agricultural production in Nigeria and Vietnam

INDICATOR	YEAR	NIGERIA	VIETNAM
Agriculture GDP (%)	2018	21.2	14.7
Cassava production value (million tons)	2018	59.5	9.8
Share of world's cassava production (%)	2018	21.4	3.6
Gross production value (US$, billion)	2018	3.2	2.1
Cassava share of agriculture GDP (%)	2018	12.7	3.3
Cassava share of agriculture production (%)	2018	13.0	6.4
Cassava harvested area (% of cropland)	2018	16.9	4.5

Sources: GDP data from World Development Indicators, World Bank; cassava production value data from FAOSTAT (Statistics Division, Food and Agriculture Organization of the United Nations).

TECHNOLOGY OF PRODUCTION

Beginning around 2000, cassava in Vietnam transitioned to an industrial crop that is mostly processed into starch, whereas in Nigeria it has remained a staple food crop used mostly to prepare traditional dishes. The transition in Vietnam was driven by industrial demand from cassava starch factories that were processing starch for exports, mainly to China. Cassava prices increased rapidly, and the ensuing supply response was remarkable as growth in production increased rapidly by more than 10 percent annually, from 1.9 million tons in 2000 to reach 9.8 million tons of cassava in 2018 (see table 7.1). The production increase was due to both expansion of area under cultivation and increased yields. New high-yielding varieties were developed through collaboration between industrial starch processors and institutes for research and development (R&D). In addition to the high-yielding varieties, farmers could also access extension services on proper crop management practices. Vietnam now ranks as the eighth-highest cassava producer in the world and third in Asia after Thailand and Indonesia. Cassava contributes about 3.3 percent to agriculture gross domestic product (GDP) in Vietnam.

Cassava yields in Vietnam leapfrogged Nigeria for the first time in 2001, and by 2018 yields in Vietnam were more than twice the yields in Nigeria. Cassava yields in Vietnam have been consistently growing over the past two decades and reached about 19 ton/ha in 2018, compared to about 8.7 ton/ha in Nigeria in 2018 (figure 7.3). In terms of yields, Vietnam ranks third in the world after Indonesia and Thailand, whereas yields in Nigeria are comparable to the Democratic Republic of Congo. Furthermore, cassava yields in Nigeria have not fully recovered from the steep drop in 2013 that was caused by drought. The adverse climatic shock affected yields across many other West African countries, primarily because farmers were not using drought-resistant varieties. Climate change is expected to increase the frequency and severity of droughts in the region, and recent estimates suggest that those effects could decrease cassava yields by about 3.5 percent by 2030.[1] With persistent low yields, production growth in Nigeria has been fueled by expansion of area under cultivation (figure 7.4). By contrast,

FIGURE 7.1

Cassava production growth soared after 1985 in Nigeria but not in Vietnam

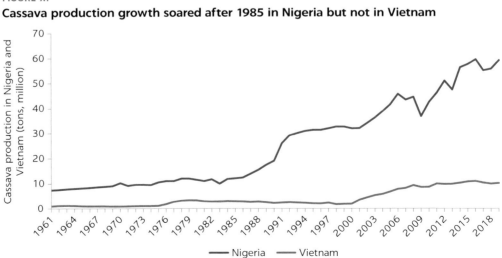

Source: FAOSTAT (Statistics Division, Food and Agriculture Organization of the United Nations).

FIGURE 7.2

Cassava production growth in Nigeria after 1985 was fueled by a rapid increase in population

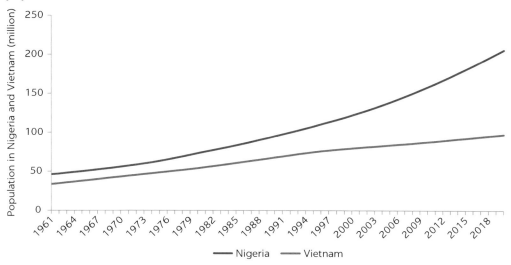

Source: World Bank Development Indicators, World Bank.

FIGURE 7.3

Cassava yields in Vietnam leapfrogged Nigeria's in 2001

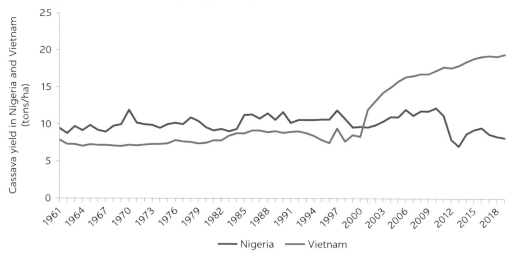

Source: FAOSTAT (Statistics Division, Food and Agriculture Organization of the United Nations).
Note: ha = hectare.

both yields and area under cultivation have provided important sources of growth in Vietnam (figure 7.5). Cassava acreage in Vietnam has been relatively stable since 2008, and yields have continued to drive production growth. Cassava acreage plateaued because of government policy prohibiting further expansion of cassava areas to avoid negative impacts on other crops and forest resources.

Because cassava is a highly perishable crop, processing is critical to maintain its value for food and nonfood uses. However, the cassava-processing subsectors in Nigeria and Vietnam could not be more different. Vietnam's processing subsector is predominantly for high-value nonfood products to meet export demand, whereas most cassava in Nigeria is processed into food products for the domestic market. Nearly 70 percent of processed cassava in Vietnam is converted to starch

FIGURE 7.4

Cassava yields have stagnated in Nigeria for decades, but acreage increased

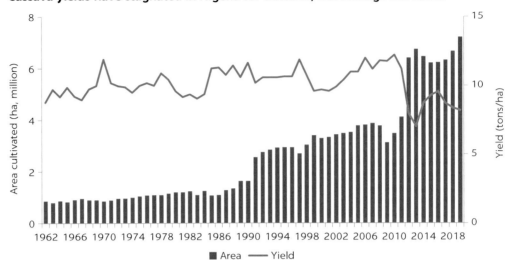

Source: FAOSTAT (Statistics Division, Food and Agriculture Organization of the United Nations).
Note: ha = hectare.

FIGURE 7.5

Since 2000, both yields and acreage in Vietnam have grown tremendously

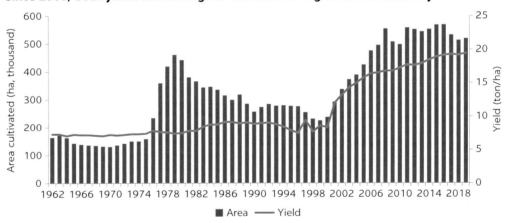

Source: FAOSTAT (Statistics Division, Food and Agriculture Organization of the United Nations).
Note: ha = hectare.

for exports, with China accounting for about 83 percent. In addition to starch, the cassava-processing industry in Vietnam generates products such as animal feeds (14 percent of processed cassava) and food products (5.6 percent of processed cassava). In contrast, about 83 percent of processed cassava in Nigeria is converted into garri—a low-value food product used to prepare traditional meals—and about 3 percent is converted to high quality cassava flour (HQCF). In 2015, the Nigerian government passed legislation that requires 10 percent of bread to be constituted of HQCF. Interviews with flour millers suggest that the industry is reluctant to use HQCF because of variable quality. Furthermore, the legislation has not been enforced, and the industry continues to make bread from wheat flour, most of which is imported by the major food agribusinesses under preferential tariff rate quotas. Nonfood cassava products account for about

7 percent of processed cassava in Nigeria, and the main products include dried cassava chips used for animal feed, ethanol production, paints, pharmaceuticals, and sweeteners.

SOURCES OF ON-FARM COMPETITIVENESS

Investments in R&D and provision of extension services have enabled cassava farmers in Vietnam to widely adopt high-yielding improved varieties. Since the early 2000s, the development and distribution of new varieties have continued to improve cassava yields in Vietnam (box 7.1). The country has invested heavily in R&D and plant protection. The investments have produced new and high-yielding cassava varieties, including the popular KM94 and KM419. These varieties are cultivated in almost 70 percent of the country's area under cassava production and produce about 29.4 ton/ha under good management practices. In addition, the investments have generated other improved varieties such as

---

Box 7.1

Policy highlights for cassava in Vietnam

Both countries have made significant policies to guide the development of the cassava subsector. The major policy highlights for Vietnam include the following:

- *Vietnam policy on sustainable cassava development.* A major policy milestone in the cassava subsector in Vietnam was the government's introduction in the early 2000s of the cassava research program, focused on distribution of high-starch-yielding varieties and extension advice. The program led to a rapid increase in yields and area under cultivation such that production growth increased by more than 10 percent annually through 2010. Demand for land to cultivate cassava grew rapidly. In some regions of the country, farmers cut down sugarcane and illegally deforested woodlands to grow cassava. The government issued a directive on sustainable cassava development in 2008, and in 2012 it directed that cassava area should be maintained at 450,000 hectares by 2020 and on land with a slope of less than 15 degrees. The directive was issued at a time when the cassava acreage reached almost 560,000 hectares. The area under cassava cultivation has remained stable since 2012.
- *Government policies in Vietnam emphasizing the needs of producers.* Because cassava can be grown in poor areas and by poor farmers, it is

viewed as an important crop to reduce income inequalities. The government's current tariff structure is mainly designed to protect farmers' interests—ahead of the interests of the processing industry. For example, in 2017 the Ministry of Finance rejected a request by the Vietnam Cassava Association to impose high export taxes on fresh cassava, which was meant to reduce direct exports by producers to China and increase supplies to the domestic processing industry. Nevertheless, there is government support for processing enterprises in the form of a tax exemption on land and subsidies for credit, research, and training.

- *Vietnam's policy mandating the use of fuel blended with ethanol (E5 biofuel) to create a market for cassava-based ethanol.* The regulation aims to make E5 biofuel cheaper than gasoline; however, the policy has so far been unsuccessful because the price differential is not high enough to create spontaneous consumer demand. In addition, there are no measures to protect the domestic industry against cheaper ethanol coming from international and regional markets. Overall, biofuel policies have had less impact on domestic cassava demand than was expected, and there is no evidence that cassava exports have reduced because of demand for biofuels.

KM98-7, SM937-26, KM140, KM98-5, and KM98. Although these varieties have relatively lower yields compared to KM94, their growing cycles are shorter and more adaptable to changing climatic conditions that often result in shortened growing seasons. Overall, improved varieties account for more than 90 percent of the cassava-cultivated area in Vietnam (CGIAR 2017). The high adoption of improved varieties is attributed to accessibility of the planting material and awareness by the farmers. For example, the Vietnam Cassava Programme distributed 10 million sticks of new varieties to various provinces between 2005 and 2018, which resulted in average yields increasing from 13 ton/ha in 2005 to 18 ton/ha in 2018.

By contrast, access to improved cassava varieties is poor in Nigeria, and adoption rates are much lower than in Vietnam. About 95 percent of farmers cultivating cassava in Nigeria are smallholder farmers growing cassava on less than 2 ha. Similarly, in Vietnam more than 85 percent of cassava is produced by small-scale farmers cultivating less than 1 ha of land. The National Root Crop Research Institute and the International Institute of Tropical Agriculture have made considerable efforts to improve cassava productivity in Nigeria. Those efforts led to the development of several improved cassava varieties, with the most recent being UMUCASS 42 and UMUCASS 43. The potential yield from these varieties is 49–53 ton/ha under research conditions, but actual yields on farmers' fields have been much lower because of improper crop management practices. Both varieties perform well in different production regions of Nigeria and contain moderate levels of pro-vitamin A with high dry matter and good disease resistance.

Despite the advancement in R&D of improved cassava varieties in Nigeria, actual yield growth is constrained by weak access to improved planting materials, low adoption, and weak extension systems. The adoption of improved cassava varieties showed a large spatial heterogeneity across the country. For example, adoption rates are estimated to be as high as 79 percent in the South West region but only about 31 percent in the South East (Wossen et al. 2017). Adoption rates are constrained by lack of awareness and weak access to improved cassava varieties. Only about 13.0 percent of farmers in 2017 obtained planting materials through research institute and extension sources, and 4.7 percent of farmers obtained them from government sources (Wossen et al. 2017). There is need to rethink the formal seed system and extension service in Nigeria because access to high-yielding improved varieties and extension services is imperative to increase productivity in smallholder systems.

A major constraint faced by farmers in Nigeria is availability of fertilizers, which leads to low fertilizer application rates and low cassava yields compared to Vietnam. Although cassava is quite resilient to varying agroclimatic conditions, the crop responds well to proper crop management practices, including fertilization. But farmers in Nigeria do not apply fertilizers directly to cassava; instead the fertilizers are applied to maize that is intercropped with cassava. About 86 percent of farmers in Vietnam apply fertilizers on cassava fields compared to 36 percent in Nigeria (Le et al. 2019; Wossen et al. 2017). Furthermore, in Vietnam, cassava is usually intercropped with leguminous crops that have the natural ability to fixate nitrogen from the air, thereby improving soil fertility. Fertilizer application rates vary greatly in Vietnam, with the highest rates in the North (about 664.17 kg/ha) and the lowest in the Central Highlands (352.7 kg/ha). In contrast, the Federal Ministry of Agriculture and Rural Development in Nigeria estimates average fertilizer application rates at 13 kg/ha, a fraction of both the lowest amounts applied in Vietnam and the 200 kg/ha recommended by the United Nations Food and Agriculture Organization (Le et al. 2019; Liverpool-Tasie et al. 2010). Evidence suggests that the primary constraint to fertilizer use in Nigeria is availability rather than affordability or farmers' lack of knowledge about the importance of using fertilizers (Banful and Olayide 2010; Liverpool-Tasie 2010). Demand far outstrips supply each year, and government fertilizer programs are fraught with several challenges that lead to late and insufficient delivery.

Cassava mosaic disease (CMD) continues to dampen yields in Nigeria, and various control measures have largely been rendered ineffective by farmers' use of contaminated planting materials. CMD is a viral[2] disease rampant in Africa and the Indian subcontinent. Despite early attempts to restrict spread through quarantine controls, the viruses behind the disease have spread rapidly with the intensification of cassava production in Africa. The practice of farmers using their own cuttings for planting or sharing cuttings with neighbors makes it hard to control the spread of the disease because farmers cannot determine if the cuttings are contaminated. The reported yield loss from CMD varies widely from complete crop loss to insignificant impacts, in part depending on the cassava varieties. As such, cassava varieties are often classified on the basis of tolerance to CMD into the following categories: susceptible, tolerant (becomes infected but with few symptoms), or resistant (difficult to infect but may be susceptible to substantial yield loss if infection occurs). Cassava plants grown from infected cuttings sustain a greater yield loss whereas plants infected at a late stage of crop growth are virtually unaffected. Therefore, the most effective control measure is a system that supplies farmers with disease-free cuttings coupled with removal of diseased plants from fields. CMD is not present in Vietnam;[3] however, cassava witches' broom disease has been a growing problem there since 2017. Like CMD, cassava witches' broom disease is propagated by diseased planting material. Unfortunately, farmers in both countries continue to use their own cuttings for several years in succeeding crops.

TRADE COMPETITIVENESS

Vietnam is the world's third-largest exporter of cassava, with export revenues exceeding US$1.3 billion in 2017.[4] In contrast, Nigeria currently plays a very minor role in cassava international trade despite being the world's largest producer. Exports of cassava products from Vietnam have grown rapidly since 2000 in response to the growing global demand and rising world market prices for starch (figure 7.6). As noted earlier, about 85.6 percent of domestic cassava production in Vietnam is exported. The main cassava products exported are starch and dried cassava. Starch exports have been growing rapidly in the country and accounted for about 72 percent of total export value of cassava products in 2017, a significant increase from zero in 2008 (figure 7.7). Dried cassava exports, however, have declined significantly from being the only product exported in 2008 to accounting for only 27.5 percent of export value in 2017. Those dynamics represent a clear transition of Vietnam's cassava processing industry from low-value product (dried cassava) to high-value cassava starch. Furthermore, Vietnam started importing dried cassava around 2014, and the imports are processed into high-value starch for exports. The value of dried cassava imports increased from about US$4 million in 2016 to US$335 million

FIGURE 7.6

Vietnam earned US$1.3 billion from cassava exports in 2017, whereas Nigeria played a minor role in the cassava trade

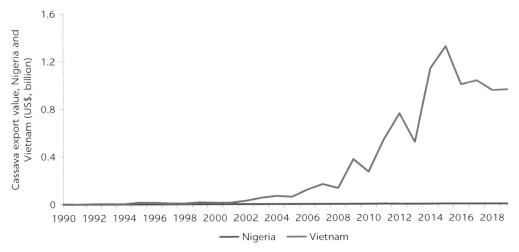

Source: FAOSTAT (Statistics Division, Food and Agriculture Organization of the United Nations).

FIGURE 7.7

Since 2008, Vietnam's exports have rapidly transitioned from low-value dried cassava to high-value starch

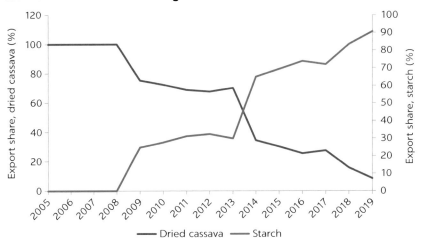

Source: FAOSTAT (Statistics Division, Food and Agriculture Organization of the United Nations).

in 2017, enabling Vietnam to increase the value of its exports from US$472 million in 2016 to US$1.36 billion in 2017. Data suggest that the quality of starch from Vietnam is also improving. For example, the Free on Board price of Vietnamese cassava starch increased from US$270/ton in 2017 to US$395/ton in 2018. That price was still relatively low compared to China and Thailand, mainly because of quality differences.[5]

Although Nigeria is still a very minor player in the cassava export market, its exports of cassava products have been growing in recent years, and there is scope to exploit the emerging opportunities. Exports of cassava products from Nigeria doubled between 2014 and 2017 to reach about US$1.26 million, but the remarkable growth started from a very low base. During that short time period, Nigeria increasingly transitioned from exporting low-value dried cassava to exporting high-value starch and cassava flour (table 7.2). Israel and China are the major

TABLE 7.2 **Nigeria is transitioning from exporting low-value dried cassava to high-value starch and cassava flour**

YEAR	EXPORT VALUE (US$, MILLION)	SHARE OF EXPORT VALUE (%)		
		DRIED CASSAVA	FLOUR	STARCH
2014	0.62	39.4	37.3	23.3
2015	0.75	32.7	40.0	27.3
2016	1.02	15.5	41.8	42.6
2017	1.26	6.6	48.1	45.4

Source: FAOSTAT (Statistics Division, Food and Agriculture Organization of the United Nations).

FIGURE 7.8

Main export markets for processed cassava products from Nigeria

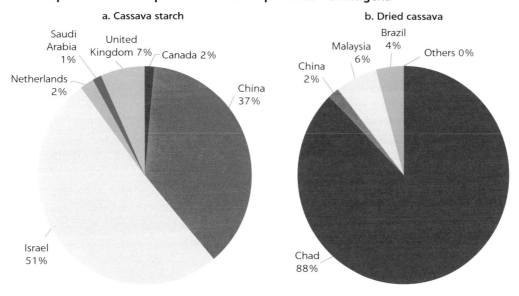

Source: United Nations Comtrade Database.

export destinations of cassava starch from Nigeria, respectively accounting for 51 percent and 37 percent of starch exports (figure 7.8, panel a). The main export destination for dried cassava from Nigeria is Chad, accounting for about 88 percent of exports (figure 7.8, panel b). Nigeria also exports dried cassava and starch to several other African countries, including Côte d'Ivoire, Niger, and Togo. Other export destinations for these cassava products from Nigeria are Belgium, Brazil, Canada, Malaysia, the Netherlands, Norway, Saudi Arabia, the United Kingdom, and the United States. Trade data suggest there is potential to increase cassava exports from Nigeria.

A strategy for export promotion would require investments in R&D to develop varieties that have high starch content and improvements in the technology of production. Key investments include effective systems to transfer clean planting materials to farmers, removing old plants contaminated with CMD and treating soils, and effective extension to ensure that farmers use correct agronomic practices and proper fertilization. In addition, private sector investments into cassava processing can be encouraged to improve coordination between organized farmers and the cassava processing industry. Interviews with small and medium enterprises in starch processing suggest that many are running below capacity and have no vertical coordination arrangements with farmers but instead rely on spot market arrangements. Industrial demand for cassava includes production of starches, paints, pharmaceuticals, sweeteners, and feed for livestock and aquaculture. However, the overall growth potential of the animal feed segment in Nigeria is not clear because aquaculture and poultry segments require highly nutritious feeds, and field surveys conducted in the course of the value chain study suggest that the problem of variable quality of cassava-based feed is the main reason the industry prefers imported feed based on noncassava products such as maize. In Vietnam, the 14 percent of cassava used for animal feed goes mostly to pig feeding, which is not an important livestock subsector in Nigeria.

CHARACTERIZATION OF CASSAVA VALUE CHAINS

The cassava value chains in Nigeria and Vietnam are organized quite differently. The main actors in cassava value chains in Nigeria are producers, processors, industrial processors, wholesale traders/transporters, retailers, and consumers. The main actors in Vietnam are producers, collectors/assemblers, processors/exporters, and consumers. In Nigeria, transactions between farmers and the next actors (intermediaries or processors) are predominantly spot and only a few processing companies have started working with farmers through vertical coordination arrangements. In contrast, in Vietnam, the relationship between farmers and village assemblers is mostly vertical coordination with some form of contracting, although spot markets also exist. Farmers living in remote areas in Vietnam with little or no access to the nearest market or city sell their produce to village assemblers, whereas farmers living close to a city sell to commune assemblers or to factory/processors, depending on volumes and prices. Because cassava is highly perishable, the distance to roads and markets plays a large part in determining a farmer's bargaining power. Furthermore, because of the high demand for fresh cassava in Vietnam, most village and commune assemblers pay in advance to secure the produce. Village assemblers procure cassava roots or dry chips from farmers and sell them to commune assemblers.

In Nigeria, farmers are typically involved in the initial processing of cassava because of the high perishability of fresh tubers and the lack of vertical coordination with organized off-takers that have advanced processing technology. There are three main value chains through which processed cassava products in Nigeria reach end users: (1) small-scale farmers that produce for direct consumption and processing into various food products, (2) medium-scale farmers that produce primarily for processing into food products, and (3) large-scale farmers that produce for industrial processing into ethanol, starch, and glucose. More than 80 percent of the fresh tubers pass through the traditional channel, with processing occurring at the village level using simple tools and techniques to convert fresh cassava into a wide array of products. This channel is wholly supplied by smallholder farmers that produce more than 90 percent of cassava in Nigeria. The industrial processing channel handles just about 10 percent of processed cassava and employs advanced processing technology.

Industrial processing capacity in Nigeria needs to expand significantly from that current share of 10 percent. The additional capacity should move closer to the production areas to stimulate transformation in the cassava subsector. The conversion ratio of cassava processing into starch is relatively low (17 percent) in Nigeria, compared with an industry average of 25 percent in Vietnam. The low starch conversion ratio suggests enormous scope in R&D to increase the starch content of cassava varieties cultivated in Nigeria. Unlike in Nigeria, demand for fresh cassava tubers is very high in Vietnam such that there is little incentive for farmers and traders to engage in processing. The scale of processing in Vietnam varies greatly and includes small-scale processors that mainly produce up to 10 metric tons of wet starch per day, medium–scale processors that produce 10–15 metric tons of starch per day, and large-scale processors generating more than 50 metric tons of starch per day. Access to electricity is fairly consistent in Vietnam's processing segment, whereas processors in Nigeria rely on power generators because of the unreliable supply of electricity.

Spot market arrangements characterize transaction relationships between cassava producers and traders in Nigeria. In contrast, most traders in Vietnam pay farmers in advance to secure supply. Nearly 90 percent of the total fresh cassava produced in Vietnam is purchased by three main types of buyers: village assemblers, commune assemblers, and large processors (factories). Village assemblers procure cassava roots or dry chips from farmers and sell them to commune assemblers. The procurement of cassava roots and dry chips is based on verbal contract and prevailing market price.

COSTS AND MARGINS OF VALUE CHAIN ACTORS

This section compares costs and margins for the actors of cassava value chains in Nigeria and Vietnam. Figure 7.9 and figure 7.10 provide a summary of the costs, selling prices, and margins for each actor along the value chains. Costs at the producer (farm) level for both countries include costs incurred by farmers to purchase various inputs, including planting materials (seedlings and cassava stem cuttings), fertilizers, chemicals, and labor. Profit margins correspond to the difference between the production costs and the sales price at each level of the value chain, which means any other costs not identified are subsumed under

FIGURE 7.9

Cassava yields have nearly tripled in Vietnam since 2000, but in Nigeria yields became more volatile and declined

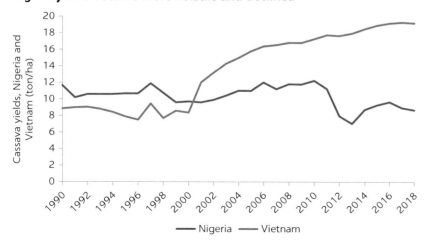

Source: FAOSTAT (Statistics Division, Food and Agriculture Organization of the United Nations).
Note: ha = hectare.

FIGURE 7.10

Cassava prices doubled in Vietnam since 2010, but prices in Nigeria remained flat

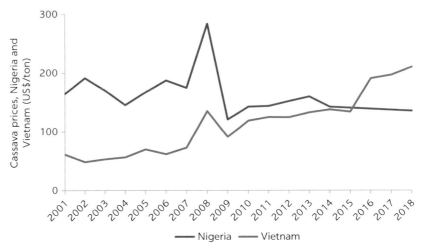

Source: FAOSTAT (Statistics Division, Food and Agriculture Organization of the United Nations).

the listed costs. Data for Nigeria were collected from farmers in the states of Ogun, Delta, and Kogi. These states were selected to represent the major cassava-growing regions in the country, which are the South West, South East, and North Central. Average cassava yields in these states are about 8.8 ton/ha. Data for Vietnam were collected in Yen Bai province of Northern Midlands and Mountains region. Because of proximity to China, most of the cassava produced in the region is processed into starch for exports to China—the major export market for starch from Vietnam. Average cassava yields in the Vietnam study area are estimated at 19.4 ton/ha. The yields are equivalent to national average yields in Vietnam. A major challenge in comparing costs and margins between Nigeria and Vietnam is that the countries process cassava into different products and sell in different markets, as noted earlier. To address this challenge, the price and cost comparisons are based on roots equivalent, which means that prices for all products correspond to the quantity of the product obtained from one kg of cassava root to enable comparison across diverse products.

Although the cost of cassava production is nearly three times higher in Vietnam, farmers' revenues are four times higher than in Nigeria because of higher yields and better farm gate prices. Cassava farm gate prices in Vietnam doubled in the last 10 years whereas prices in Nigeria remained flat. The total variable cost of cassava production per ha in Vietnam was US$696 compared to US$235 in Nigeria, which translates to US$0.036/kg in Vietnam and US$0.014/kg in Nigeria because of higher yields in Vietnam. The relatively low cost of production in Nigeria is mainly attributed to low input use, especially low use of fertilizers and agrochemicals.[6] However, the combination of higher yields and better farm gate prices makes cassava farming more profitable in Vietnam—with profit margins of US$683/ha compared to US$147/ha in Nigeria. Labor is the major cost component in Nigeria with a cost share of nearly 60 percent. But, in Vietnam, the major cost component is fertilizers with a cost share of about 51 percent. The relatively higher cost share for labor in Nigeria is not surprising because production is mainly through smallholder farmers that lack access to mechanization services. Tractor services are used in about 10 percent of cultivated area, typically in medium- and large-scale farms that produce for industrial processing. The average labor requirement in one cassava season in Nigeria is estimated at about 260 person-days/ha, compared to 66 person-days/ha in Vietnam. On aggregate, production costs account for a relatively larger share of farm gate prices in Nigeria (62 percent) than in Vietnam (51 percent), which means that profit margins for farmers in Vietnam comprise a relatively higher share of farm gate prices than for farmers in Nigeria.

Farmers participating in starch value chains in Vietnam earn higher profit margins than those participating in the starch value chain in Nigeria. The higher profit margins can be traced to higher yields, better farm gate prices, and a higher starch conversion ratio of the cassava varieties grown in Vietnam. The difference in the cassava starch conversion ratio (25 percent in Vietnam compared to 17 percent in Nigeria) is mainly attributed to differences in the starch content of cassava varieties cultivated in the two countries and the conversion efficiency in the processing segment. As noted earlier, the estimated profit margin for producers (farmers) in starch value chains is US$0.035/kg in Vietnam and US$0.019/kg in Nigeria (figure 7.11). The profit margins for farmers in Vietnam account for 72 percent of total margins in the starch value chain, which is higher than the 50 percent share of margins earned by farmers in Nigeria.

Although farmers in both countries earn the highest margins per kg relative to other actors, total margins are by far the lowest at the producer level because farmers cultivate small plots with low volumes of production. This suggests that profits for farmers in Nigeria can be increased through raising yields and forming producer organizations that can deliver the agglomeration economies of scale. In both countries, the starch processors capture the highest total margins. The estimated margins for a large-scale starch processor in Vietnam with installed capacity of 40 million tons annually are about US$4.3 million. A large-scale starch processor in Nigeria with installed capacity of 32 million tons annually would earn profit margins of about US$2.8 million. The margins of intermediate actors (traders and assemblers) depend on the aggregate number

FIGURE 7.11

Buildup of costs, prices, and margins for starch value chain, Nigeria and Vietnam

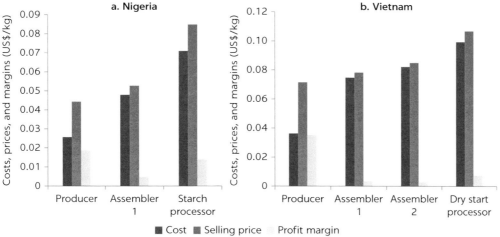

Sources: Dankers and Ott 2021; JMSF Agribusiness 2020.

FIGURE 7.12

Buildup of costs, prices, and margins for garri value chain, Nigeria

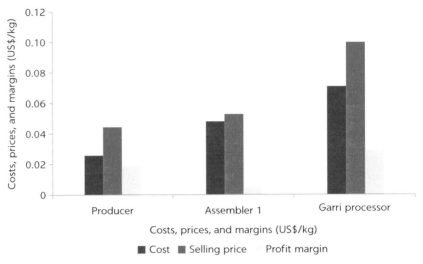

Sources: Dankers and Ott 2021; JMSF 2020.

FIGURE 7.13

Farmers in Nigeria's garri value chain earn a relatively smaller share of value chain margins

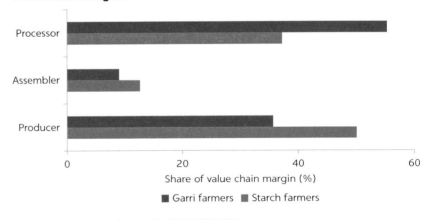

Sources: Dankers and Ott 2021; JMSF 2020.

of actors in the value chain (length of the value chain) and the volumes traded. These intermediaries tend to earn higher margins when they participate in shorter value chains or handle higher volumes.

Farmers in Nigeria's garri value chain earn a relatively smaller share of total profit margins compared to those in the starch value chain, but the relatively small share is offset by higher total margins in the garri value chain. A comparison of the total profit margins in cassava value chains in Nigeria shows that the garri value chain has higher margins (US$0.053/kg) compared to US$0.038/kg in the starch value chains (see figure 7.12 for garri value chain costs, prices, and margins in Nigeria). The share of value chain profit margins accruing to the farmers (producers) in garri value chains is 36 percent (figure 7.13), which is lower than the 50 percent received by farmers in the starch value chain. However, the starch and garri value chains in Nigeria are not differentiated at the producer level, so farmers earn the same margins regardless of the value chain. The lack of differentiation points to the underdeveloped nature of the value chain for industrial starch. The same varieties for food products are processed into starch because there are no specialized varieties with high starch content. Investment costs for garri processing are estimated to be relatively lower than starch processing.

CONCLUSIONS

Nigeria has been the world's largest producer of cassava for the past one and half decades. However, cassava has remained a staple crop used mostly to prepare traditional dishes and has not transitioned to an industrial crop. This is despite government efforts to develop the cassava subsector—for example, the Presidential Cassava Initiative (2001–07) and more recently the Presidential Agricultural Transformation Agenda (2011–15). The slow progress in transitioning cassava to an industrial crop is a missed opportunity to generate jobs as the value chain ranks high in terms of potential for jobs creation. In contrast, the transition of cassava as an industrial crop in Vietnam happened around the year 2000, and the crop is mostly processed into starch for exports to China and other countries. The transition was driven by industrial demand from cassava starch factories that were processing starch for exports. The supply response was remarkable: production increased rapidly by more than 10 percent annually between 2000 and 2018, driven by both rising yields and increased area under cultivation.

The government of Vietnam created the enabling environment to facilitate the transformation of the cassava subsector. In particular, the government invested in strategic R&D, plant protection, and provision of extension services so that cassava farmers could adopt high-yielding, improved varieties. The results were staggering. Cassava yields in Vietnam surpassed those in Nigeria for the first time in 2001, and, by 2018, yields in Vietnam were more than twice the yields in Nigeria. In contrast, cassava yields in Nigeria have barely changed in the past two decades because of farmers' poor access to improved varieties, low adoption, weak extension systems, and crop diseases—especially the CMD. The drought of 2013 depressed cassava yields in Nigeria (and other West African countries) primarily because farmers were not using drought-resistant varieties. Clearly, there is an imperative to address the delivery systems for planting materials, inputs, extension, and plant protection services in Nigeria because R&D advances have not translated to yield growth in farmers' fields.

Nigeria may pursue a two-pronged strategy for transformation of the cassava value chains to (1) increase the competitiveness of the industrial starch value chain and (2) modernize the food products value chains to deliver improved garri and HQCF. Both aspects of the two-pronged strategy could focus on meeting the huge domestic demand for industrial cassava products and food items, before pursuing export markets. Recent data suggest that exports of cassava products from Nigeria have been growing rapidly, and there is scope to exploit the emerging opportunities. For example, exports of cassava products from Nigeria doubled between 2014 and 2017 to reach about US$1.26 million, although the remarkable growth started from a very low base. During that short time period, Nigeria increasingly transitioned from exporting low-value dried cassava to exporting high-value starch and cassava flour.

A strategy for developing the industrial starch value chain would require coordinated investments between researchers, farmers, and the processing sector—so that farmers can access varieties that yield high starch content and produce for the specific needs of starch processors under vertical coordination schemes. The conversion ratio of cassava processing into starch is relatively low in Nigeria (17 percent), compared with an industry average of 25 percent in Vietnam. This low ratio suggests enormous scope in R&D to increase the starch content of cassava varieties cultivated in Nigeria. The research work will need to be complemented with effective systems to transfer clean planting materials to the farmers while removing old plants contaminated with CMD, treating soils, providing effective extension to ensure farmers apply the correct agronomic practices and proper fertilization, providing business incentives for private sector investments into cassava processing, linking organized farmers with the cassava processing industry, and effectively promoting exports. Interviews with many small and medium enterprises in starch processing suggest that many are running below capacity and have weak vertical coordination with farmers. The industry needs to transition from spot transactions and develop dedicated supply chains through vertical coordination arrangements with growth-oriented farmer organizations. To stimulate transformation in the cassava subsector, the capacity would need not only to expand significantly but also to move closer to production areas.

A strategy for modernizing the value chains for cassava food products should aim to deliver quality garri and HQCF to support healthy diets and meet the needs of higher-income consumers and the milling and baking industry. Although demand for garri remains high among low-income consumers, it is not growing among middle- and higher-income consumers, partly because of a lack of product differentiation. In particular, urban consumers demand differentiated and branded garri products, with superior attributes in terms of taste, color, and texture. Expanding the market for high-quality differentiated garri products would require coordinated investments between the milling sector and upstream segments of the value chains—farmers and researchers—to produce cassava that is healthy (perhaps low in starch) and with better taste and color. Such coordinated investments would also improve the quality of HQCF, which is critical to enforcement of the 2015 legislation that requires bread to be constituted from both cassava and wheat.

NOTES

1. According to projects from the International Fund for Agricultural Development's Climate Adaptation in Rural Development (CARD) Assessment Tool, cassava yields in Nigeria will decrease as a result of climate change by about 3.5 percent by 2030—albeit less than rice yields, which are projected to decrease by 5.7 percent (https://www.ifad.org/en/web /knowledge/-/publication/climate-adaptation-in-rural-development-card-assessment -tool).
2. The disease is caused by one, or a mixture, of about 10 species of cassava mosaic geminiviruses.
3. See the Centre for Agriculture and Bioscience International (CABI) datasheet on CMD (https://www.cabi.org/isc/datasheet/2747), part of CABI's Invasive Species Compendium.
4. Data from 2017 are used because it is the latest year for which data are available.
5. The quality demands are higher in starch for consumption relative to industrial use. The main quality attributes are white color, fine texture, neutral taste, and absence of odor.
6. An estimated 86 percent of farmers in Vietnam apply fertilizers to cassava compared with 36 percent in Nigeria (Le et al. 2019; Wossen et al. 2017).

REFERENCES

Banful, A. B., and O. Olayide. 2010. "Perspectives of Selected Stakeholder Groups in Nigeria on the Federal and State Fertilizer Subsidy Programs." Nigeria Strategy Support Program (NSSP) Report 8, International Food Policy Research Institute, Washington, DC.

Bentley, J., A. Olanrewaju, T. Madu, O. Olaosebikan, T. Abdoulaye, T. Wossen, V. Manyong, P. Kulakow, B. Ayedun, M. Ojide, G. Girma, I. Rabbi, G. Asumugha, and M. Tokula. 2017. "Cassava Farmers' Preferences for Varieties and Seed Dissemination System in Nigeria: Gender and Regional Perspectives." IITA Monograph, International Institute of Tropical Agriculture. Ibadan, Nigeria.

CGIAR (Consortium of International Agricultural Research Centers). 2017. "Assessment Reveals that Most Cassava Grown in Vietnam Has a CIAT Pedigree." CGIAR Research Program on Roots, Tubers, and Bananas. http://www.rtb.cgiar.org/2016-annual-report/assessment-reveals-that-most-cassava-grown-in-vietnam-has-a-ciat-pedigree/.

Dankers, C., and A. Ott. 2021. "Nigeria–Viet Nam Value Chain Benchmarking Cassava Synthesis Report." Background paper for this book. Unpublished.

Forsythe, L., H. Posthumus, and A. Martin. 2016. "A Crop of One's Own? Women's Experiences of Cassava Commercialization in Nigeria and Malawi." *Journal of Gender, Agriculture and Food Security* 1 (2): 110–28.

JMSF Agribusiness. 2020. "Sources of Growth in Agribusiness Small and Medium-Sized Enterprises (SMEs): Cassava Report." Unpublished manuscript.

Le, D. P., R. A. Labarta, S. de Haan, M. Maredia, L. A. Becerra, L.T. Nhu, T. Ovalle, V. A. Nguyen, N. T. Pham, H. H. Nguyen, H. T. Nguyen, K. Q. Le, and H. H. Le. 2019. "Characterization of Cassava Production Systems in Vietnam." CIAT Publication No. 480, International Center for Tropical Agriculture, Hanoi. https://hdl.handle.net/10568/103417.

Liverpool-Tasie, S., B. Olaniyan, S. Salau, and J. Sackey. 2010. "A Review of Fertilizer Policy Issues in Nigeria." Nigeria Strategy Support Program (NSSP) Working Paper 19, International Food Policy Research Institute, Washington, DC.

Wossen, T., G. Tessema., T. Abdoulaye, I. Rabbi, A. Olanrewaju, J. Bentley, A. Alene, S. Feleke, P. Kulakow, G. Asumugha, A. Abass, M. Tokula, and V. Manyong. 2017. "The Cassava Monitoring Survey in Nigeria: Final Report." Ibadan, Nigeria: International Institute of Tropical Agriculture.

8 Competitiveness and Policy Priorities in the Poultry Value Chain

The gross production value of chicken was comparable between Nigeria and Vietnam in 2007. But, in the past 10 years, the gross production value increased rapidly in Vietnam and fell sharply in Nigeria, such that it is now at least nine times higher in Vietnam. Nigeria's chicken population has been declining since 2010 (figure 8.1), dragging down the gross production value, which recorded average annual growth of about –2.4 percent. The negative growth is a significant drop from the 1.9 percent annual growth achieved between 2000 and 2008 (figure 8.2). The drop was caused by an escalated influx of poultry meat from Benin between 2008 and 2011 and the 2006–08 outbreak of the High Pathogenic Avian Influenza (HPAI) epidemic, which was followed by another outbreak in 2014. Data suggest that the poultry sector in Nigeria has not been able to recover from the impacts of the HPAI shock. Currently, production value of chicken meat in Nigeria is about US$315.5 million, nearly a 10th of the US$2.9 billion value of production in Vietnam. The chicken population in Vietnam is estimated at 317 million birds producing meat output of 839.6 thousand tons annually and contributing 6.7 percent to agricultural gross domestic product (GDP). In comparison, Nigeria has about 139 million birds[1] producing about 192.7 thousand tons of chicken meat (figure 8.3). Although poultry production is one of the most commercialized subsectors in Nigerian agriculture, the share of chicken meat in agricultural GDP is relatively low at only 1 percent.

In the early 1990s, chicken meat productivity in Vietnam was lower than in Nigeria, but it is now 50 percent higher thanks to two decades of steady growth (figure 8.4). The lack of growth in Nigeria reflects weak ability to recover from shocks, slow technical change at the farm level, and weak access to extension and advisory services. For example, less than 15 percent of poultry farmers accessed extension services in 2015 in Oyo state (Oladeji 2011). In contrast, poultry farmers in Vietnam receive regular extension support from central and local government, including annual transfer of new technologies such as new breeds, biosafety protocols, and so on. Without growth in productivity and as a supply response to the 2002 government policy of restricting importation of poultry products, the population of birds (flock size) in Nigeria increased by about 5.4 percent annually between 2000 and 2010 compared to 3.9 percent in Vietnam

FIGURE 8.1

Since 2010, Nigeria's chicken population has dropped, but Vietnam's has continued to increase

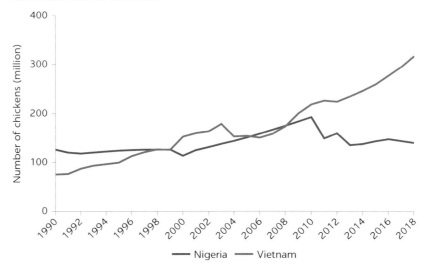

Source: FAOSTAT (Statistics Division, Food and Agriculture Organization of the United Nations).

FIGURE 8.2

Since 2008, chicken meat production value dropped rapidly in Nigeria but increased steadily in Vietnam

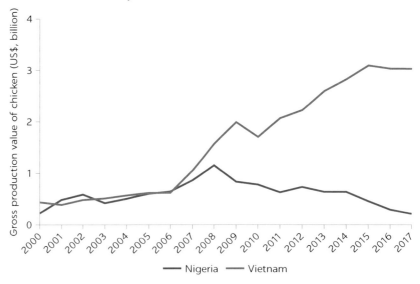

Source: FAOSTAT (Statistics Division, Food and Agriculture Organization of the United Nations).

(see figure 8.1). But the growth era was short-lived; the flock size has been on a declining trend, and the current flock size is comparable to 2000 levels. The declining trend is related to several factors, including weak enforcement of the 2002 import ban, heightened smuggling of imported chicken through the Benin border, and the 2014 HPAI outbreak. Part of the government's response to the epidemic involved culling about 1.4 million birds within the first 6 months of the epidemic (January to June 2015) (Sahel Capital 2015).

FIGURE 8.3

Chicken meat production growth accelerated in Vietnam after leapfrogging Nigeria in 1996

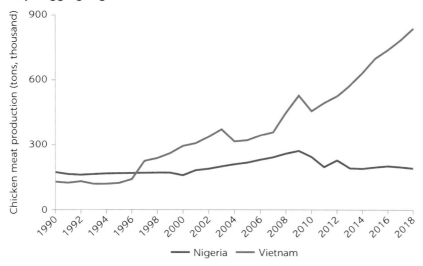

Source: FAOSTAT (Statistics Division, Food and Agriculture Organization of the United Nations).

FIGURE 8.4

Chicken meat productivity in Nigeria is about 57 percent lower than in Vietnam

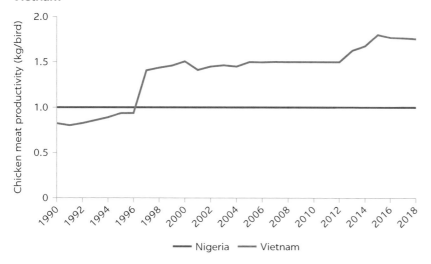

Source: FAOSTAT (Statistics Division, Food and Agriculture Organization of the United Nations).

TECHNOLOGY OF PRODUCTION

In both countries, most chickens are raised in people's backyards and in poultry farms of less than 1,000 birds. Indigenous breeds account for 80 percent of birds in Nigeria and 70 percent in Vietnam. The scale of production in Nigeria is very similar to Vietnam. About 83 percent of chicken meat production in Nigeria occurs in small-scale farms with flock sizes ranging between 100 and 600 birds; in Vietnam about 86 percent of chicken farms have fewer than 600 birds.

Large-scale chicken farms with flock size of more than 1,000 birds make up about 4 percent of chicken meat production in both countries. Commercial poultry farming in Nigeria is concentrated in the South West region—close to Lagos with its large market of nearly 17.5 million people. There are also significant poultry production operations in the northern parts of the country, near the city of Kano, the second-largest market in the country. The systems of production can be classified as free range/backyard (extensive), semicommercial (semi-intensive), and commercial (intensive), depending on the size of investments and technology of production in breeding, feeding, and disease control (table 8.1). About 44.4 percent of chickens in Nigeria are raised in extensive systems by

TABLE 8.1 **Technology of poultry production in Nigeria and Vietnam**

PRODUCTION SYSTEM	NIGERIA	VIETNAM
Extensive (backyard/ free-range)	• Mixed breed flocks with birds roaming freely, mainly in rural areas • Low capital investment and operational costs (labor, feed, etc.) • Biosecurity measures are poor or nonexistent in many instances • Most common in northern region • Accounts for about 44.4 percent of chickens	• Practiced by about 92 percent of poultry farmers • Small scale with low capital investment. Average of 50–60 birds with high mortality rate (45–50 percent) • Different animal species raised together in residential areas • Minimal biosecurity
Semi-intensive	• Combines traditional practices in the extensive system with improved technology • Accounts for about 33.3 percent of chickens • Flocks size is 50–2,000 birds, including both improved and local breeds • Most common in the southern regions and characterized by wooden/metal/brick houses with deep litter farming system • Mostly used by outgrowers and contract farmers • Biosecurity measures may range from low to midlevel • Capital investment lower than intensive system but operation costs usually higher	• Combines traditional practices with improved technology, improved breeds, and quality feed • Practiced by about 6 percent of poultry farmers • Flock size is 150–2,000 birds and includes mixed breed flocks • Farms typically integrate meat production with breeding and hatching. • Mostly used by outgrowers • Poultry houses are small and simple • Biosecurity is medium • Capital investment higher than extensive system
Intensive	• Characterized by full automation with exact temperature control, high biosecurity level, with minimal labor costs • About 22.3 percent of chickens are raised in the system, consisting of 55 percent layers and 45 percent broilers, mostly exotic breeds • Unit sizes are large depending on the technology used and can reach 20,000 birds per pen house (either caged or open floor) • Investment costs are high and pen houses are 100 percent imported with no local manufacturing. • Efficient feeding and watering systems, low wastage, high feed conversion ratio, and optimum live weight achieved within 42 to 45 days	• Practiced by about 2 percent of poultry farmers • 37 percent broilers, 30 percent layers, 23 percent ducks and geese, 10 percent breeding stock • Facilities are well equipped and relatively mechanized, including both semiautomatic and automatic equipment with high biosecurity measures • Mainly improved or exotic breeds supplied by foreign companies or national breeding centers • Flock size ranges from 2,000 to 100,000 • High capital investment and short production period (up to 4–5 batches of birds per year)

Source: World Bank staff compilation.

6.6 million households. The semi-intensive system accounts for 33.3 percent of chickens raised by 1.3 million households, and the remaining 22.3 percent are raised in intensive systems by 17 thousand commercial farms (ASL 2050 2018). The most prominent breeders (including Ajanla farms, Chi farms, Olam farms, Shonga farms, and Tuns farms) have licenses to import day-old chicks (DOCs). Breeder farms are mainly concentrated in the South West, with Olam and Shonga in the North West. Vietnam has 219 registered breeding farms (mainly concentrated in Red River Delta and Southeast regions). As in Nigeria, the extensive system predominates in Vietnam and accounts for about 92 percent of poultry farmers, followed by the semi-intensive system (6 percent of farmers) and the intensive system (2 percent of farmers) (Nguyen and Long 2008).

TRADE COMPETITIVENESS

Formal imports of poultry meat have been remarkably low in Nigeria, primarily because of a government policy restricting imports since 2002. The policy restricts traders from accessing foreign exchange permits issued by the Central Bank to import chicken, eggs, turkey, and processed poultry meat products. Traders could still import with own financing but at a higher exchange rate. DOCs are excluded from the import restrictions. Also excluded from the policy are poultry equipment, vaccines, drugs, antibiotics, vitamins, and additives; however, these equipment and inputs are subject to import tariffs ranging from 5 to 10 percent, value added tax ranging from 7.5 to 15.0 percent, and an additional levy.[2] Enforcement of the restrictions on importation of chicken has been a challenge, and at times imports of poultry meat have increased rapidly through both official channels and smuggling. For example, imports soared during 2008–10 because the HVAI epidemic of 2006–08 reduced local supply, creating room for an influx of imports. The imports arrived in Nigeria from Benin (figure 8.5) but were produced in a third country. It is estimated that about 3 million tons of

FIGURE 8.5

Imports of chicken meat in Nigeria closely track exports from Benin

Source: FAOSTAT (Statistics Division, Food and Agriculture Organization of the United Nations).

poultry products were imported into Benin between 2009 and 2011 and then reexported to Nigeria (Sahel Capital 2015). A comparison of data shows that imports of chicken meat in Nigeria closely track exports from Benin.

The price incentives to import chicken through Benin are remarkably high, enough to pay for rents associated with the smuggling business. Frozen chicken from Benin often arrives at the Nigerian market at a cost of US$2.50–US$3.50/kg (JMSF Agribusiness 2020) whereas the farm gate price of locally produced frozen chicken costs US$5.00–US$ 5.50/kg at retail locations and approximately US$3.39/kg at the farm gate (Sahel Capital 2015). The cost disadvantage between imported and locally produced poultry can be traced to the high cost of feed—locally produced maize and soybeans—and wide fluctuations in those commodity prices during the year. In contrast to Nigeria, where the government closed all land borders to the movement of goods in a bid to tackle smuggling, there are no poultry import restrictions in Vietnam. The country receives chicken from low-cost producers such as the United States (figure 8.6), but also exports to China and Japan. Vietnam's chicken exports to those destinations increased rapidly from about –57 percent between 2010 and 2012 to 268 percent between 2013 and 2018, reaching US$30.2 million in 2018.

The policy of banning chicken imports has contributed to slow growth in demand for chicken meat. The annual per capita consumption of chicken meat in Nigeria has barely increased during the past two decades and lags countries with comparable per capita incomes. Furthermore, the annual per capita consumption of chicken meat has fluctuated over the years as follows: 1.4 kg per capita between 1995 and 2002, 1.7 kg per capita between 2003 and 2013, and 1.0 kg per capita between 2014 and 2017. Those consumption levels lag behind other middle-income countries with comparable per capita incomes (figure 8.7 and figure 8.8). For example, per capita consumption in Nigeria is, respectively, seven and three times lower than in neighboring Ghana and Cameroon—and 12 times lower than in Vietnam. A back-of-the-envelope calculation suggests that the consumption market for chicken

FIGURE 8.6

Chicken meat imports are low in Nigeria because of import restrictions

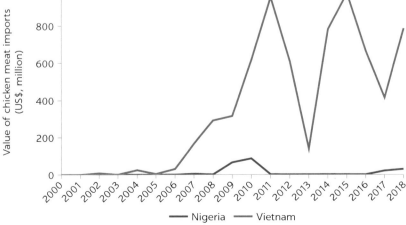

Source: FAOSTAT (Statistics Division, Food and Agriculture Organization of the United Nations).

FIGURE 8.7

Consumption of chicken meat in Nigeria is a fraction of demand in comparable middle-income countries

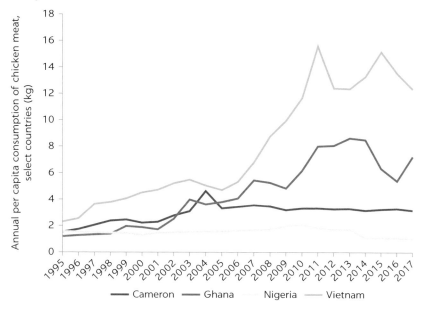

Source: FAOSTAT (Statistics Division, Food and Agriculture Organization of the United Nations).

FIGURE 8.8

Sources of chicken meat imports for Nigeria before and after import ban, 2000–16

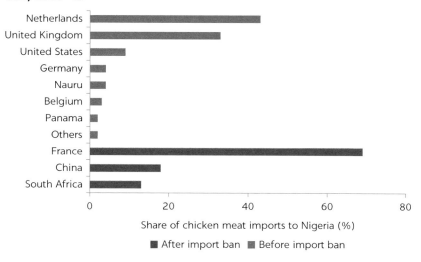

Source: United Nations Comtrade Database.

would have increased by at least US$4.6 billion per annum (equivalent to 2.3 million tons) if Nigeria had the same per capita consumption as Vietnam and no import restrictions. Enormous opportunities exist to grow the consumption market for chicken meat with targeted interventions to provide better genetics, increase productivity and quality of feeds (maize and soybean), provide vaccination programs to reduce mortality, and encourage efficient waste management to manufacture fertilizers.

CHARACTERIZATION OF CHICKEN MEAT VALUE CHAINS

The chicken meat value chains in Nigeria and Vietnam have similar actors; however, most of the chickens in Vietnam are marketed live. The main actors in Nigeria's chicken meat value chains are breeders and input suppliers, producers/farmers, aggregators, processors/slaughterhouses, retailers, and consumers. In Vietnam, the main actors are breeders and input suppliers, producers/farmers, aggregators, wholesalers, processors/slaughterhouses, retailers, and consumers. In Nigeria, breeders import grandparent stock from the pure-line breeds in Europe, as well as DOCs. The importation of DOCs is not subject to the 2002 ban on poultry imports. In addition to DOCs, other key inputs to poultry production include feed, equipment, and veterinary supplies. Some breeders also provide these inputs. About 80 percent of DOCs in the country are produced and used in the South West region. Feed millers are also mostly located in the South but rely on maize and soybean farmers in the North for up to 75 percent of their raw materials. But there are also significant investments in milling and breeding in the North. For example, Olam International has made major investments in integrated inputs supply in Kaduna, including a poultry breeding farm, DOC hatchery, and animal feed mill. The company supplies inputs to farmers in the North West region (especially Kano). Olam International operates another integrated poultry feed mill in Kwara State that supplies to farmers in the North Central region.

Contract arrangements between processors/slaughterhouses and farmers/producers account for less than 5 percent of chicken meat production in Nigeria and less than 10 percent in Vietnam. Contract farming eliminates all actors between farmers and processors, including aggregators/collectors and wholesalers. The main benefits of contract farming include traceability of birds and inputs, which mitigates the risk of contamination and enables early detection and control of diseases; integrated credit arrangements by which farmers receive quality inputs such as DOCs, feeds, and vaccines; and transfer of technology and knowledge to farmers, which leads to improved productivity. The limited growth in contract farming means that most transactions in chicken meat value chains are carried out under spot transactions and weak forms of vertical coordination such as verbal purchase agreements. The processors practicing contract farming in Nigeria include Amobygn, Tuns Farms, Zartec Farms, Ajanla Farms, Olam Farms, and Shonga Farms (Sahel Capital 2015). Similar arrangements are implemented in Vietnam by firms such as CP Group Company of Thailand and Japfa Comfeed Company. Horizontal coordination at the industry level is stronger in Vietnam than in Nigeria. Vietnam has many livestock associations with the mission to support trade and market promotion. In Nigeria, poultry farmers/traders are generally not organized, and only an estimated 20 percent belong to farmers/traders' associations (Oladeji 2011). The Poultry Association of Nigeria (PAN) is an industry-level organization for the poultry sector.

The poultry sector in Nigeria provides opportunities for regional collaboration because feed production (maize and soybean) occurs mainly in the North to serve poultry production in South. Maize is the main ingredient in poultry feeds, and most requirements in Nigeria are met through domestic production (figure 8.9). The leading maize producing states—Borno, Kaduna,

FIGURE 8.9

Most of the raw materials for poultry feeds in Nigeria (maize and soybean) are met through domestic production

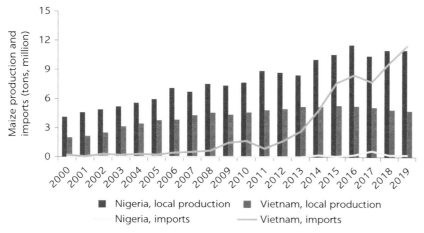

Source: FAOSTAT (Statistics Division, Food and Agriculture Organization of the United Nations).

Niger, Plateau, and Taraba—are all in the Northern region. They account for nearly 60 percent of total maize production in Nigeria. Feed millers, mostly concentrated in the South West region, secure supplies of raw materials through contracts. However, there are concerns among poultry farmers and producer companies that feed quality is variable because of poor quality of the main raw materials—maize, soybean, and sorghum. Considering that feeding costs account for 50–70 percent of the cost of production, there is need to improve the quality of the ingredients through vertical coordination arrangements that go beyond feed millers and the farmers to include the relevant research and extension organizations involved in breeding and dissemination to farmers. Furthermore, the movement of the raw materials from North to South is costly primarily because of high transportation costs and the poor road networks.

Nigeria and Vietnam differ significantly in terms of the trade policy environment on raw materials for livestock feeds. Nigeria's ban on maize imports was lifted in 2017 but without allowing foreign exchange permits for maize imports. Nevertheless, data suggest that maize imports to Nigeria have increased rapidly since 2016 and that local maize production declined beginning around the same year, perhaps reflecting competition with imported maize. In contrast with Nigeria, Vietnam's poultry feed mill segment relies on imports for up to 75 percent of the raw materials (mostly maize grains). Since 2010, Vietnam has considerably lowered import tariffs of important feed ingredients. For example, tariffs on maize and soybean were reduced by 10 percentage points in 2010 from 28 percent and 30 percent, respectively, to 18 percent and 15 percent, with a further reduction of the soybean tariff to 8 percent (figure 8.10). Those measures to increase animal feed millers' access to imported raw materials have been accompanied by strategic measures to increase competitiveness of the domestic maize and soybean sector by developing and disseminating improved varieties to increase yields.

FIGURE 8.10

Vietnam has adopted a two-pronged policy to increase imports of raw materials for poultry feeds while increasing productivity by lowering tariffs on ingredients

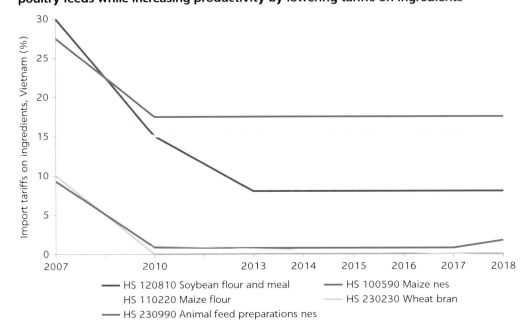

HS 120810 Soybean flour and meal — HS 100590 Maize nes
HS 110220 Maize flour — HS 230230 Wheat bran
HS 230990 Animal feed preparations nes

Source: ITC Access Map.
Note: HS codes reflect the international Harmonized System (HS) six-digit code system for classifying goods, which allows participating countries to classify traded goods on a common basis for customs purposes. nes = not elsewhere specified.

FIGURE 8.11

Buildup of costs, prices, and margins for chicken meat value chain, Nigeria and Vietnam

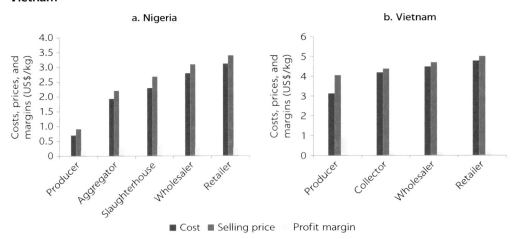

■ Cost ■ Selling price   Profit margin

Source: World Bank staff compilation; JMSF Agribusiness 2020.

COSTS AND MARGINS OF VALUE CHAIN ACTORS

This section compares costs and margins for the actors in chicken meat value chains in Nigeria and Vietnam. Figure 8.11 provides a summary of the costs, selling prices, and margins for each actor along the value chain in Nigeria (panel a) and Vietnam (panel b). The costs at the producer (farm) level for both countries include costs incurred by farmers to purchase various inputs, including DOCs, feed, veterinary services (vaccines, drugs, and so on), labor, and energy. The profit margins correspond to the difference between production costs and the sales price at each level of the value chain, which means that any other costs not identified are subsumed under the listed costs. Data for Nigeria were collected from farmers in Ogun state (JMSF Agribusiness 2020), one of the leading states in poultry production. The average chicken size from the sample was 3.3 kg.[3] Data for Vietnam were collected in Hanoi,[4] and the average chicken size was about 1.8 kg.

The cost of chicken meat production is lower in Nigeria than in Vietnam, across all cost items except veterinary costs (mainly vaccines and drugs). The total cost of production is at least four times higher in Vietnam—US$3.14/kg in Vietnam compared to US$0.70/kg in Nigeria. The main driver of the relatively higher costs is feed, which is US$2.38/kg of chicken meat in Vietnam and US$0.36/kg of chicken meat in Nigeria, accounting for 76 percent of the costs in Vietnam and 51 percent[5] of the costs in Nigeria (table 8.2). The high cost of feed in Vietnam is related to high dependence on imports of major input (grains) used by feed millers in the formulation of poultry feed (figure 8.12). In contrast, poultry feed in Nigeria is constituted from local production of the key ingredients such as maize, cassava, sorghum, soybean, and millet. There are restrictions on imports of these commodities, including outright bans and exclusion from foreign exchange permits awarded by the Central Bank. The second most important component of the cost of production is DOCs, which cost US$0.40/kg of meat in Vietnam (13 percent of the cost) and US$0.14/kg of meat in Nigeria (20 percent of the cost). That DOCs are more expensive in Vietnam is rather surprising because of the remarkable private sector investments in the breeding segment. Labor accounts for a relatively small share of the cost of production in both countries, and the absolute costs are similar.

Despite the higher cost of production, chicken meat producers in Vietnam earn higher margins than in Nigeria and capture a higher share of the total margins in the value chain. The farm gate price of chicken meat is about four times higher in Vietnam (US$4.10/kg) than in Nigeria (US$0.91/kg), allowing producers to earn higher margins in Vietnam (US$0.92/kg) than in Nigeria (US$0.17/kg) (see table 8.2). Producers in Vietnam earn nearly 60 percent of the total value chain margins (figure 8.13, panel b) whereas in Nigeria they earn

TABLE 8.2 **The cost of production of chicken meat is lower in Nigeria than in Vietnam**

	NIGERIA	VIETNAM
Day-old chicks	0.14	0.40
Feed	0.36	2.38
Veterinary (vaccine, drugs, and so on)	0.11	0.09
Labor	0.04	0.06
Other costs (fuel, electricity, water, and so on)	0.05	0.21
Total costs	0.70	3.14
Sales price	0.91	4.10
Losses from mortality	0.05	0.04
Profit	0.17	0.92

Source: World Bank staff compilation; JMSF Agribusiness 2020.
Note: All amounts are in US dollars.

FIGURE 8.12

Vietnam relies heavily on imports of major poultry feed ingredients

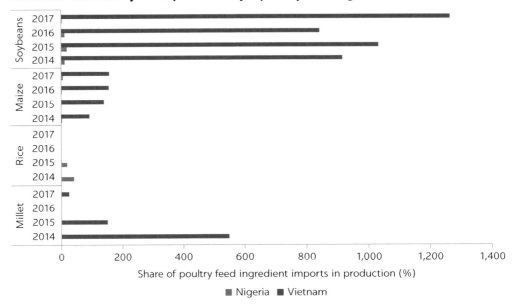

Source: FAOSTAT (Statistics Division, Food and Agriculture Organization of the United Nations).

FIGURE 8.13

Profit margins in the chicken meat value chain, Nigeria and Vietnam

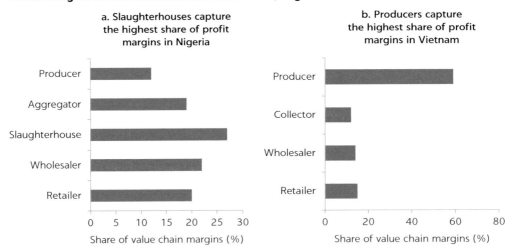

Source: World Bank staff compilation; JMSF Agribusiness 2020.

about 12 percent of the margins—with the highest share of the margins in Nigerian value chains (about 27 percent) accruing to slaughterhouses (figure 8.13, panel a). However, the producers in the typical chicken meat value chain in both countries tend to work with smaller volumes relative to other actors; therefore, their total profit margins are lower.

CONCLUSIONS

Nigeria's policy of banning chicken imports has slowed down growth of chicken meat consumption without offering the expected protections to producers. Implementation of the policy has been a challenge because of porous borders that have for years allowed smuggling of chicken from Benin and neighboring countries, and that smuggling denies producers the intended protections from the import ban. The rents from smuggling are captured by the smugglers, thus denying consumers lower prices of imported chicken and dampening growth of consumption. As a result, the annual per capital consumption of chicken meat in Nigeria is significantly lower than in countries at the same level of development: 7 times lower than in neighboring Ghana, 3 times lower than in Cameroon, and 12 times lower than in Vietnam. A back of the envelope calculation suggests that the consumption market for chicken would have increased by at least US$4.6 billion per annum (equivalent to 2.3 million tons) if Nigeria had the same per capita consumption as Vietnam and no import restrictions.

The quality of domestically produced poultry feeds varies significantly such that poultry producers (and other livestock producers) prefer imported feeds. The variability of quality is primarily due to weak regulatory enforcement of standards and lack of vertical coordination between farmers producing feed ingredients in the North and poultry producers in the South. The main ingredients in poultry feeds are maize, soybeans, and sorghum, mainly produced in northern states such as Borno, Kaduna, Niger, Plateau, and Taraba. Because poultry production occurs predominantly in the southern parts of the country, there are unexploited opportunities for regional coordination to organize the value chain with the aim to improve the quality of locally manufactured feeds and substitute imports. Coordination arrangements should include, in addition to the farmers producing the feed ingredients and the poultry producers, the relevant research and extension organizations involved in crop breeding to develop crop varieties that supply nutrients required for poultry production and extension departments to disseminate new varieties and crop management practices to farmers.

A robust policy and regulatory framework is needed to enable growth of the feed industry. Enabling policies that have helped spur growth in Vietnam include specification and enforcement of standards to ensure the quality of feeds, including standards for maximum allowable levels of mycotoxins, heavy metals, and microorganisms in feed ingredients and compound feeds; and regular inspection, sampling, and testing of feeds by the Ministry of Agriculture and Rural Development and Market Inspection Agency. Taken together, the animal feed sector is more than US$2 billion, and there is enormous scope for competitive investments to improve the quality and quantity of feed, reduce the costs of production in the livestock sector, and create jobs.

In addition to improving the animal feeds segment, there is scope for improving collaboration between private investors and public veterinary health authorities to unlock investments to produce vaccines and drugs. There are important lessons to draw from the experience of how Vietnam spurred investments in vaccines and drugs after its own outbreak of HPAI in 2004. The impact of the epidemic was worse in Vietnam compared to Nigeria, leading to the death/culling of 38.3 million birds, representing about 15 percent of the poultry population (of which 50 percent were chickens) (Anh 2004). In response, private enterprises in Vietnam started experimenting with vaccines in 2005, supported by the Department of Animal Health, continually testing vaccine efficacy against emerging strains of the virus (WHO 2017). In 2016, the

Vietnamese Ministry of Agriculture and Rural Development signed Decision #1756/QD-BNN-TY to establish a high-level steering committee to promote in-country veterinary vaccine manufacturing for major livestock diseases. The decision highlighted the need for improved domestic production of poultry H5 vaccines as a national priority and has led to the establishment of five major veterinary vaccine development institutions in the country.

Access to power is critical in poultry production and processing, and it is a major constraint faced by Nigeria's poultry industry. There are, however, enormous investment opportunities in efficient waste management to generate biogas energy. The electricity grid in Nigeria has limited reach, and rural areas where most production occurs do not have regular access to electricity. The poultry subsector largely depends on micropower generated by poultry farms, which is costly compared to electricity. The most common sources of power are solar lamps and generators to provide light and heat. The power challenges can be alleviated through microenergy projects that convert waste from poultry production into sources of energy. It is estimated that only 46 percent of poultry waste in Nigeria is managed in an environmentally sound and economical manner (Okai 2019). Most waste materials[6] are burned, used as compost, dumped in pits and wastelands, or flushed into streams and other water bodies—causing widespread air, water, and land pollution.

The conversion of farm waste into energy is yet to take off in Nigeria. An assessment of the biogas potential from solid waste and livestock excrement in 1999 suggests minimum output of 1.382×109 cubic meters of biogas per year, equivalent to 4.81 million barrels of crude oil (Adeniran et al. 2014). In addition to biogas fuel, the biofertilizers generated from biogas plants have commercial value. It's a win-win solution that generates clean and cheaper energy, provides for environmentally safe waste management, provides additional income to farmers, creates job opportunities, and decentralizes energy generation and environmental protection. The economic use of poultry waste is more advanced in Vietnam. According to the General Statistics Office, Vietnam produced 84.5 million tons of solid waste and 50 million cubic meters of liquid waste in 2016. Nearly 60 percent was treated, and 20 percent was used for biogas, composting, worm farming, and feeding fishes.

NOTES

1. Nigeria has the second-largest chicken population in Africa after South Africa (Sahel Capital 2015).
2. For example, equipment for scaffolding, shuttering, propping, or pit-propping of iron and steel attracts a 15 percent levy, in addition to import duties and value added tax, amounting to a total of 27.5 percent import charges. Antibiotics for poultry are subject to 5 percent import duty, but vaccines are exempt from import charges.
3. In contrast, data from FAOSTAT (Statistics Division, Food and Agriculture Organization of the United Nations) indicate that the average size has been 1 kg since 1990, raising doubts about the accuracy of FAOSTAT data.
4. Data collected by the Institute of Policy and Stragey for Agriculture and Rural Development.
5. Based on sample from farmers in Ogun state. Other studies have returned much higher feed costs in Nigeria—up to 70 percent of the cost of production (see USDA 2019).
6. Waste materials include droppings, dead birds, hatchery waste, litter, offal, water from processing waste, and biosolids.

REFERENCES

Adeniran, K. A., K. O. Yusuf, M. O. Iyanda, and O. A. Alo. 2014. "Relative Effectiveness of Biogas Production Using Poultry Droppings and Swine Dung." *Ethiopian Journal of Environmental Studies and Management* 7 (4): 371–78.

Anh, B. Q. 2004. "Bird Flu Prevention and Poultry Development Planning in Viet Nam." Workshop of Solutions for Developing Poultry Industries after Eliminating Bird Flu in Viet Nam, Ministry of Agriculture and Rural Development, Ha Noi. (In Vietnamese)

ASL 2050 (Africa Sustainable Livestock 2050). 2018. "Livestock and Livelihoods Spotlight, Nigeria: Cattle and Poultry Sectors." Food and Agriculture Organization of the United Nations, Rome. http://www.fao.org/3/CA2149EN/ca2149en.pdf.

JMSF Agribusiness. 2020. "Sources of Growth in Agribusiness Small and Medium-Sized Enterprises (SMEs): Poultry Report." Unpublished manuscript.

Nguyen, V. D., and T. Long. 2008. "Poultry Production Systems in Viet Nam." GCP/RAS/228 /GER Working Paper No. 4, Food and Agriculture Organization of the United Nations, Rome. http://www.fao.org/3/a-al693e.pdf.

Okai, E. K. 2019. "How Nigeria's Young Poultry Farmers Are Turning the Problem of Waste on Its Head." The Poultry Site, December 13, 2019. https://thepoultrysite.com/articles/how-ni gerias-young-poultry-farmers-are-turning-the-problem-of-waste-on-its-head.

Oladeji, J. O. 2011. "Sources and Utilization of Poultry Production Information among Poultry Farmers in Oyo State." *International Journal of Livestock Production* 2 (2): 011–016.

Sahel Capital. 2015. "An Assessment of the Nigerian Poultry Sector." Sahel newsletter, Vol 11. https://sahelconsult.com/wp-content/uploads/2019/06/Sahel-Newsletter-Volume-11.pdf.

USDA (United States Department of Agriculture). 2019. "Nigeria: Animal Feed Sector Snapshot—2019." Global Agricultural Information Network Report NG-19005, USDA Foreign Agricultural Service. https://apps.fas.usda.gov/newgainapi/api/report /downloadreportbyfilename?filename=Nigeria%20Animal%20Feed%20Sector%20 Snapshot_Lagos_Nigeria_5-20-2019.pdf.

WHO (World Health Organization). 2017. "Made in Viet Nam Vaccines: Efforts to Develop Sustainable In-Country Manufacturing for Seasonal and Pandemic Influenza Vaccines." Consultation held in Viet Nam, April–June 2016.

APPENDIX A

Estimating the Size and Structure of the Agribusiness Sector

The agribusiness sector includes primary agriculture and all upstream and downstream off-farm agriculture-related activities, including input supply, trading and transportation, processing, food services, and so on. (figure A.1). The agribusiness off-farm components expand as part of agricultural transformation that is associated with economic development. The transformation is driven by higher farm productivity, commercialization, and increased demand for processed and ready-to-eat foods, which in turn create new opportunities for value added and job creation. As transformation accelerates, more farm output is processed and traded, and farmers demand more modern inputs.

Although the importance of primary agriculture in the economy declines as countries develop, the importance of the entire agribusiness sector declines at a slower rate and remains a major part of high-income countries' economies (figure A.2, panel a). Eventually, the value added or gross domestic product (GDP) generated beyond the farm (off-farm agribusiness) exceeds what is generated on the farm (primary agriculture) (figure A.2, panel b). These dynamics lead the focus of food policy to gradually shift from raising farm productivity to also promoting food industries and markets.

Agricultural GDP is captured by national accounts data and includes all value added generated by crops, livestock, forestry, and fishing. National accounts also report GDP for nonagricultural sectors, some of which are related to agriculture. For example, food processing is part of manufacturing GDP, and trading and transporting food products are part of services GDP. Some farm inputs are also produced by manufacturing (for example, fertilizers and feed) or services (for example, banking and extension).

The exchange of goods and services between sectors is an important part of the economy and is tracked in national accounts using input-output tables (IOTs) or, more recently, supply-use tables (SUTs). Statistical agencies periodically update (rebase) national accounts to use the most recent available data. Rebasing typically involves building a new SUT with detailed sectors and product categories.[1] This book uses the information contained in SUTs to measure the size of a country's agribusiness sector, including on-farm and upstream/downstream components.

FIGURE A.1

Components of the agribusiness sector

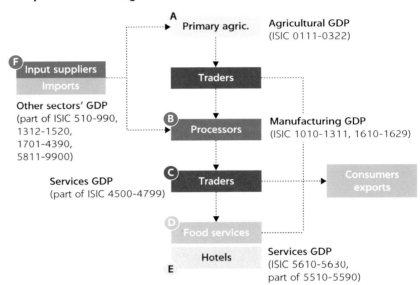

Source: International Food Policy Research Institute.
Note: ISIC refers to the International Standards Industrial Classification, which is the United Nations system to classify all economic activities. Agric. = agriculture.

FIGURE A.2

Economic importance of agribusiness and off-farm agribusiness

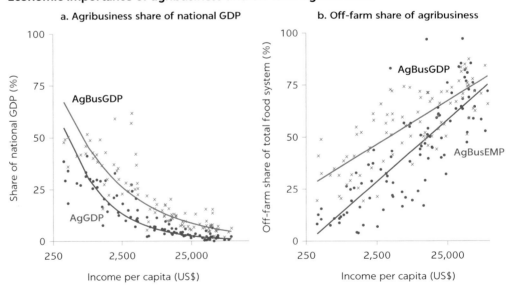

Source: International Food Policy Research Institute estimates using supply-use tables from 98 countries covering 96 percent of global gross domestic product (GDP) circa 2015.
Note: Off-farm agribusiness includes agro-processing, input supply, trade and transport, food services, and hotels and accommodation. Income per capita is measured by gross national income (GNI), which is GDP plus net foreign transfers. Both GDP and GNI are measured in constant 2011 US dollars. AgBusEMP = employment in the agribusiness sector comprising primary agriculture (on-farm) and off-farm agribusiness; AgGDP = agricultural GDP from primary agriculture, including crops, livestock, forestry, and fishing; AgBusGDP = the sum of GDP from agriculture (AgGDP) plus off-farm agribusiness (agro-processing, input supply, trade and transport services, and food services). In panel a, x's and o's are observations from the countries on AgBusGDP and AgGDP, respectively; in panel b, they are observations from the countries on AgBusGDP and AgBusEMP, respectively.

The definition of AgBusGDP is the sum of the following five agribusiness components, with the amount of value added in each component calculated directly from SUTs:

1. *Agriculture.* Includes all GDP generated in the agricultural sector, including all crops, livestock, forestry, and fishing (ISIC 0111–0322).[2]
2. *Agro-processing.* Includes all food and agriculture-related GDP within the manufacturing sector, including the processing of meat, fish, dairy, grains, animal feed, beverages, tobacco, yarn and natural fibers, and wood and timber products (ISIC 1010–1311 and 1610–1629).
3. *Input supply.* Includes all GDP generated during the production of inputs used directly by farmers and agro-processors (for example, fertilizer and banking services). Inputs produced by farmers and processors themselves are excluded to avoid double-counting. Only the portion of GDP generated by *local* input producers is included in AgBusGDP, and this portion is calculated as the share of agriculture and processing's input demand in total economy-wide demand. For example, if agriculture uses a third of all petroleum in the economy, then a third of the *local* petroleum sector's GDP is considered part of the agribusiness sector. If all petroleum is imported, then this input does not contribute to AgBusGDP because the value added occurs outside the country.
4. *Trade and transport services.* Includes all GDP generated by the domestic transporting and trading (retailing and wholesaling) of agri-food products between farms, firms, and final points of sale (markets). National accounts data do not separate the trade sector's GDP into its food and nonfood components, but this GDP is estimated using SUT product-level data on transaction cost margins (that is, the gap between producer and consumer prices, less any taxes). Transaction costs are the main source of demand for trade services, so a portion of trade sector GDP can be attributed to the agribusiness sector on the basis of the share of trade margins on agri-food products relative to the margins on all marketed products.
5. *Food services.* Includes all GDP generated in the food services sector (ISIC 5610-5630) and a portion of the GDP in the hotels and accommodation sector (ISIC 5510-5590). Producers of food services (that is, meals prepared outside the home) are usually standalone operations (for example, restaurants and street vendors), whereas hotels often run restaurants in addition to providing accommodation. The portion of hotels and accommodation GDP attributed to agribusiness is based on the share of agri-food inputs in the sector's total input purchases. This assumes that labor and capital costs (that is, worker remuneration and operating profits) in the hotel sector are proportional to intermediate input costs, and that the food and nonfood services supplied by hotels are proportional to the cost of food and nonfood inputs. This assumption likely results in underestimation of the contribution of agribusiness to the hotels and accommodation sector.

A series of SUTs measured in current prices was constructed for Nigeria using national accounts and other data. Nominal estimates of AgBusGDP are converted to constant prices by adjusting sectoral GDP for inflation using sectoral deflators from national accounts data. Because 2017 is the baseline year, real AgBusGDP estimates are expressed in constant 2017 prices and dollar exchange rate.

The estimation of AgBusEMP follows a similar procedure to AgBusGDP and uses the same SUT data, but with three additional steps to estimate employment in the five components of the agribusiness sector:

- *Base year employment by sector.* The number of workers employed during 2017 in each of the SUTs' 86 sectors is estimated using data on labor value added from the SUT and employment data for 14 broad sectors published by the International Labour Organization (ILO).[3] Average wages are calculated for the 14 sectors and applied to their corresponding sectors in the SUT to derive employment for each of the 86 sectors.
- *Historical employment estimates.* Average total GDP per worker is estimated for each of the SUTs' 86 sectors. Changes in real sectoral GDP over time are assumed to lead to proportional changes in sectoral employment (that is, average GDP per worker is initially assumed to be constant over time). These constant employment-to-GDP ratios are applied to sectoral GDP estimates from the Institute for Food Policy Research Institute's historical time series of SUTs.
- *Corrected employment estimates.* Initial sectoral employment estimates are scaled to match ILO employment numbers. The final AgBusEMP indicator reflects annual changes in employment-to-population and employment-to-GDP ratios, is consistent with official employment statistics, and has the same definition and agribusiness components as the AgBusGDP.

ILO triangulates information from labor force surveys and other data sources in order to derive sectoral employment estimates that are consistent across time and countries. ILO employment data may deviate from official sources, but they permit comparisons across Global Field Support Strategy countries and adopt a global definition of the labor force (for example, workers must be at least 15 years of age).

NOTES

1. IOTs and SUTs can be extended to include interactions between industries and institutions (for example, households, government, and rest of the world). The resulting database is called a social accounting matrix, or SAM.
2. ISIC codes refer to the International Standard Industrial Classification (Revision 4).
3. ILO employment data are available at https://www.ilo.org/ilostat.